Local Identities and Transnational Cults within Europe

CABI Religious Tourism and Pilgrimage Series

General Editors:

Dr Razaq Raj, Leeds Business School, Leeds Beckett University, UK
Dr Kevin Griffin, School of Hospitality Management and Tourism, Dublin Institute of Technology, Ireland

This series examines the practical applications, models and illustrations of religious tourism and pilgrimage management from a variety of international perspectives. Pilgrimage is not only a widespread and important practice in Islam, Judaism and Christianity, but also in other major religious traditions such as Buddhism, Hinduism and Sikhism.

The series explores the emergence and trajectories of religious tourism and pilgrimage. Inclusive of all denominations, religions, faiths and spiritual practices, it covers evaluations of religious tourism and pilgrimage, management guides, economic reports and sets of represented actions and behaviours within various cultural, management and marketing contexts. A key strength of the series is the presentation of current and diverse empirical research insights on aspects of religious tourism and pilgrimage, juxtaposing this with state-of-the-art reflections on the emerging theoretical foundations of the subject matter.

The series illustrates the principles related to religion, pilgrimage and the management of tourist sites. It aims to provide a useful resource for researchers and students of the subject, and increase understanding of this vital aspect of tourism studies.

Titles Available

Pilgrimage and Tourism to Holy Cities: Ideological and Management Perspectives
Edited by Maria Leppäkari and Kevin Griffin

Conflicts, Religion and Culture in Tourism
Edited by Razaq Raj and Kevin Griffin

The Many Voices of Pilgrimage and Reconciliation
Edited by Ian S. McIntosh and Lesley D. Harman

Local Identities and Transnational Cults within Europe
Edited by Fiorella Giacalone and Kevin Griffin

Titles in Preparation

Religious Pilgrimage Routes and Trails: Sustainable Development and Management
Edited by Anna Trono and Daniel Olsen

Religious Tourism in Asia
Edited by Shin Yasuda, Razaq Raj and Kevin Griffin

Risk and Safety Challenges for Religious Tourism and Events
Edited by Maximiliano Korstanje, Kevin Griffin and Razaq Raj

Islamic Tourism: Management of Travel Destinations
Edited by Ahmad Jamal, Kevin Griffin and Razaq Raj

Managing Religious Tourism
Edited by Maureen Griffiths and Peter Wiltshier

Local Identities and Transnational Cults within Europe

Edited by

Fiorella Giacalone

University of Perugia, Italy

and

Kevin Griffin

Dublin Institute of Technology, Ireland

CABI is a trading name of CAB International

CABI
Nosworthy Way
Wallingford
Oxfordshire OX10 8DE
UK

Tel: +44 (0)1491 832111
Fax: +44 (0)1491 833508
E-mail: info@cabi.org
Website: www.cabi.org

CABI
745 Atlantic Avenue
8th Floor
Boston, MA 02111
USA

Tel: +1 (617)682-9015
E-mail: cabi-nao@cabi.org

A catalogue record for this book is available from the British Library, London, UK.

Library of Congress Cataloging-in-Publication Data

Names: Giacalone, Fiorella, editor. | Griffin, Kevin A., editor.
Title: Local identities and transnational cults within Europe / edited by Fiorella Giacalone and Kevin Griffin.
Description: Wallingford, Oxfordshire, UK ; Boston, MA : CABI, 2018. | Series: CABI religious tourism and pilgrimage series | Includes bibliographical references and index.
Identifiers: LCCN 2017054581 (print) | LCCN 2018008086 (ebook) | ISBN 9781786392534 (pdf) | ISBN 9781786392541 (ePub) | ISBN 9781786392527 (hardback : alk. paper)
Subjects: LCSH: Tourism--Europe--Religious aspects. | Pilgrims and pilgrimages--Europe.
Classification: LCC G156.5.R44 (ebook) | LCC G156.5.R44 L63 2018 (print) | DDC 263/.0424--dc23
LC record available at https://lccn.loc.gov/2017054581

ISBN-13: 9781786392527 (hbk)
        9781786392534 (PDF)
        9781786392541 (ePub)

Commissioning editor: Claire Parfitt
Associate editor: Alexandra Lainsbury
Production editor: Tim Kapp

Typeset by SPi, Pondicherry, India
Printed and bound in the UK by CPI Group (UK) Ltd, Croydon, CR0 4YY

Contents

List of Contributors

Alfonsina Bellio, anthropologist, is a visiting research fellow at the Institute of Advanced Studies (Nantes, France) and a postdoctoral researcher working with the Groupe Sociétés, Religions, Laïcités (GSRL) (EPHE-CNRS) of Paris, under the direction of Philippe Portier. She is in charge of teaching anthropology of Europe at the University of Bordeaux and introduction to sociology of religion at the Catholic University of the West (UCO), University of Angers. She has worked in the Department of Humanistic Studies of Calabria (Cosenza, Italy), where she defended her thesis for a doctorate in anthropology and literature, after a Masters in social and historical anthropology of Europe, at the School for Advanced Studies in the Social Sciences (École des Hautes Études en Sciences Sociales) in Paris, under the direction of Daniel Fabre. As a laureate of the programme 'Research in Paris', she has benefited from an annual scholarship from the City of Paris. During her activity within the Department of Humanistic Studies at the University of Calabria, as well as with the Ministry for Cultural Heritage and Activities, for the Historical, Artistic, and Ethno-anthropological Patrimony (PSAE) superintendence of Calabria and other institutions, she has been entrusted with various teaching and research responsibilities. The results of her findings have been presented at several international scientific conferences (in Italy, France, Canada, Romania, Russia, Serbia, Bulgaria, Lithuania, Belgium, Portugal, Spain and Croatia). Email: alfonsina.bellio@gmail.com

Riccardo Cruzzolin is a researcher in the Department of Political Science, University of Perugia. He teaches political and economic anthropology. He has focused his more recent research activity on the popular piety and folklore of Catholic immigrants from Ecuador and Peru. Some of his recent publications include: 'Fare comunità nelle periferie: San Sisto e oltre', in *Santambrogio Ambrogio, a cura di, Giovani a Perugia. Vissuti urbani e forme del tempo* (edited by S. Ambrogio, 2014); 'Costruzione di località e utilizzo dello spazio pubblico da parte dei migranti', in *Popolazioni mobili e spazi pubblici. Perugia in trasformazione* (edited by S. Roberto, 2014); and 'Complicità e dissonanze nella ricerca di campo', *Mondi Migranti*, 3 (2014). Email: riccardo.cruzzolin@unipg.it

Paola de Salvo is an assistant professor in sociology of environment and territory at the Department of Political Science, University of Perugia. She teaches sociology and communication of tourism. Her main research interest is focused on the study of local development and tourism, in particular the study of territorial development as a process that links socio-economic and cultural aspects to sustainable development, which gives value to the sense of place, local identity, narrations and values. Email paola.desalvo@unipg.it

Guillaume Etienne is an ethnologist, assistant professor at the University of Tours, France and member of the Citeres Laboratory. He defended a PhD in ethnology in 2013, about a local pilgrimage and his adoption by different migrations. He focuses on the following research fields: heritage, construction of a sense of belonging and ethnicity. Email: guillaume.etienne@etu.univ-tours.fr

Laurent S. Fournier completed his PhD at the University of Montpellier in 2002 on the revitalization of local festivals in Mediterranean France. From 2005 to 2015 he was an assistant professor at the University of Nantes, where he investigated English and Scottish traditional games and sports. He also served as an expert in intangible cultural heritage for the French Ministry of Culture. He is now an assistant professor at the University of Aix-Marseille and a researcher at the Institut d'ethnologie méditerranéenne, européenne et comparative à Aix-en-Provence (IDEMEC UMR 7307 CNRS et Aix-Marseille-Université). Laurent S. Fournier is the president of the FER-Eurethno network (Council of Europe) and has served as a board member of the Société International d'Ethnologie et de Folklore. Email: laurent.fournier@univ-amu.fr

Fiorella Giacalone is an associate professor of cultural anthropology in the Department of Political Science, University of Perugia (Italy). She is head of the degree courses in social work and social policy. She is a member of two international associations of anthropologists (FER Eurethno du Conseil de l'Europe and European Association of Social Anthropology (EASA)). She has taught at the universities of Florianopolis (Brazil), Valladolid (Spain), Paris and Marrakech (Morocco). She is interested in the holy feminine, the bodily symbols in Catholicism and Islam, and the forms of construction and definition of the female body in the monotheistic religions. She is concerned also with the relationship between medical anthropology and social services for immigrants. Recently, she has studied the daily life of young Muslim immigrants in a secular Western culture. She has published seven books and 70 essays in books and Italian and foreign scientific reviews. Email: fiorella.giacalone@unipg.it

Kevin Griffin, PhD, is a lecturer in tourism at the Dublin Institute of Technology, where he teaches students from undergraduate to PhD level. His research interests are broad, but primarily encompass a range of tourism themes such as heritage, culture, social tourism, the pedagogy of fieldwork and, in particular, religious tourism and pilgrimage. He is co-founder of the *International Journal of Religious Tourism and Pilgrimage*, and has published widely. His main recent publications include: *Cultural Tourism* (2013, edited with Raj Razaq and Nigel D. Morpeth); *Religious Tourism and Pilgrimage Management: An International Perspective*, second edition (2015, edited with Raj Razaq); *Conflicts, Challenges, Religion and Culture* (2017, edited with Raj Razaq). Mailing address: School of Hospitality Management and Tourism, Dublin Institute of Technology, Cathal Brugha Street, Dublin 1, Ireland. Email: kevin.griffin@dit.ie

André Julliard has a PhD in anthropology (University Paris V – René Descartes). He is a researcher at the Institute of Mediterranean, European and Comparative Ethnology (IDEMEC, CNRS/Aix-Marseille Université, Aix-en-Provence). His most recent research crosses three fields of study: individual and collective devotion; the transcendence of systems (religious, political) of thought; and manufacturing of heritage in policies of territorial development. They concern three anthropological domains: European and Mediterranean Christianities (Catholicism and orthodoxy); religions of country in western Africa; and patrimonial politics. One of his most recent publications is 'Saint Nicolas: du tombeau à la place publique. Modernité des fonctions de saint patron dans les politiques régionales et les relations internationales entre l'Europe et la Turquie (2009–2013)', in *En orient et en Occident le culte de saint Nicolas en Europe Xe–XXIe siècle* (edited by V. Gazeau, C. Guyon and C. Vincent, 2015). Email: pamjulliard@wanadoo.fr

Tony Kiely is a lecturer and researcher in the College of Arts and Tourism, Dublin Institute of Technology, Ireland, lecturing in the areas of business finance, marketing and strategic management. His research interests incorporate the relationships between traditional music and tourism, church tourism and pilgrimage, festival tourism and identity, and their related social histories. Tony has presented at a range of international conferences. His most recent publications include: *From Tullycross to La Rochelle: Festival Food, French Connections, and Relational Tourism Potential* (2017); 'Why Rita? Devotional practice and pilgrimage intent towards a medieval Italian saint in central Dublin', *International Journal of Religious Tourism and Pilgrimage*, 4, 2 (2016); '"We managed"; Reflections on the culinary practices of Dublin's working class poor in the 1950s', in

Tickling the Palate; Gastronomy in Irish Literature and Culture (edited by E. Maher and M. Mac Con Iomaire, 2014); 'Resurrecting Harry Clarke; Breathing life into stained glass tourism in Ireland', *International Journal of Religious Tourism and Pilgrimage*, 2, 2 (2014); 'Tapping into Mammon; Stakeholder perspectives on developing church tourism in Dublin's liberties', *Tourism Review*, 68, 2 (2013); with M. Brophy 'Competencies: A new sector', *Journal of European Industrial Training* 26, 2, 3, 4 (2002). Email: tony.m.kiely@dit.ie

Inga B. Kuźma PhD is a lecturer at the Institute of Ethology and Anthropology of Culture, University of Łódź, Poland. First, her field research concerns the methodological problems of anthropological/ethnological study on a phenomenon and includes women's studies, gender theory and history. She has worked on the religious habits, beliefs and rituals of the Polish Catholic communities (rural and urban) – particularly on women's religious experiences, the cult of Our Lady, the pilgrimage and the cult of female saints. Second, she has been studying social exclusion due to urban homelessness in the context of the involved anthropology (the main topics: a methodological framework of the involved action research and participatory action research; an empowerment and bottom-up inclusion of the excluded and 'muted' group; and 'just' and 'unjust/not equal' urban spaces). Email: inga.kuzma@uni.lodz.pl

Mathilde Lamothe has a PhD in ethnology, with joint international supervision of her doctoral thesis (cotutelle) between Université Laval (Quebec, Canada), the University of Pau and Pays de l'Adour (France). Her fieldwork is focused on heritage and sport in Gascogne (France) and Quebec (Canada), their transformations and their relationships to look beyond the classical binary pattern of tradition/modernity. These studies analyse the production of new cultural activities from traditional practices and how local actors position themselves with relation to their cultural heritage. Email: mathilde_lamothe@hotmail.com

Gaëlla Loiseau is a doctoral student in sociology at the University of Le Havre. Her research focuses on the identification processes of mobile populations, conflicts of uses in the context of mobility and the running of living spaces of travellers in France. She co-edited the digital book *Actualité de l'Habitat Temporaire. De l'habitat rêvé à l'habitat contraint*, published by Terra-HN editions in 2016 (free access online: www.shs.terra-hn-editions.org/Collection/?-Actualite-de-l-habitat-temporaire-1-). Email: gaellaloiseau@gmail.com

Daniele Parbuono has a PhD in ethnology and anthropology from the University of Perugia (Italy), where he teaches courses in museum anthropology and cultural anthropology. He is a full professor at Chongqing University of Arts and Sciences (China), where he teaches Italian anthropology and cultural heritage, and ethnographic methodology. Together with Liu Zhuang, he directs the China-Europe Cultural Heritage Centre (inside which the Italian Language and Culture Institute was also set up) of the Chongqing University of Arts and Sciences. His research interests include political, religious and migration anthropology, linguistics heritage and folkloric phenomena with particular attention to the processes of cultural 'patrimonialization' in Italy and China. Some of his recent books are: with Francesca Sbardella, *Costruzione di patrimoni. Le parole degli oggetti e delle convenzioni* (2017); '*Storie' e feste. Un'etnografia della comunicazione politica* (2013); with Ester Bianchi, *L'Umbria guarda la Cina* (2013); *Folclorismi medievali, rinascimentali e barocchi. Riflessioni antropologiche sulla contemporaneità 'storica'* (2012); with Giancarlo Baronti and Giancarlo Palombini, *Séga seghin' segamo… Studi e ricerche su 'Sega la vecchia' in Umbria* (2011). Email: daniele.parbuono@hotmail.com

Gianfranco Spitilli (Teramo, 1975), has a degree in Ethnology and a PhD in ethnoanthropology; is research fellow at the University of Rome 'La Sapienza', Department of History, Cultures, Religions. He conducts research in the fields of religious ethnology, ethnomusicology and anthropology of memory in south-central Italy, Belgium and Romania. He is a member of the Société Française d'Ethnomusicologie (SFE), Réseau EURETHNO of Scientific and technical cooperation in European ethnology and historiography of the Council of Europe, International Society for Ethnology and Folklore (SIEF), Italian Association for Ethno-anthropological Sciences (AISEA) and the Italian Society for the Museum of Design and Heritage Demoethnoanthropological (SIMBDEA). He collaborated for several years through teaching and research activities with the teaching of visual anthropology (with Professor A. Ricci) at La Sapienza University of Rome. He is a visiting lecturer in the history and culture of popular traditions at the University of the Studies of Molise (Professor V. Spera), and in anthropology and cultural anthropology at the Intercultural University 'D'Annunzio' in Chieti (Professor L. Giancristofaro). He has published books and essays in Italian and foreign scientific journals, documentaries and audio CDs with research materials. In 2009 he won the Nigra Prize for anthropological research. Email: gianfrancospitilli@gmail.com

1 Introduction: Local Identity and Transnational Cults

Fiorella Giacalone[1]* and Kevin Griffin[2]
[1]University of Perugia, Perugia, Italy; [2]Dublin Institute
of Technology, Dublin, Ireland

Religious Tourism, between Local Identity and the International Dimension[1]

Before it became a political entity, Europe had long been a place where the movement of pilgrims and merchants made the knowledge of different languages and cultures possible. This was especially true in the case of the fairs held to celebrate the festivals associated with holy sites.

Pilgrimage, in its traditional sense, and in historic references, is a journey, often long and complex, which is performed out of devotion – a spiritual quest for the fulfilment of a votive. It is a necessary sacrifice that is made in order to arrive at a 'holy' place. This perspective renders the process of secularization witnessed today even more interesting, as it has an effect on all religious phenomena, and thus also the sense of what it means to undertake a pilgrimage.

The latest figures released by the United Nations World Trade Organization (UNWTO) (2011) estimate that annually there are 330 million travellers to places of worship, of which there are 40 million in Italy alone. About half of this total can be defined as pilgrims in the strictest sense. Travel to places of worship, from the more established to the more recent pilgrimages, some of which have yet to be approved by the appropriate Church, appears to have reclaimed its position among the destinations available to the urban traveller, in the search for old and new forms of spirituality. This demonstrates how religious dynamics can surprise even academics, who might have expected to observe aspects of increasing secularization of society, more so than new forms of religiosity, which have, to varying extents, been codified by the Church (such as Medjugorje, or other sites associated with Marian apparitions).

There has been a long tradition of pilgrimage studies in Italy, with the aim of investigating the diverse expressions of popular religiosity, in a country where the Catholic culture has profoundly influenced the manner of worship. This has historically been expressed in terms of conflict, at times implicit, at times more explicit, between official forms of worship and expressions of popular Catholicism (Lombardi Satriani, 2000; Buttitta, 2002), also in relation to Marian apparitions (Apolito, 1990; 2002) and the study of miracles (Gallini, 1998). Since the United Nations Educational, Scientific and Cultural Organization (UNESCO) directives (1997 and 2003), the devotional sphere has been augmented with the study of tangible and intangible heritage (objects, festivals and rituals). Votive aspects have been included as part of valorization

---

*Corresponding author. E-mail: fiorella.giacalone@unipg.it

© CAB International 2018. *Local Identities and Transnational Cults within Europe*
(eds F. Giacalone and K. Griffin)

and renewal projects, with the aim of capitalizing on them and the development of a territorial brand that promotes local resources, such as the environment, landscape, food and wine production, and religious aspects (Mariotti, 2013; Ranisio and Borriello, 2014). This also occurs in a critical sense, taking into account the political and institutional dimensions (Palumbo, 2003).

The political dimension and local identity are particularly intertwined with the concept of pilgrimage, as they imprint the identity of a territory, and qualify and define it, not only by supporting and directing the development of the local economy and tourism, but also through encouraging community and aggregative social practices.

In recent decades, reflections on religious tourism, in particular in English (after the study by Turner and Turner in 1978), have developed following a multidisciplinary approach, involving anthropology, geography, sociology and history, with interesting theoretical developments. It must be said, however, that scant attention has been paid to studies in French and Italian, as noted by Albera (Albera and Blanchard, 2015).

It appears, for some authors, that pilgrimage has become a form of criticism of the urban and occupational lifestyle, interpreted as time dedicated to travel, naturalistic aspects and the personalization of faith. The debate, in recent decades, has centred on the ambiguous and polyvalent nexus between pilgrimage and religious tourism, often combining the two aspects, or observing the prevalence of touristic aspects over the religious. Pilgrimage has become a plural and polysemic context, in which social and private practices, public and political discourse and marketing, and consumer dynamics are brought together, involving multiple and contradictory viewpoints, such as ethnicity, local identity, transnational dynamics and inter-religious relations (Albera and Blanchard, 2015, pp. 7–8).

MacCannell (1973) sees travel for tourism as a kind of pilgrimage, a search for an authentic existence; through a semiotic reading he reflects on the relationship between social imagination, intellectual construction and the desire for authenticity. Tourism, from his perspective, is a type of secular religion based on the search for the self, beyond the context of the everyday. It has a ritualistic dimension, moving towards another place, associated with the multiform productions of the social imaginary. In this sense he considers tourism to be a 'search for authenticity', beyond the heavily polluted urban context, in a perspective of self-realization. Simonicca, who has often addressed the approach of MacCannell in his works, and appears to be in agreement, believes that the search for motivation and direction is at the core of tourism-related behaviour, almost as if this could indicate different forms of moral integration, in contrast with the alienation of urban life: tourism produces objects, and transforms them to the extent that they become inauthentic, representing an ethnography of modernity (Simonicca, 2011, pp. 72–74). While the theoretical perspectives offered by MacCannell are stimulating, in particular the aspects critical of contemporary society, it would be misleading to think of tourism as a religion, above all because of the different motivations and practices associated with the two activities. Religion can be modified, transformed into a ritual and communicative dimension, in hierarchical or genre forms, and even secularized, but the search for authenticity seems more influenced by urban life than by religion. Religion involves worship, rituals, ceremonies and mediators of the sacred; the expressive search for subjectivity in certain forms of mysticism, which is sometimes considered heretical or criticized by religious institutions. Those who undertake a pilgrimage cannot be an 'observer' in the sense of adherence to institutional and theological forms, and while they can express this path in subjective and personalized forms, they are seeking a sacred dimension, not authenticity. Nevertheless, it is possible to consider the phenomenon as a journey to another place, where this other place offers the opportunity to reach a higher level of consciousness than the context of origin.

Cohen (1992) describes tourism as an experience, in terms of the relationship between the subject and otherness, between the centre and elsewhere, and between the authentic and false, in relation to the awareness of the traveller. In this sense, there are different levels of satisfaction or dissatisfaction with regard to the place of arrival, which are associated with different levels of awareness. He differentiates those heading to a religious centre from those who travel for art tourism, even though religious sanctuaries are often also museums, and the two roles appear to have become blurred, to the extent that the tourist sees the religious sites from a historical-artistic point of view. Eade and Sallnow consider it essential to define the specificity of individual pilgrimages and the diverse historical perspectives that are contextual to the sites, and maintain that these sites have become the subject of diverse interests, an 'arena of competitive discourse' between the various social actors, be they civic, religious or economic authorities (1991, pp. 5). Gastrell and Reid (2002), Albera and Eade (2015), and Albera and Blanchard (2015) affirm that economic processes are part of the same socio-cultural space, and that the differences depend on perceptions and expectations at the local level; therefore, the theoretical perspective cannot be generalized without taking the ethnographic aspect into account.

It appears that the debate tends to identify pilgrims with tourists, although with some degree of nuance, seeing in the former the dimension of the consumption of the sacred, a form of consumption understood in relation to both the place of worship and visits to cities of art. Collins-Kreiner has underlined the difference between the perspective of the religious organization, which also sees the pilgrim as a tourist-consumer, and the contrasting point of view of the traveller; in her view, religious motivation should be distinguished from its economic-tourist counterpart (2010).

One of the cardinal concepts is that of *heritage*, a concept that seeks to combine the different expressions of the traditions associated with a site, in its overall dimension, blending together nature and culture, landscape and works of art, forms of human activity and respect for the environment. In this sense, modernity does not develop based on new forms of industrialization, but the 'recovery' of crafts activities, historical traditions and landscape protection. The site and its history are identified as elements in commodification and economic and tourism activities. In this new role, tourism is strongly linked to *terroir*, in terms of the natural environment, food and wine production, and the historical and artistic dimension. In this new meaning, tourism is directly tied to sites, and the repository of significance associated with the site, its saint. The historical context serves tourism, and tourism takes on religious, artistic, naturalistic and ecological aspects.

At least four viewpoints are involved in the 'city-sanctuary system': that of the institutions and their proposal for the 're-evangelization' of Catholics, who today have a very superficial popular knowledge of Christianity; that of economic organizations that target the pilgrim-tourist as a supporter of local businesses (restaurants, hotels and shops); that of local authorities, who aim to promote a form of tourism that also involves locations associated with art, and the promotion of local food and wine; and, finally, that of the pilgrims, who are mainly motivated by the religious element, but are inevitably immersed in a consumer mechanism related to the experience of the journey itself. In the dimension of popular religiosity, such travellers are not only pilgrims hoping for answers to their problems, but also consumers of the sacred and souvenirs, such as in the case of Lourdes (Reader, 2014).

It appears that religious organizations, while aware that pilgrims are 'consumers' of the sacred, even in the economic sense, concentrate on the task of religious education, with regard to the masses of pilgrims and travellers, who are increasingly secularized, and appear more attracted by a personal dimension than the official dimension the institutions promote and support.

The development of religious/environmental/cultural tourism is a recent development, the result of the rediscovery of nature trails and renewed attention to the landscape, the value of which is finally being recognized, as is the risk caused by urban sprawl. This is a new postmodern consciousness, which was quite alien to pilgrims until a few decades ago. In the past, they travelled to 'touch the sacred', and paid little or no attention to the landscape. Even in sanctuaries located in mountainous and scenic areas this aspect was somewhat taken for granted, and not perceived as having added value because the value was attributed to the Virgin Mary or patron saint.

In religious tourism, the sacred seems less present, at the expense of the cultural and secular, and if the tourist has an emotional experience it will be when they encounter a work of art or a panoramic view. The secular tourist sees art and nature as exceptional, while the pilgrim associates the exceptional with the sacred.

In highlighting specific local features, they are presented as 'special' and 'unique' icons, and equated with the sanctity of the site and the saint, as if they were signs of the extended power of the saint. In this syncretism, food and wine, the landscape and places of worship are combined as part of the exceptional local features that establish the identity of the location; therefore, generating its own *brand* can mean increasing the power of the site, in terms of both the local economy and religious tourism.

It is interesting to observe how new forms of religious tourism associate works of art with holy sites, and offer nature trails associated with the saints. This is the case of the Way of St Francis in Assisi. Since 1994 the Way of St Francis has been recognized by the Council of Europe as a cultural route, much like the *Camino de Compostella*. In this sense, the Region of Umbria promotes the paths of St Francis, the saint known throughout the world, in order to encourage visitors to travel to certain landscapes and cultural sites in Umbria. The association with the best-known Italian saint and his hymns to nature (Sister Moon, Brother Sun) is clear. While this has helped make the Way of St Francis a route of naturalistic pilgrimage, Assisi is also associated with Giotto, culture and landscape.

Certainly, compared to the past, more attention is paid to the political and economic context, in which various interests and diverse contemporary perspectives collide: the use of the media, aspects of tourism related to the journey, the dynamics of commercialization, the requirements of local identity and the widespread phenomenon of secularization. These are certainly concepts worthy of consideration, as they appear to have moved the focus of pilgrimage from a purely religious experience to an art tourism experience, which disregards a particularly widespread permanent 'sacred need', even in Catholic Europe.

The Structure of the Book

This volume collects together a selection of papers from the XXVIII Colloque Eurethno du Conseil d'Europe, the European network of Francophone anthropologists, which was held in Perugia and Assisi from 12–14 September 2014, with the title 'Le tourisme religieux en Europe'. The aim is to offer an overview, albeit partial, of the different forms taken on by pilgrimage and religious tourism today, as a means to interpret the complexity of the religious practices that bring together institutional dynamics, votive practices, and migration and intercultural dimensions in differentiated contexts. The organization of the book serves to weave a common thread between practices that are traditional, to various extents, in terms of local and transnational dimensions, and offer a variety of interpretive keys to this complex phenomenon, from religious, historical, political and touristic perspectives, bringing together the work of academics from many geographical areas.

Blending theoretical constructs with solid investigative research, the first part of the book: 'From Local to International, the Development of Devotion', provides a selection of chapters that interrogate the development of devotional practices and cults. While the cases are essentially local in nature, they clearly illustrate the origins and evolution of ritualistic practices, presenting a range of perspectives on this human activity, some being quite ancient, others being relatively new in origin. Chapter 1, by Giacalone and Griffin contextualizes the book with a reflection on pilgrimage studies and their evolution in European literature. Following this, the chapter presents an overview of the book, outlining the overall structure and detailing the contributions of the various authors.

Chapter 2 by Spitilli analyses the cult of the Madonna del Alno di Canzano, based in a rural town in the province of Teramo, Abruzzo (Italy). The mediators of this supernatural encounter were oxen, joined in the following days by a horse, which knelt in the presence of the Virgin. The history of this local cult reveals the complexity of the symbolic procedures and social strategies that govern the progressive definition of devotional practices, translating into ritual language the succession of political struggles and power relations between the urban elites, the local church and the rural population, the continuity between liturgical and folk rituals, and the semantic logic that organizes the universe.

The objective of religious tourism involves not only sites associated with faith, but also visits to historical and cultural sites, environments and landscapes. The contribution by Paola de Salvo (Chapter 3) reflects on new forms of religious tourism, at both the theoretical and scientific levels, in examining the Way of St Francis, which, through the involvement of political and religious authorities, was awarded the 'pilgrim's licence'. In 2011 a new entrepreneurial initiative was created, the 'Umbria and Francesco's Ways' consortium, co-financed by the Region of Umbria (Italy). It consists of enterprises offering hospitality and dining services located along the entire route, whose activity is dedicated exclusively to the enhancement, promotion and marketing of the Way of St Francis. The pilgrim is awarded a certificate at the end of the official route: the *Testimonium Viae Francisci*. This is a religious travel document that accompanies each pilgrim along the path, and attests to their identity and intentions.

In Chapter 4, Bellio analyses how Calabria has witnessed an interesting phenomenon – the construction of new places of worship associated with forms of fortune telling that characterize the contemporary religious landscape. Pilgrimage and religious tourism are issues that can be investigated in light of the transformations that characterize the religious practices of southern Italy, where there are significant examples of the popularity of mystical figures leading to a process involving hospitality facilities being constructed to accommodate the thousands of faithful who characterize the perimeter of action.

In Chapter 5, Fournier analyses a number of local pilgrimages in Provence (France), where excesses and rivalry among the parishioners were evident, to the extent of violent combat, as they fought for the honour of serving the saint. The ritual battles have now become an instrument of tourism development, with religious and civil authorities finding ways to make use of this historical and ritualistic heritage.

Part 2, containing Chapters 6–11, presents an eclectic set of papers discussing various aspects of 'Popular Pilgrimage Development'. In Chapter 6, Parbuono investigates the role played in the Chinese community by the Temple of the Buddhist Association of the Chinese community in Prato, which hosts a range of important festivals and welcomes pilgrims from other cities. This is both a social meeting place, and a place of 'complementarity cultural worship' with regard to the religious practices that the Chinese officiate during their journey to the monasteries in their country of origin.

The conflict between institutions and popular practices emerges in the cult of Saint Sarah in Saintes Maries de la Mer, in the Camargue (France), where the gypsy saint, who is not officially recognized by the Catholic Church, is the subject of strong devotion. This is particularly true during her feast, in June, which also serves

as a gathering for various Roma communities. In this case, the religious tourism attracts tourist-photographers, who search for a gypsy folklore dimension along the streets of the French city. The cult of Sarah, as described by Gaëlla Loiseau in Chapter 7, has also been exported by tourist-pilgrims to Brazil, and has become an element of Umbanda rituals, as a black saint of the marginalized.

Cruzzolin (Chapter 8) reflects on the worship of the Señor de los Milagros by Peruvian immigrants in Italy, and the related pilgrimages held in Perugia and Rome. His contribution is intended to illustrate the way in which the members of a specific diaspora, in this case the Peruvians, have been able to propose a counter-hegemonic discourse that redefines the boundary between visibility and invisibility in Italian society, giving rise to a discussion on the relationship between Catholicism and migration. Devotional images are the means by which Catholic Peruvian migrants can regain a sense of narrative, and the ability to articulate and relate their own experiences, thus, enabling a community dimension at the moment when a symbolic centre is established (represented by a venerated painting).

In Chapter 9, Guillaume writes about the cult of Saint Solvang, which is celebrated by Portuguese immigrants in France on Pentecost Monday. This festival has become a really important element of life for the Portuguese community, through which they display community membership via rituals and dance on French soil.

Lamothe, in Chapter 10 explores how travelling through Landes (France) offers a surprising connection between religion and sport. This manifests itself in road signs indicating the 'Chapel of Our Lady of Rugby' at Larrivière-Saint-Savin, the 'Chapel of Our Lady of the *Course Landaise*' in Bascons or the 'Chapel of Our Lady of the Cyclists' at Labastide-d'Armagnac. These chapels constitute authentic places of worship, dating from the mid-twentieth century, which represent a two-fold tribute to sports and athletes. They attract numerous visitors, in particular during the pilgrimage on Whit Monday, during which a tribute to departed athletes is held. The study attempts to understand what has enabled or favoured the creation of this unique syncretism, which allows the shirts of rugby players and cyclists to be placed together with statues of the Blessed Virgin in religious shrines rich in sporting memory.

In Chapter 11, Julliard brings to light the transnational nature of the cult of St Nicholas of Bari (Italy), which attracts Catholic and Orthodox pilgrims (Italians and Slavs), due to the particular appeal of the saint, a native of Myra. The analysis highlights the perspective of a French 'foreign traveller' who analyses the cult through an external ethnographic vision of local dynamics.

The third element of the book, Part 3, provides a focus on Saint Rita. The worship of St Rita of Cascia, one of the most widespread Catholic icons of the twentieth century, extends not only across Europe and Latin America, but also into the Middle East (such as in Lebanon). Three chapters are presented that deal with various aspects of this saint's worship. The first of these contributions dealing with St Rita, by Inga Kuzma (Chapter 12), emphasizes the emergence of the cult of the saint in Poland, in Krakow in particular, where the post-communist era has seen the development, especially in Catholic areas, of new processional routes associated with transnational cults. In the second chapter, her veneration is interpreted with reference to local perspectives: the relationship between the saint and the town of Cascia, with which she is identified. Giacalone in Chapter 13 continues with an analysis of the pilgrimage to Roccaporena, with a reflection on the boundaries between pilgrimage and tourism. The analysis seeks to investigate the meaning of the relationship between pilgrims, the saint and local identity. The third offering by Kiely (Chapter 14) explores the evolution and anatomy of devotional practice among a predominantly female congregation, who attend a weekly novena mass in Dublin, Ireland, to seek favours and support from a saint who is simultaneously a figure from medieval Italy and an ordinary woman like them, who understands their ongoing practical worries.

Chapter 15 by Griffin and Giacalone presents some concluding comments, reflecting on the various challenges provided by the chapter authors, and drawing together some final thoughts. This is followed by Discussion Questions for each chapter. These are provided to foster discussion and reflection on the individual chapters, and encourage readers to engage with further study and investigation.

Note

1 Liam Boyle provides English translation for the work of Fiorella Giacalone.

References

Albera, D. and Blanchard, M. (eds) (2015) *Pellegrini del nuovo millennio. Aspetti economici e politici delle mobilità religiose*. Mesogea, Messina, Italy.

Albera, D. and Eade, J. (eds) (2015) *International Perspective on Pilgrimage Research: Itineraries, Gaps and Obstacles*. Routledge, London, New York.

Apolito, P. (1990) *Dice che hanno visto la Madonna. Un caso di apparizione in Campania*. Il Mulino, Bologna, Italy.

Apolito, P. (1990, 2002) *Internet e la Madonna. Sul visionario religioso in Rete*. Feltrinelli, Milan.

Buttitta, I. (2002) *La memoria lunga. Simboli e riti della religiosità tradizionale*. Meltemi, Rome.

Cohen, E. (1992) Pilgrimage and tourism: convergence and divergence. In: Morinis, A. (ed.) *Sacred Journeys: The Anthropology of Pilgrimage*. Greenwood Press, Westport, Connecticut, and London, pp. 47–61.

Collins-Kreiner, N. (2010) The geography of pilgrimage and tourism: Transformations and implications for applied geography. *Applied Geography* 30, 153–164.

Eade, J. and Sallnow, M.J. (eds) (1991) *Contesting the Sacred: The Anthropology of Christian Pilgrimage*. Routledge, London.

Gallini, C. (1998) *Il miracolo e la sua prova: un etnologo a Lourdes*. Liguori, Napoli, Italy.

Gatrell, J.D. and Reid, N. (2002) The cultural politics of local economic development: the case of Toledo jeep. *Tijdschrift voor Economische en Sociale Geografie* 93(4), 397–411.

Lombardi Satriani, L.M. (ed.) (2000) *Santità e tradizione. Itinerari antropologico-religiosi in Campania.* Meltemi, Rome.

MacCannell, D. (1973) Staged authenticity: arrangements of social space in tourist settings. *American Journal of Sociology* 79(III) 589–603.

Mariotti, L. (2013) La Convenzione sul patrimonio intangibile e I suoi criteri tra valorizzazione, tutela e pprotezione. *Voci* X, 88–97.

Palumbo, B. (2003) *L'Unesco e il campanile.* Meltemi, Rome.

Ranisio, G. and Borriello, D. (eds) (2014) *Linguaggi della devozione. Forme espressive del patrimonio sacro.* Edizionidipagina, Bari, Italy.

Reader, I. (2014) *Pilgrimage in the Marketplace.* Routledge, London, New York.

Simonicca, A. (2011) Turismo e autenticità riconosciuta. In: Nocifera, E., De Salvo, P. and Calzati, V. (eds) *Territori lenti e turismo di qualità. Prospettive innovative per lo sviluppo di un turismo sostenibile.* Franco Angeli, Milan, Italy.

Turner, V. and Turner, E. (1978) *Image and Pilgrimage in Christian Culture. Anthropological Perspective.* Columbia University Press, New York.

UNWTO (2011) *Religious Tourism in Asia and the Pacific.* UNWTO, Madrid, Spain.

2 Continuity from Local Cult to 'Accepted' Ritual

Gianfranco Spitilli*

La Sapienza University of Rome, Rome, Italy

Introduction[1]

This chapter explores a rural cult in central Italy through an interpretation inspired by European religious ethnology and the anthropology of Christianity. The field research, carried out in the two-year period of 2014–15 and still in progress, is sustained by the meticulous exploration of historic civil, religious and family archives – as if carrying out consultation with ethnographic interlocutors. The close historical examination opens the spectrum of the ethnological investigation to an interpretation stratified by the present-day context of the research topic revealing otherwise invisible aspects of current behaviour and practice.

According to the legend on the founding of the church of the Madonna of Alno in Canzano, a rural village in the province of Teramo in Abruzzo, the Madonna appeared upon a white poplar tree to a farmer named Floro on 18 May 1480. Non-human intermediaries to this supernatural encounter were oxen, and in the following days a horse, kneeling in the presence of the Virgin. A herbal substance, to which miraculous powers are attributed, gushed from the tree. This gave origin to the tradition of pilgrimage in the form of a duplicate procession that brings the faithful worshippers and the statue of the Madonna from an urban church to a rural one built on the site of the apparition.

In the perspective of analysis initiated by Robert Hertz, the history of this local cult reveals the complexity of symbolic procedures and social strategies that preside over the progressive definition of devotional practices, translating into ritual language the succession of political struggles and relations of power between the urban elites, the local church and the farming population as well as the continuity between liturgic and folk rites, the semantic logic that organizes the universe.

The Tree of Perdono

On 3 August 1849, Francesco Taraschi the Mayor of Canzano and President of the local Charity Commission received a plea for help. A certain Floro di Giovanni, a farmer, declared himself to be in a serious state of poverty and requiring economical support in order to face his needs and those of his immediate family. The request is in written form and the handwriting is awkward and strained, perhaps that of an of an old parish priest who drew it up on the farmer's behalf.

In the opening, Floro presents himself 'humbly', qualifying himself as a descendant of

*E-mail: gianfrancospitilli@gmail.com

'an old and honourable family of farmers and certain traditions, that in 1480 another Floro while working with his oxen was called upon by an angelic voice and chosen to carry out a celestial order'.[2]

This communication, discovered in the course of research at the State Archive of Teramo opens up an unexpected possibility of observation on the ancestry of farmers, which the source materials link to the origins of the cult of the Madonna of Alno in Canzano, a rural town situated above a hill ridge between the valleys of the Tordino and Vomano rivers in northern Abruzzo. Halfway through the nineteenth century, at a distance of almost 400 years from the apparition of the Virgin among the branches of a tree, as narrated by written text and oral tradition, the family descendants of the direct witness to the event still live in the countryside surrounding the residential area in the same place as the scene of the miraculous epiphany: the contrada called Perdono (Forgiveness).

Floro di Giovanni was almost 21 years old at the time. He lived in a 'small hovel together with his elderly mother and a sister of tender age', working a 'small piece of adjoining land' necessary for survival.[3] The same plot of land cultivated by his forebear Tore di Flore di Giovanni Angelo, as found in the Land Register of 1619, inherited in uninterrupted sequence by a Floro and a Giovanni (Palma, 1832)[4]: a vineyard, olive grove and a plot of land with trees located in Colle Vitto, in the area of Perdono, ancient property of the Cappella di S. Giacomo.[5]

A brief genealogical examination introduces the perspective of investigation followed in the present work: it tries to tightly combine the ethnographic exploration of the present-day devotion and the historical reconstruction of the cult of the Madonna of Alno, on the basis of the applied methodological model of Robert Hertz for the study of San Besso, the first monographic research in the field dedicated to a Christian rite and cult (Hertz, 1994; Charuty, 1995; Isnart, 2008, 2014). For this purpose it is necessary to try and give importance to the location of diverse centres of worship distributed throughout the territory and the forms assumed by the religious practices in a contemporary context, trying to outline the correspondence to hagiographic legend, the social structures and the tensions that they have undergone over the course of centuries (Charuty, 1995).

The contrada of Perdono is a grouping of a few sparse homes in a rural area downhill from the town of Canzano, towards the Vomano River. The small church dedicated to the Madonna was rebuilt more than once after landslide disasters and is situated in the vicinity of the first apparition, where it was originally built in all probability during the sixteenth century (Di Nicola, 1979). Some tens of metres away there are two chapels of similar workmanship, called cunette, erected in correspondence to the points that the aetiological narration designates as the scene of the second and third apparition.

The present-day Canzanesi, in particular those that reside in Perdono, do not retain a direct recollection of the family descending from Floro di Giovanni; they do however have a precise awareness of the house in which Floro lived when he had the prominent role in the Marian vision while working in the nearby fields. Italo Marsilii has always lived in the contrada, like his ancestors; he keeps an eye on the small church, he takes care of the vegetation, removing underbrush or planting new trees. He organizes celebrations in his role as a member of the Deputazione di Maria SS. dell'Alno (Deputation of Saint Mary of Alno), in which he has taken part many times as had his family and relatives over the past century. 'Floro lived here' recounts Italo, 'then our grandparents bought that house, our cousins lived in that house' (I. Marsilii, 2015).

Italo Marsilii doesn't know the identity of the previous owner and hypothesizes that the family of Floro has been extinct for centuries. Memories find more precision however in the deeds. A purchase agreement was made in 1918 between Giovanni di Floro and the grandfather Domenicantonio Marsilii: a two-room house with an opposing stall and barnyard adjacent to the place of the apparition.[6] But the change of ownership didn't merely regard the material property and imply *de facto* the transfer of specific roles and functions: the new lineage of the Marsilii took over the supervision of the space sacralized by the legendary topography assisted by the special attention that all of the inhabitants of Canzano, especially those who grew up in the countryside, reserve to this day for the area of Perdono. A safeguard under farmer's pertinence uninterrupted for 500 years, which has allowed us to accomplish the reweaving of Floro's genealogical fabric, not limiting his figure to a purely mythical existence and giving us the concrete image of a family lineage aware of their prerogative sanctioned by the miraculous events of 1480. Therefore it is not an indefinite past (Albert-Llorca, 1994) but a historically determined existence that has been linked to a narrative scenario, on the basis of recurrent models that have transformed them into legendary personifications (Donà, 2015).

In the month of May the rural church is attended daily, enlivened by daily functions celebrated by the parish priest of Saint Mary of Alno and by the participation of numerous devotees busy with the recitation of the rosary and the prayers dedicated locally to the Virgin.

The worshippers say mass for the defunct and stand with others facing an impressive wooden altar in front of a large painting depicting the miracle of the apparition: the scene represents Floro as an elderly farmer with white hair and beard genuflecting with his oxen in front of the Virgin set between the leafy branches of a magisterial tree among the hills of the contrada.

The arboreal element places the Canzanese legend in relation to a specific narrative complex – that of the appearance of Madonnas or of Marian effigies on trees – interwoven with other mythical themes in the hagiographic story and stated in numerous devotional forms both in a local setting and that of the more extensive regional territory (Salvatore, 2002; Gasparroni, 2011). White poplar or alder, according to the ambivalent captions shown on the historical documents and in the prevalent appellation practice (alvano, albano, albero, alno)[7] are the legendary plants that unequivocally connote the devotional geography, thus designating Perdono as the location of the Marian event. In addition, an added thaumaturgic qualification: a correspondence that the ritual language translates in the analogical relation between the mythical tree and the altar and in the presence, just a few metres away, of the very tree from which gushed a curative substance right up until after the Second World War.

The sphere of activity of the miraculous balsam must have been quite wide, if we abide by what is reported in 1786 in a double report from the Parish Priest Francesco Antonio Taraschi and of the Mayor Vincenzo Santarelli, which describes the cure of a young blind, mute and 'rigid'[8] girl originating from Fano a Corno located in the Gran Sasso mountain area.[9] The account

provides details of the kinds of action by an elderly lady and 'devoted woman' named Anastasia, resident in the contrada and 'custodian of the church' who had the task of collecting the 'rather odoriferous liquid' and sprinkling it on the bodies of pilgrims. According to Taraschi, the emanation of the substance involved different trees, the oil was collected in 'vessels for devotion' and 'if they annointed people's illness', differently for Santarelli, 'they originated from another *alno* which grew majestically in the same place as the apparition of the first tree'. This coinciding *de facto* with the legendary plant, a permanent plant *substitute* that presentificates *in loco* the Virgin of the Canzanesi by means of the aromatic essence and its effects, and subject therefore to the ritual manipulation by the cult (Albert-Llorca, 1994; Albert *et al.*, 2013; Robin Azevedo, 2013).

But the assimilation between the resinous tree of Perdono and the particular local entity called the Madonna of Alno seems to lead further, reopening the examination of the identity of the plant imparted by the oral account just as with the ecclesiastic and civil documents of administrative nature or literary and historical production. Which arboreal species in fact does it regard? And what relation can be established between the Virgin and the plant species of the Canzanese cult?

Rita Salvatore, in agreement with what seems to emerge from the majority of sources, identifies the location of the mariophany with the *Populus alba*, or white poplar, adducing motivations of linguistic, iconographic and botanical order (Salvatore, 2002). The line of investigation seems productive, but requires integration of symbolic and ritual nature. Let us try to follow a further interpretive step by linking together the elements that have emerged thus far.

The hagiography of the Madonna of Alno has shown us the identity of a mythical intermediary called Floro, a name that seldom appears in the registers and coincides in exclusive terms with a legendary lineage placed under the custody of the epiphanic scenario. In this place, dominated by nature that is at once wild and domesticated and known for centuries as Perdono, the flora has assumed a wide range of cultural significance as a result of the Marian apparition becoming the bearer of miraculous healing by means of the oleaginous secretions from the trunk of a tree. The mythical-ritual tree, identified by the white poplar still widespread in the area, appears in the oldest representation of the miracle, that of the painted bas relief in the care of the Sanctuary of Canzano, which depicts the Virgin of Alno accommodated between the tree's leafy branches, encircled by four angels in flight: an image that closely recalls the iconography of the tree of life of terrestrial Paradise.

The olfactory characterization of the miraculous tree and its copious resinous component recall the Edenic flora, which medieval sources describe as richly aromatic, or the odorous resin reported in the vicinity of the Garden (Albert, 2006). In the analysis of the second and third chapter of *Genesis* Albert shows the interdependence that subsists between the two mysterious trees of Eden in the Christian story of salvation, the tree of life and that of knowledge of good and bad, or of sin. The Hebrew exegesis and the medieval imagination hesitate in the identification of the second one, combined in the sources with diverse plant species such as the grapevine, grain, date palm, banana; a widespread opinion converges to the contrary towards the recognition of the first in the balsam tree of Judea, a resinous plant also called the poplar of Galaad, or *Populus candicans*, belonging to the same family of *Populus alba* of Canzano, the *Salicaceae*. Its 'fruit' identified *de facto* as the oil of mercy, was a substance containing fragrances and aromas endowed with therapeutic and miraculous virtues capable of stopping the decay of the body.

The connection between the two Edenic trees finds its basis in the legend of the invention of the Holy Cross referred to in the Gospel according to Nicodemo, reproposed in a more articulate version by Jacopo da Varagine in the *Legenda Aurea* (Saintyves, 1922; Albert, 2006). Albert identifies in this legendary elaboration the fusion of the two parallel aetiological traditions, which in one narrative unites Eden and Golgota, the curative properties of the fruit from the tree of life and the redemptive power of Christ's cross and baptism. The oil of benevolence in this way becomes an instrument of spiritual immortality for Christianity – and not corporeal like the fruit of the tree of life – rejoining it to the baptismal sacrament, bearer of an analogous promise of immortality and salvation following the sacrificial death of Christ on the Cross. In the liturgical practice of baptism the symbolic reasons are translated in the use of two holy oils, the oil of the catechumen and the holy chrism, a mixture of olive oil, and historically, the oil of the Balsam of Judea tree. In turn the tree of sin, basis and cause of the fall from terrestrial Paradise and the consequent *forgiveness* transformed by Redemption into the tree of life becomes the symbol of the cross in the person of the Virgin in her function as supreme mediator (De Montfort, 1712; Albert-Llorca, 1994, 2002; Albert, 2006).

We can reinterpret what happened in Canzano in the countryside of Perdono under a different light. Is it only about coincidence? This seems improbable. The hagiographic logic and ritual construction explored until now seem to be respondent to precise metaphoric coordinates that find justification inside the multiform and stratified Christian symbolic architecture.

The twentieth century signals the progressive decadence of the cult and its ceremonies, sanctioned by an event that seems to belong to a diabolic order: 'bad dogs', 'that bit' (I. Marsilii, 2015) were led to the miraculous poplar to anoint them with resinous oil and heal them from rabies (G. Stortone, 2014). From that time on 'the Madonna had finished making miracles, inasmuch as she was scorned' (B. Marsilii, 2015).

This is a process of inversion that singles out an animal category, that of the dog, accompanied by an ambivalent or more often negative connotation, frequently translated in the hagiography as demonic expression, concretization of the malignant spirit in the disorienting form of rabid dogs that bite (Profeta, 1993; Anti, 1998).

The tree of Perdono 'dried out', then dried up and was cut down.

Town and Countryside: A Dual Model?

The residential area of Canzano, at one time enclosed by a fortified wall, is positioned on a precipitous hill at an altitude of 448 m, 'about one third of a mile' from the site of the apparition (Palma, 1832), which happened towards the southwest, 'just beneath the castle' (Di Nicola, 1979). The architectonic configuration of Canzano is still today marked by the presence of refined buildings that define the main road in the direction of the central square, testimony to an asset that is social, political and economic, strongly hierarchicalized and a visible sign of its recent history and of that coeval to the foundation of the Marian cult (Di Nicola, 1979; Salvatore, 2002). Nearby, on the hill and the wide valleys, hamlets and rural contradas dot the territory with farmhouses that are isolated and gathered in circumscribed settlements where the farming families and their present-day heirs, in part, still live today.

If Perdono is assembled around the rural church, the historical nucleus of Canzano is characterized by its sanctuary, which arose in the sixteenth century in an outlying area called Piano del Castellano, absorbed in the past century by new construction that situated it inside recent urbanization. According to what is reported in the aetiological narration, the perimeter of the building was outlined by a tamed horse, mounted by Floro di Giovanni, which became docile by Marian intervention.

We shall examine therefore at this point the overall contents of the legend of the foundation of the cult of Madonna of Alno and its urban and rural sanctuaries, hence how it was transmitted by means of a multiplicity of oral and written sources of cultured and popular origin, in a dialectical process of circularity and continuity determined, even among the strongest tensions, 'in the circle of "shared culture"' (Schmitt, 2000).[10]

On 18 May 1480 at about 12 noon 'a bumpkin named *Floro di Giovanni*, living in the immediate surroundings of Canzano', saw oxen on their knees while he was trying to plough the soil. Raising his glance he noticed a 'majestic Lady' prostrate on a white poplar tree. Then he heard her say: 'I am the Queen of Heaven: go to Canzano and tell the people that it is my wish that they build a Church in my honour in *Piano del Castellano*'. Floro immediately obeyed and ran to Canzano, 'but far from being believed' was derided and offended, and he returned sadly to work. The following day at the same time, the Virgin appeared on the same piece of soil; having listened to Floro's story about what happened she disappeared without speaking. On 20 May the Madonna appeared on the ground for the third time and obliged the farmer to return to

the town and mount, until he was believed, an 'untamed' horse belonging to Falamesca de Montibus, a horse so ferocious that it was fed through a hatch-door; therefore, to let the horse guide Floro to the designation of the site in which She intended to be honoured. Floro went once again to Canzano reporting what the Virgin had already communicated to him; overcoming the resistance of the owner and the hostility of the local people, he approached the horse, which suddenly became docile and let him ride it, being conducted to Piano del Castellano, where the horse 'turned three times around an area, finally kneeling, bending its head to the ground' to the amazement and joy of the crowd that followed it. Brought back to the stable by Floro, the horse became untamed as before (Palma, 1832).

The narrative structure of the foundational legend interweaves a multiplicity of hagiographic themes. Non-human intermediaries in the supernatural encounter were the plough oxen, on their knees to reveal to Floro the presence of the Virgin and as such, discoverers, inventors of the Marian figure in accordance with the hagiographic model exceptionally widespread in all of the central Italian area both in the legendary configuration and to a lesser extent in the ritual sphere (Di Nola, 1976; Donà, 2003; Spitilli, 2011). The mariophany is fulfilled therefore by the intercession of an animal species, that of the bovine, subject of a profound and centuries-old process of Christianization that attributes to bulls, oxen, cows and calves operative functions and metaphoric qualities, therefore assimilating them to 'good Christians' and even to 'saints' (Anti, 1998; Spitilli, 2012). In a story reported by Fabre referring to the area of the Pyrenees, L'arbre du bœuf, we find an even more intimate connection between the 'discoverer' of the Virgin and the tree: an ox endowed with nutritive properties by means of its own blood becomes wild and elusive in order not to be felled, in the end dying of old age asks to be buried by the youth who fed it – a male Cinderella – near his house. On the site of the burial-ground a miraculous tree is born of its carcass and produces different fruit for every season and finally, all the fruit of Creation (1993).

The revelatory path of Floro conjoins on the third day with a further non-human intermediary, the horse belonging to the soldier

Falamesca,[11] which introduces in turn a mythical theme of the guiding animal and of animal-like constitution (Donà, 2003, 2008). The horse is referred to at times as untamed, wild, ferocious, untouchable, skittish, wicked, arrogant, proud, tremendous, furious; Davide Di Basilio and Renato De Nigris, indicating the state of alteration, define it as 'out of phase' and 'overcome with madness' (2014). All this contributes to the idea that this is a beast with an aberrant personality and of completely adulterated behaviour: a *wild* beast, possessed by a negative or demonic agent.[12]

The sources describe an especially attractive white coloured animal (Palma, 1832; Di Nicola, 1979). The strict relation between untameability, beauty and the 'pure white coat', understood according to different contexts as a sign of the diabolic or of regality, good tidings, peace (Centini, 1990; Sensi, 2014; Lombardi Satriani and Meligrana, 1996), contributes in highlighting the ambivalence of the horse – white or pale – in terms of demonic vehicle or bearer of good will, representative of antithetical and contradictory forces linked to sorcery, oppressive dreamlike representations, the chthonic dimension, or intermediary of charismatic revelations, dreams and visions (Sauzeau and Sauzeau, 1995; Praneuf, 2001; Bridier, 2002; Wagner, 2005).

The intervention by Floro of Marian intercession caused an immediate inversion: the animal became tame, timid and docile, only to return just as quickly to its original state of untameability at the end of the foundational path. The lexicon of the myth and its local declensions suggest to us that from the moment of contact between Floro and the horse, the Virgin assumed total control of the animal by means of the farmer, directing him in the preselected places. The semantic unity formed in this way makes Floro di Giovanni into a being inhabited by supernatural power that acts on its own by means of putting him into a state similar to that of a *trance*.

From a topographic point of view, the legend delineates the places of worship and their localization in the territory (Hertz, 1994). Variations on the foundational story tell us that the horse mounted by Floro traced the perimeter of the future sanctuary kneeling at every corner (D. Di Basilio; A. Mascella; M. Felpa, 2014),[13] or that it genuflected at the point where the main altar was constructed making three rounds to define the area of the edifice (Palma, 1832). After this it returned to the stable, or differently, steered to the site of the apparition, where it found the oxen 'bowing down and genuflecting' under the tree which 'cast splendor'[14]; according to some witnesses the horse went, on the contrary, first to Perdono and then to Piano del Castellano, tracing the perimeters of both churches (G. Stortone, 2014).

The order of execution of these founding actions is not secondary, because it contributes contemporaneously to the hierarchy of the sanctuaries. Nevertheless, it is not possible to tend to one hypothesis or the other. That which appears evident on first analysis is the emergence of a dual model of the cult based on a polarization of the domains, of the ritual configuration between the two churches and the substitute figures associated with them – the simulacrum of the Virgin and the tree of Perdono (Albert *et al.*, 2013), whose interdependence is further ratified by a prodigious dual event narrated in the same report by Parish Priest Taraschi and Mayor Santarelli of 1786. The document does not limit itself to precisely designating Perdono as the elective place of the requests for grace and healing, but contextually associates the origin of the thaumaturgic secretions from the tree and a supernatural auditory event verified inside the sanctuary in an epoch shortly following the apparition and the completion of the church: for 5 or 6 days one could hear 'the organ playing by itself to the amazement of those entering to make prayer' causing uncontainable emotion among the devotees; 'at the same time', at the rural contrada, 'the odoriferous resinous oil' used for miraculous cures started gushing from the tree for the first time.[15]

The countryside and the town, the ox and the horse, the farmer and the soldier, the healings and the audio-visual vivacities are the terms of a legendary subject constructed on the axis of differential identification and on the definition of their points and transactions of conjunction. If Floro with his oxen represents the mobile element of the story, originating from the rural world, the white horse is certainly an indicator of a higher social class, that of his noble and military landlord, incapable of taming an animal that symbolizes the *status*.

The union Floro–horse takes part in the shaping of a social, political and religious state of contraposition and of poverty through the institution of a new cult by direct initiative of a celestial being (Albert-Llorca, 2005), shared between the town and the surrounding rural area. It is the tangible sign of a renewed ability of the ecclesiastic structure to perceive the religious life of rural settlements and to take into consideration the needs and behaviour towards an acceptance to the official religion. A process of integration governed by its evolution in the ruling class, common to many legends of Marian foundation, which coagulate around the figure of the Madonna – as demonstrated by Adriano Prosperi – 'an encounter between the official proposal of the Church and the production of exceptional and miraculous events by the humble' (1984).

However, on more detailed examination the situation seems not immediately ascribable all inside of the Marian cult to a linear bipolarism between the sanctuary near the residential area and the one displaced in the countryside. In the religious history of Canzano, the devotion to the Madonna of Alno is affirmed beginning with a will to decentralization, originating from the need for full recognition of the community and its territory by means of the singularity of its sanctuaries, put into play by the legend and actions of the foundational miracle (Christian, 1981; Albert, 2005). The new centres of worship both arose outside of the town walls – *extra moenia* – accredited to miraculous forces and functionally distinct from the central authority of the ancient parish of Saint Blase, consecrated by the liturgy of the universal Church and incardinated at the heart of the town's historical centre (Albert-Llorca, 2005; Isnart, 2008).

With the emergence of the new cult and its 'non-indifferent'[16] income from census, offerings and bequests, the parish church of Saint Blase was subject to progressive marginalization over the course of centuries that brought it to a state of dilapidation (Di Nicola, 1979). The church of Saint Mary of Alno, rich in fine decor, altars and chapels on the contrary became the seat of the parish at the beginning of the nineteenth century.

The Return of the Virgin

Canzano, 18 May 2014. At approximately 11:30 a.m. the simulacrum of the Virgin exits the church of Saint Mary of Alno led by the parish priest. A crowd of worshippers are waiting outside to form the procession and to accompany the effigy along the tortuous path that will take her towards the rural church of Perdono.

If every image, including a statue, is in a certain sense an apparition, at Canzano it is precisely an apparition that translates into an image: an individual visionary experience transforms itself this way into a public representation, governed by specialists but accessible to the entire community. During the days that precede the celebration, some women from the town connected to relatives of members of the Deputazione take care of the preparation of the Madonna for the celebration: a mannequin made up of a body-frame of wood and fabric, painted head and hands, of the type of effigy to 'be dressed' (Silvestrini, 2003). This practice of ritual manipulation reaffirms the heavenly force of visible bodies and the efficacy of simulacra as an instrument of the concretization of divine beings in present times (Charuty, 2001) – an attitude inherited from the evolution of the post-tridentine Catholic Church, committed to the counter-reformist defence of the veneration of images protracted up to Vatican Counsel II and still greatly widespread in contemporary festive structure. The effigy of the Madonna of Alno used for the procession is in fact a perennial representation of the foundational miracle, periodically brought back to life by the faithful by means of the annual care that precedes the celebration, the cyclic renewal of clothing and the cloak in white silk, dotted with stars and motifs of fitomorphic inspiration. The Virgin is set on a base of a painted tree trunk, with branches and leaves in decorated iron from which hang small angels in flight; she seems to levitate in the air, suspended between the branches as on the day of the apparition. The farmer Floro appears in miniature at the feet of the Madonna, kneeling with the oxen.

In the past the dress and the cloak were made locally: there was an age-old school of embroidery in Canzano that was established in 1880 by the Sisters of Sant'Anna, taken on in turn by the Sisters of Divine Providence up until the beginning of the 1960s when the baton was passed to some women of the town. The close relationship between the conventual world and the host community of Canzano over the decades favoured the transfer of the prerogative of this repetitive, methodical and typically contemplative art to the female micro-society of the town, which was committed to the realization of the gown of the Virgin as well as the decorated fabric intended to adorn the altars of the church.

All of the Canzano embroiderers evoke the virtue of patience, which is an essential condition of the practice: you either have it or learn it through constant reiteration, point after point, in solitude or in company, implementing a formative process that in addition to manual training is accompanied by the definition of interior character and attitude, orienting it towards calmness and silent reflection. This is a way of constructing female Christian identity actuated by the practice of dressmaking and embroidery, which Marlène Albert-Llorca links to the long theological development of the doctrine of the Immaculate Conception, identifying with this the connections to the figure of the Virgin in the widespread representations of Maria in the act of weaving and embroidery for Jesus and the Temple, perhaps instructed by her mother Sant'Anna herself (Albert-Llorca, 1995a).

The interaction of the women with the effigy of the Madonna of Alno also calls for the arrangement of the long head of hair; on top of the hairstyle there is a crown and halo storied by luminous electric stars to complete the outfitting of the Virgin's head.

Embroidered with gold and silver thread, the gown is in fact a work of jewellery. Up until about 20 years ago, before the theft of the 'treasure' accumulated over centuries thanks to donations by the faithful, the entire garment was at one time covered in small chains, rings, pins, bracelets and necklaces in gold or coral. These, together with the cloak and protruding arms, in accordance with a manner of sacralization that associates all of Mediterranean Europe and characterizes these Marian portrayals as 'miraculous', contribute to constructing the identity of extraordinary beings by means of the proliferation of precious objects (Albert-Llorca and Ciambelli, 1995; Ciambelli, 2002).

Reconstituted following the renewed offerings by the devoted, the 'treasure' of the Madonna is now exhibited inside of a display case connected to a pedestal that supports the Virgin during the cortège and the days of its stay in the church of Perdono. The jewels, often donated as *ex voto* for grace received or to ask for special protection or benefit, correspond in accordance with a recurring logic to the entrustment of the prerogative of the personage and the existence of the individual and finite donor as well as the immutability and inalterability itself of the miraculous image straddling the territorial and celestial worlds able to assure contact between one and the other (Albert-Llorca and Ciambelli, 1995): 'the most precious thing belonging to a person' recalls Benito Marsilii, 'is generally left to the Madonna' (B. Marsilii, 2014).

The preciousness of the 'treasure' and its locally attributed high symbolic value define by analogy the essential qualities considered indispensable for one to take part in the Deputation, renewed every 3 years and assigned to safeguard the bequested jewels along with the correct management of the revenue for the organization of the celebrations and the maintenance of the places of worship. At the end of the mandate, explains Italo Marsilii, every member 'speaks to someone who is up to the job' (I. Marsilii, 2015): honest people are required, those who know the traditions of the Madonna well and are devoted to them; people who have attained trust from the community and carry out their entrusted task *as an honour* (B. Marsilii, 2015). They are the honest and respectable like Floro and his ancestry in a practice of constant reactualization of legendary moral prototype modelled on ritual learning for the male community of believers.

If the jewels of the Virgin in their entirety represent the wealth of the collectivity and the ideal unity of the community, the intimacy of donation underlines once again the exclusivity of a relationship that familiarizes non-human entities according to categories of interpersonal and domestic relations (Albert-Llorca, 1995b). Bride and queen, the Madonna of Alno is called 'Signora' by the devoted of the Deputation who touch her, undress and redress her: an individualized and personified Virgin, who chose to stay at Canzano, as highlighted by the seamstress Aurora Mascella (2014).

The ceremonial protocol put into act to stimulate an effective vitalization of the Marian simulacrum has prodigious antecedents remembered from sources, like the one of the appearance of a luminous star on the chest of the Madonna's image that lit up the church for about half an hour. This took place during the bishopric of Monsignor Visconti in 1614 (Palma, 1832).

A miraculous animation that renews the relationship between the effigy and its celestial prototype and highlights the multiform interaction with the devotees in accordance with a process in which the history of western Christianity is studded: changes in expression, movement of the eyes, face, and hands, perspiration, tears, luminous and dazzling irradiations are written in the articulated history of *living* images, especially numerous from the fourteenth to the seventeenth centuries but already widely attested in the Middle Ages (Faeta, 1997, 2000; Ricci, 1999; Sansterre, 2015).

The return of the Virgin of Alno is fully revealed in the processional disposition when the clothed statue complete with its festive trousseau leaves the sanctuary in which it rested during the preceding year to physically rejoin the place where she was seen to have appeared in 1480. An itinerary practised for centuries takes her out into the open countryside to the first bend, under the imposing mother-church, lifted on the hard flat surface of a wooden canopy; in front, the local band leads the way. Preceded by the parish priest with a multitude of worshippers following, the Madonna welcomed by festive bells reaches Perdono. For 2 days and 2 nights, the Virgin 'reappeared' in the rural contrada is watched over constantly: 'never leave the Madonna by herself' is the rule in force during the time of stay at the site of the first epiphany (B. Marsilii, 2015).

The turnout of pilgrims is today circumscribed to an essentially local setting coinciding for the most part with the community of Canzanese, either residents or those who return to town for the occasion. A need for rooted reunion, decodified by means of the analysis up to now, is anchored to a subplot of otherwise indecipherable conformities of the modern-day festive structure.

Thanks to the rite, the Madonna of Alno seems therefore to come every year to incarnate her image: on the third day of the celebration, corresponding to the third apparition, the effigy leaves the contrada and returns in procession to the town retracing the path made by Floro towards the residential area. The effigy enters Canzano and passes in front of the building that at one time kept the legend's untamable horse in its cellars. With a stop in front of the hills, the Madonna is welcomed and acknowledged by the jubilation of fireworks. She then completes the last passage towards Piano del Castellano where the church stands today, her resting place.

Notes

[1] John Oslansky provides English translation for the work of Gianfranco Spitilli.
[2] Archivio di Stato di Teramo (henceforth indicated as ASTe), *Luoghi pii laicali – Corrispondenza*, Canzano, b. 52, fasc. 44, 1849.
[3] ASTe, *Luoghi pii laicali – Corrispondenza*, Canzano, b. 52, fasc. 44, 1849.
[4] The data have been confirmed by genealogical research carried out at the ASTe and the Archivio Storico Diocesano di Teramo (henceforth ASDTe).
[5] Archivio Storico Comunale di Canzano, *Libro del Catasto*, 1619, f. 58v e f. 86v.
[6] ASTe, *Catasto Provvisorio Napoleonico*, Canzano, vol. 8, partita 2079.
[7] White poplar: *Populus alba* (Linnaeus, 1753) or from late Latin, *albarum* (Zingarelli, 1984); Alder: *Alnus*.
[8] Stiff-limbed.
[9] ASDTe, Canzano, *Attestato per quella Chiesa extra menia*, 1786, Faldone 3, Varie 1700.
[10] See also, among others: Ginzburg, 1976; Burke, 1980; Gurevič, 2000; Schmitt, 2000; Charuty, 2001; Brown, 2002.
[11] ASDTe, Sante Visite del Vescovo G.B. Visconti, 1609.
[12] We refer to the altered state, described by Ernesto de Martino, which results from 'malignant forces of people or mythical entities' versus other 'people or mythical entities' (2003), whose negative action also involves non-human realities such as that of the animal world (Sibilla 1980, 1985; Ravis-Giordani, 2001).
[13] ASDTe, Canzano, *Attestato per quella Chiesa extra menia*, 1786, Faldone 3, Varie 1700.
[14] ASDTe, Canzano, *Attestato per quella Chiesa extra menia*, 1786, Faldone 3, Varie 1700.
[15] ASDTe, Canzano, *Attestato per quella Chiesa extra menia*, 1786, Faldone 3, Varie 1700.
[16] ASTe, *Luoghi pii laicali – Corrispondenza*, Canzano, b. 50, fasc. 3, 1817.

References

Albert, J.-P. (2005) Les montagnes sont-elles bonnes à penser en termes religieux? In: Brunet, S., Julia, D. and Lemaitre, N. (eds) *Montagnes sacrées d'Europe*. Actes du colloque 'Religion et montagnes', Tarbes, 30 May–2 June 2002. Publications de la Sorbonne, Paris, pp. 65–71.

Albert, J.-P. (2006) La fortune d'un texte: Genèse 2–3, France.

Albert, J.-P., Jamous, R. and Molinié, A. (2013) Introduction: figures et substituts du saint. La fabrique rituelle. *Archives de sciences sociales des religions* 161, 165–173.

Albert-Llorca, M. (1994) La fabrique du sacré. Les vierges 'miraculeuses' du pays valencien. *Genèses* 17, 33–51.

Albert-Llorca, M. (1995a) Les fils de la Vierge. Broderie et dentelle dans l'éducation des jeunes filles. *L'Homme* 133, 99–122.

Albert-Llorca, M. (1995b) La Vierge mis à nu par ses chambrières. *Clio. Histoire, femmes et sociétés* 2, 201–228.

Albert-Llorca, M. (2002) *Les Vierges miraculeuses. Légendes et rituels*. Gallimard, Paris.

Albert-Llorca, M. (2005) La Vierge et les montagnes: l'exemple catalan. In: Brunet, S., Julia, D. and Lemaitre, N. (eds) *Montagnes sacrées d'Europe*. Actes du colloque 'Religion et montagnes', Tarbes, 30 May–2 June 2002. Publications de la Sorbonne, Paris, pp. 207–213.

Albert-Llorca, M. and Ciambelli, P. (1995) *Parures de femmes, parures de Vierges*. Ministère de la Culture, Direction du Patrimoine – Mission du Patrimoine Ethnologique (rapport de recherche).

Anti, E. (1998) *Santi e animali nell'Italia Padana. Secoli IV–XII*. Clueb, Bologna, Italy.

Bridier, S. (2002) *Le cauchemar. Étude d'une figure mythique*. Paris, Presses de l'Université de Paris-Sorbonne.

Brown, P. (2002) *Il culto dei santi. L'origine e la diffusione di una nuova religiosità*. Einaudi, Torino, Italy [1981].

Burke, P. (1980) *Cultura popolare nell'Europa moderna*. Mondadori, Milan, Italy [1978].

Centini, M. (1990) *Animali uomini leggende. Il bestiario del mito*. Xenia, Milan, Italy.

Charuty, G. (1995) Logiques sociales, savoirs techniques, logiques rituelles. *Terrain* 24, 5–14.

Charuty, G. (2001) Du catholicisme méridional à l'anthropologie des sociétés chrétiennes. In: Albera, D., Blok, A. and Bromberger, C. (eds) *L'anthropologie de la Méditerranée*. Maisonneuve & Larose-MMSH, Paris, pp. 359–385.

Christian, W. (1981) *Local Religion in Sixteenth Century Spain*. Princeton University Press, Princeton, New Jersey, USA.

Ciambelli, P. (2002) *Bijoux à secret*. Éditions de la Maison de Sciences de l'Homme, Paris.

de Martino, E. (2003) *Sud e magia*. Feltrinelli, Milan, Italy [1959].

de Montfort, L.M. (1712) *Le Secret de Marie*. § 70 e 78.

Di Nicola, G. (1979) *Canzano. Storia – Folclore – Turismo*. Edizioni Eco, S. Gabriele (TE).

Di Nola, A.M. (1976) *Gli aspetti magico-religiosi di una cultura subalterna italiana*. Boringhieri, Turin, Italy.

Donà, C. (2003) *Per le vie dell'altro mondo. L'animale guida e il mito del viaggio*. Rubbettino, Soveria Mannelli (CZ).

Donà, C. (2008) Animali guida e santi. In: Giaveri, M.T., Frediani, F., Zorini, A.O., Salerno, V. and Scotti, M. (eds) *Los guardo azzurro. Costanti e varianti dell'immaginario mediterraneo*. Mesogea, Catania, Italy, pp. 187–210.

Donà, C. (2015) Meroveo, Basina e il mito dinastico dei Franchi. *Rhesis* 5(2), 42–85.

Fabre, D. (1993) L'ours, la vierge et le taureau. *Ethnologie française* 23(1), 9–19.

Faeta, F. (1997) Qualche appunto sulle immagini e la santità in un contesto popolare moderno. In: Boesch Gajano, S. (ed.) *Santità, culti, agiografia. Temi e prospettive*. Viella, Rome, pp. 241–253.

Faeta, F. (2000) 'Mirabilis imago'. Simboli e teatro festivo. In: Id., *Il santo e l'aquilone. Per un'antropologia dell'immaginario popolare nel secolo XX*. Sellerio, Palermo, Italy, pp. 31–58.

Gasparroni, A. (2011) Il fascino delle Madonne arboree. Tra natura e cultura tradizionale alcuni esempi abruzzesi. In: De Santis, M. (ed.) *Credere la luce. Per una nuova iconografia della Madonna dello Splendore*. Edizioni Fondazione Piccola Opera Charitas, Giulianova, Italy, pp. 14–17.

Ginzburg, C. (1976) *Il formaggio e i vermi. Il cosmo di un mugnaio del '500*. Einaudi, Turin, Italy.

Gurevič, A. Ja. (2000) *Contadini e santi. Problemi della cultura popolare nel Medioevo*. Einaudi, Turin, Italy [1981].

Hertz, R. (1994) San Besso. Studio di un culto alpestre. In: Id., *La preminenza della destra e altri saggi*. Einaudi, Turin, Italy, pp. 165–216 [1913].

Isnart, C. (2008) *Saints légionnaires des Alpes du Sud. Ethnologie d'une sainteté locale*. Éditions de la Maison des Sciences de l'Homme, Paris.

Isnart, C. (2014) (ed.) Hertz, R., *Œuvres publiées*. Classiques Garnier, Paris.

Linnaeus, C.N. (1753) *Species Plantarum*. XXXI, Imprensis Laurentius Salvius, Stoccolma, Sweden.

Lombardi Satriani, L.M. and Meligrana, M. (1996) *Il ponte di San Giacomo. L'ideologia della morte nella società contadina del Sud*. Sellerio, Palermo, Italy [1982].

Palma, N. (1832) *Storia Ecclesiastica e Civile della Regione più settentrionale del Regno di Napoli. Detta dagli antichi Praetutium, ne' bassi tempi Aprutium. Oggi Città di Teramo e Diocesi Aprutina*. Vol. II, Presso Ubaldo Angeletti Stampatore dell'Intendenza, Teramo, Italy.

Praneuf, M. (2001) *Bestiaire ethno-linguistique des peuples d'Europe*. L'Harmattan, Paris.

Profeta, G. (1993) *Un culto pastorale sull'Appennino*. Libreria dell'Università Editrice, Pescara, Italy.

Prosperi, A. (1984) Madonne di città e Madonne di campagna. Per un'inchiesta sulle dinamiche del sacro nell'Italia post-tridentina. In: Boesch Gajano, S. and Sebastiani, L. (eds) *Culto dei santi, istituzioni e classi sociali in età preindustriale*. Japadre Editore, L'Aquila, Italy, pp. 615–647.

Ravis-Giordani, G. (2001) *Bergers corses. Les communautés villageoises du Niolu*. Albiana/PNRC, Aiaccio, France.

Ricci, A. (1999) Gli occhi, le luci, le immagini: le madonnelle. Spazio del sacro e pratiche devozionali delle edicole religiose. In: Lombardi Satriani, L.M. (ed.) *La sacra Città. Itinerari antropologico-religiosi nella Roma di fine millennio. Meltemi*, Rome, pp. 33–75.

Robin Azevedo, V. (2013) 'Avec saint Louis on s'est fait respecter'. *Archives de sciences sociales des religions* 161, 175–188.

Saintyves, P. (1922) *Essays de folklore biblique. Magie, mythes et miracles dans l'Ancien et le Nouveau Testament*. Librairie critique Émile Nourry, Paris.

Salvatore, R. (2002) *Sante Marie degli alberi. Culti mariani arborei in Abruzzo*. Andromeda Editrice, Colledara, Italy (TE).

Sansterre, J.-M. (2015) Vivantes ou comme vivantes: l'animation miraculeuse d'images de la Vierge entre Moyen Âge et Époque moderne. *Revue de l'Histoire des Religions* 232(2), 155–182.

Sauzeau, A. and Sauzeau, P. (1995) Les chevaux colorés de l'Apocalypse'. II: Commentaires, iconographie et légendes de l'Antiquité au Moyen Age. *Revue de l'histoire des religions* 212–4, 379–396.

Schmitt, J.-C. (2000) *Religione, folklore e società nell'Occidente medievale*. Editori Laterza, Bari, Italy.

Sensi, M. (2014) 'Madonna a cavallo' in un santuario mariofanico della Valnerina (sec. XV). In: *Omaggio a Vauchez*. www.aisscaweb.it (Associazione Italiana per lo Studio della Santità, dei Culti e dell'Agiografia), pp. 1–15.

Sibilla, P. (1980) *Una comunità Walzer delle Alpi. Strutture tradizionali e processi culturali*. Olschki Editore, Florence, Italy.

Sibilla, P. (1985) *I luoghi della memoria. Cultura e vita quotidiana nelle testimonianze del contadino valsesiano G.B. Filippa (1778–1838)*. Fondazione Monti, Anzola d'Ossola, Italy.

Silvestrini, E. (2003) Abiti e simulacri. Itinerario attraverso mitologie, narrazioni e riti. In: Silvestrini, E., Gri, G.P. and Pagnozzato, R. (eds) *Donne madonne dee. Abito sacro e riti di vestizione, gioiello votivo, 'vestitrici': un itinerario antropologico in area lagunare veneta*. Il Poligrafo, Padova, Italy, pp. 16–65.

Spitilli, G. (2011) *Tra uomini e santi. Rituali con bovini nell'Italia centrale*. Squilibri, Rome.

Spitilli, G. (2012) Il santo e il bue. Contributo all'analisi di un complesso rituale. *Voci*, anno IX, 155–174.

Wagner, M.-A. (2005) *Le cheval dans les croyances germaniques. Paganisme, christianisme et traditions*. Champion, Paris.

Zingarelli, N. (1984) *Il nuovo Zingarelli. Vocabolario della lingua italiana*. Zanichelli, Milan, Italy.

3 Developing Pilgrimage Itineraries: The Way of St Francis in Umbria as Case in Point

Paola de Salvo*

Department of Political Science, University of Perugia, Perugia, Italy

Introduction

Travelling for spiritual and religious reasons is nothing new and indeed may be considered one of the oldest forms of tourism. Religion has long underlain the main urges impelling mankind to undertake journeys, especially non-economic travel (Jackowski and Smith, 1992). Furthermore, even though religion has always played a key role in the development of leisure time and has influenced how the individual enjoyed it, the growth of religious motivations coincided with the development of modern tourism. Pilgrimages have become much more widespread in the past decades. They now constitute a large sector of international tourism, are more organized and standardized in format (Timothy and Olsen, 2006), and are today one of the most popular displays of human mobility (Shinde, 2008; Nyaupane and Budruk, 2009). The latest data from the World Tourism Organization (WTO, 2011) estimated that 330 million travellers visited holy places, with 40 million visiting Italy alone. Holy places strongly attract not only tourists who are interested in their spiritual awakening, but also people who are motivated by an interest in history (Shinde, 2008; Olsen, 2009). As more and more religious or spiritual destinations associate well-known holy places with their rich historical and artistic heritage, the two-fold attraction of a holy place and its cultural framework is often the main reason for making a trip (Ramirez, 2011).

These new reasons for travelling make it even more difficult to distinguish the features of pilgrims and tourists. Recent interpretations of this complex debate maintain they are not one and the same person, that is, they are not '*one in the same*' (Nyaupane *et al.*, 2015, p. 344), because their travel experience (Griffiths, 2011) and reasons are diverse and dissimilar (Turner, 1973; Cohen, 1992). The term 'pilgrimage' in today's world is associated with a religious trip, a journey to a sanctuary or holy place. It derives from the Latin word *peregrinus*, which had much wider connotations, including for example, the stranger, the wanderer, the traveller, even the new arrival, foreigner and so forth. The word 'tourist' also derives from the Latin *tornus*, which originally referred to a circular trip, usually for pleasure and amusement, which ended with a return to its starting point (Smith, 1992).

Pilgrimages have recently shifted their focus towards post-modern themes, with clear discrepancies emerging between the old paradigm that emphasized only the religious aspects of the pilgrimage and recent studies that tended to support more secular models. Pilgrimages are not, in fact, only religious in nature. Collins-Kreiner

---

*E-mail: paola.desalvo@unipg.it

(2010) argued that the religion-only pilgrimage was no longer a valid model as the secular should also be included. Major changes in travel in the last decades, a renewed search for physical and psychological well-being and the growth of a new tourism that emphasizes the cultural and spiritual dimensions of a trip are modifying the paradigms and theories of pilgrimages and religious tourism. As tourism and religion intersect ever more closely, they attract the attention of experts who try to analyse the relationship from diverse points of view. Bremer (2005) identified three approaches: the spatial, which attributes different behaviour patterns to pilgrims depending on the modality of the religious space thay have decided to visit; the historical, which studies the links between religious- and tourist-related types of trips; and finally the cultural, which identifies pilgrimages and tourism as activities in the post-modern era.

New Paradigms for Pilgrimages and Religious Tourism

The origins of contemporary tourism, one of the newest social phenomena worldwide, can be traced back to the earliest forms of pilgrimage. One of the oldest reasons for travelling is the compelling urge to satisfy religious reasons (Griffin, 2007). Studies on the links between religion, pilgrimages and tourism often focused separately on religion or tourism, neglecting to examine co-relations or conduct comparative studies of the two sectors (Collins-Kreiner, 2010). This initial approach did not seem to realize the development of tourism could be studied with no link to religion or that pilgrimages have been carried out from time immemorial (Vukonić, 2002; Timothy and Olsen, 2006).

Pilgrimages and tourism may be associated with connotations that vary with the analytical perspective. Timothy and Olsen (2006) identified the following perspectives: religious only, the pilgrims' point of view, the tourist industry and finally a more scientific perspective. In the pilgrimage vs. tourism debate Collins-Kreiner (2010) detected two levels of analysis: (i) the vision of the religious organizations, and (ii) the travellers' point of view. She claimed that pilgrims were different to tourists and were generally not considered tourists, because they travelled for purely spiritual reasons, while tourists travelled or visited places out of secular interest, curiosity and/or just pleasure. On the other hand, religious organizations display a more entrepreneurial approach, considering pilgrims as tourists who should be treated as such. This perspective played a major role in the development of all pilgimage-related business activities, that is, accommodation, supply of food and drink, shopping and commerce, and even the religious centres themselves.

From a more scientific point of view the earliest theories on the relationship between pilgrimages and tourism focused mainly on the different types of tourists and pilgrims (MacCannell, 1973; Cohen, 1979, 1992; Smith, 1992) and on their discrepancies. Among others, Turner and Ash (1975), Armanski (1978) and Prahl and Steinecke (1979), emphasized that the significance of a journey or a pilgrimage in the past had been debased in modern tourism and the superficiality of tourism was a symptom of alienation in modern society. Conversely MacCannell (1973, 1976), one of the first to note the convergence of tourism and pilgrimages, pointed out and reinforced the view that modern tourism held the same significance as traditional pilgrimages. He suggested everyday life was a profane time, attributed a sacred value to holidays and identified tourist attractions as modern sanctuaries. Alienation from modern society meant that tourists sought a more genuine, real lifestyle elsewhere, and they activated their search in socio-cultural environments that had been the destinations of traditional pilgrimages (Cohen, 1992). Moreover, pilgrim–tourist differences were most marked in very holy places while they were weaker in places of 'popular pilgrimage' where features overlapped in both groups (Cohen, 1992 in Collins-Kreiner 2010, p. 156). The difficulties in outlining the borders between pilgrimages and tourism were also addressed by some religious sociologists in terms of shrine visit modalities (Davie, 2000). Davie showed that even tourists from a secular background displayed a different approach to the visit precisely because they were aware they were standing before holy buildings and sites. In his view, even though cathedrals, churches and diverse holy places were considered open and freely accessible to the public, attitudes when visiting them were different to visiting places of general culture.

Scientific reports focused on comparing tourists and pilgrims, highlighting their similarities or differences (Cohen, 1998; Collins-Kreiner and Kliot, 2000; Digance, 2003, 2006; Timothy and Olsen, 2006). It is not, however, correct to demarcate them so clearly because of the rapid convergence of the religious and secular sectors of tourism. Several types of relationships between pilgrimage and tourism are found in the morphology of religious tourism. Sharpley and Sundaram (2005) reported that the link between religion and tourism could be conceptualized with reference to the intensity of religious reasons. This theory depicted an ideal continuum with the sacred and the profane at opposite ends and diverse possible combinations of the holy and the secular, with the middle ground being held by what is generally defined as religious tourism (Smith, 1992; Vazquez de la Torre *et al.*, 2012) (Table 3.1).

The relationships that emerged reflect the traveller's diverse, changing reasons. Their interests and activities may slide from tourism to pilgrimage and vice versa even though the individual may not perceive the change. Vazquez de la Torre *et al.* (2012) suggested the spectrum ran from the devout, pious pilgrim with a prevalently religious interest ('pilgrim > tourist'), through another individual where religious and tourist reasons are equally balanced, to the person who is prevalently a tourist ('pilgrim < tourist') and finally to the entirely secular tourist. Different forms of religious tourism develop in the central area of this ideal continuum where diverse interests may prevail, ranging from religious and cultural to knowledge acquisition. In this context Nolan and Nolan (1989), in particular, had already shown religious tourism was an individual search for sanctuaries and holy places where, instead of prayers, visitors sought understanding of the place's identity and meaning and its historical and cultural significance.

Widening out this insight to research into economic, sociological, cultural and behavioural patterns (Vukonić, 1996; Timothy and Olsen, 2006) characterizes modern scientific research into pilgrimages and religious tourism. Experts are stimulated by interesting comparisons that lead away from the old paradigm that placed, as we have already stated, only religious

reasons at the centre of a pilgrimage. New meanings, new points of view and renewed interests helped the tourist trip converge on the pilgrimage and gave rise to even completely secular pilgrimages (Kong, 2001). There was growth of tourist trips with the exterior forms of pilgrimages (Nocifora, 2010) but without their intrinsic interior content, that is, the religious experience and the idea of the sacred and the devotional.

The secular society speaks more correctly of religious tourism. The holy nature of the place does not inspire religious devotion but rather a secular approach to a cultural or even spiritual visit with no reference to the religious links that gave rise to the original pilgrimage. This new approach reduces differentiation, draws pilgrims and tourists closer together and tends to add value to the individual's experience as he or she searches for a new spirituality. According to Eberhart (2005) this desire for spirituality, which is not limited to religion despite using its methods, is what drives modern pilgrims on their travels. Religion-free spirituality helps pilgrims find themselves and activate 'neo-aggregation social rites' (Eberhart, 2005, p. 97). Pilgrims and tourists became inter-dependent in a new social space that is simultaneously sacred and profane (Gatrell and Collins-Kreiner, 2006).

The very word 'pilgrimage' entered more widespread use in the mass media and spoken language, assuming different meanings with the different contexts. Common usage indicates journeys and visits in profane contexts. A modality of reciprocal contamination between pilgrimage and tourist trip was established, varying only in how the trip was experienced rather than in how it was defined. As Dupront (1967, p. 103) wrote: 'we should not fall into the temptation to put them into a hierarchy as we risk impoverishing one as we put the other into the limelight'.

Developing Holy Places: Religious Itineraries

New forms of tourism feature active experiences that help the tourist rediscover the cultural and spiritual dimensions of his journey (Palmer, 2004; Uriely, 2005). They produce more responsible consumer models that characterize growing demands for variety, quality, contents that induce experiences and emotions as well as

Table 3.1. Continuum from pilgrims to tourists. (From Vazquez de la Torre *et al.*, 2012.)

Pilgrims	Religious tourism	Secular tourism
Sacred	Sacred-secular	Secular

sense-making. Ever more stimulated to become part of the atmosphere and impressions the place evokes, tourists want to feel as though they are actively living there. In this context religious heritage tourism is one of the most common forms of tourism not only because of its underlying spiritual reasons and the historical, artistic and architectonic importance of the places that are visited but also because it satisfies the post-modern tourist's desire for cultural growth and experiences. In contemporary society religious reasons are enriched by the meanings and values of a secular society. Religious tourism draws faith, history, culture and knowledge of the place closer together, uniting pure spirituality with a broader individual well-being. The common denominator in the pilgrimage seems to be the need to reconcile spirit, mind and body with the need for knowledge.

The reason for visiting holy places is changing into something more cultural and/or ethical or social. Visits to holy places are flanked by requests to follow religion-related paths and itineraries. A well-known religious heritage that is shared by diverse areas is, in fact, essential when planning a religious itinerary programme where tourists/pilgrims move along their themed pathway, visit different sights and live through experiences that are linked to their search for culture, authenticity and spirituality. Thus, profound relationships are created between people and places. Alderman (2002) adopted the term 'pilgrimage landscape' to define a space that, by involving a multitude of material and immaterial elements, stimulates culture and experiences (Andriotis, 2011), strengthening the bonds between the religious attractor and the places that are visited. Although tourists often choose a destination and journey along a pathway with religious connotations and mystical significance, religion is not the motivating force behind their journey. More and more often a renewed interest in works of art and the landscape where they are sited are the reasons for visiting holy places or wanting to travel along a religious pathway.

A more tourism-orientated interpretation of cultural/religious itineraries considers them as a form of tourism that respects the natural environment. They offer great opportunities to encounter other cultures, socialize with them and bond with the communities that are visited (Parkins and Craig, 2006). The relationship dimension becomes pre-eminent, spreading out from the merely personal to the links between man and the environment, and the bonds between man and the local community. Journeying along religious itineraries, in harmony with the environment and local culture, paying attention to the quality of the land, gives rise to a tourist consumerism that is extremely sensitive to the layout of the area and the dynamics of local development. This in turn generates alternative forms of tourism such as the ecological, food and wine tours, slow journeys, well-being and so forth.

Holy places and religious inineraries attract well educated, top-class tourists. They are interested in visiting and learning about religious buildings and places of historic and artistic significance. They are also interested in the landscape where these religious places are sited, and actively participate in local events and religious festivals, which are perceived as signs of local identity (Morazzoni and Boiocchi, 2013). This vision means that tourism along religious and cultural itineraries safeguards the area yet is a means of development. It becomes a tool that promotes responsibility, sustainability and awareness, recognizes the value of authenticity and local culture, and contributes to the individual's personal enrichment and growth (Rizzo et al., 2013). Many sacred and devotional pathways and itineraries bear testimony to the culture of the area, its landscapes, expressions of local identity and experience of man's knowhow. Value is added to the scenery, as the significance of its environment, history, nature and production is interpreted and appreciated. The area is enjoyed linearly by finding out about all its aspects until understanding is reached of its particular economic value. The itineraries thus become an opportunity for development and support for local communities, bringing culture, typical products, the local environment, accommodation and restaurants together in one single integrated system. Pilgrims/tourists benefit from a system that offers them the local area with its religious dimension still playing a central role but enhanced by the history, environment, culture and society in which the cult of the holy place developed and grew.

The rediscovery and development of religious itineraries also focus on the spiritual and cultural value of journeying on foot, which is considered an alternative form of tourism.

It strongly features slowness, the tourists' new sense of responsibility for the environment and the search for experiences. Walking along a religious itinerary means pilgrims/tourists have all the time they need to understand, observe, and communicate with other travellers and the resident population (Canestrini, 2001).

The features of modern religious tourism compel the diverse stakeholders in the area to be very careful about programming initiatives to develop its religious, artistic and cultural heritage. For religious tourism they should include only a cross-section of top quality proposals for the historic–artistic, the theological–teaching and the pedagogical–anthropological domains (Mazza, 1996; 2005). As far as regards the historic–artistic domain, rereading the religious history of the place and its heritage appears essential for acquiring in-depth knowledge to assist in the search for its cultural roots and value, and uncover a new stimulus to live it in the present. Respect for, and development of, the religious and spiritual aspects (i.e. the theological–teaching domain) of the sites and ecclesiastical architecture is important to satisfy the demands of pilgrims and tourists. Finally, developing the pedagogical–anthropological domain is essential to ensure tourists/pilgrims have the opportunity to appreciate and understand the works of art as signs of faith that bear witness to the sacred nature of the place and the expressive capacities of the civilization in which they arose. Thus, itineraries may become significant aesthetic, religious and cultural experiences.

The Way of St Francis

In their description of religious tourism in Europe, Nolan and Nolan (1992) distinguished between pilgrimage destinations that exert a strong attraction for the faithful but hold little appeal for tourists with secular interests; holy places with marked historical and artistic features that attract both the devout and religious tourists because of emerging information about their history, works of art and their landscapes; and finally places that are used only for encounters and religious festivities. Falling within the second category of this classification is the Way of St Francis, an itinerary that runs through Umbria, Tuscany and Latium, linking places

that played a part in the life and preaching of St Francis. It integrates strongly religious aspects with an extremely valuable cultural and environmental heritage (Fig. 3.1).

Close adherence to the story of St Francis makes the Way an authentic itinerary. The diverse stages conserve memories of the saint's activities, reproposing the experience of where the saint walked and lived, that is, in places which thus become new tourist attractors. Following the Way in the footsteps of St Francis constitutes 'an authentic spiritual journey which satisfies the desire in mankind, even in modern humans, to look for the meaning of life deep within oneself' (Giuletti and Bettin, 2012, p. 17). It is coherent with the needs/demands of post-modern pilgrims/tourists, who are in search of authentic experiences, renewed relationships with the surrounding environment and psycho-physical well-being. The Way of St Francis, which was financed by Inter-Regional Funds for the development of religious itineraries, was inaugurated in Umbria in 2008. Pilgrims/tourists move in stages from La Verna to Assisi and from Greccio to Assisi (Fig. 3.2).

The Way is still under construction and local authorities intend linking Assisi up with with other places and symbols that played major roles in the life of St Francis. Proposals include connecting with the Lauretana and Francigena pilgrim routes. The Way, which unfolds through enchanting countryside, is closely connected to the message of St Francis. Although a spiritual form of itinerary, it responds to the needs and demands of curious pilgrims/tourists, who can concentrate on the multiple layers of expression in the area. Travelling along the Way of St Francis on foot or by bicycle enables expression of the spiritual values of walking or travelling slowly, which strengthen modalities of sustainable, responsible tourism (Savoja 2011; Clancy, 2014).

The Way of St Francis encompasses features and details that create a multiple interest place for tourism. First, its spiritual and religious vocation rings out loud and clear as a pilgrim route in an area that is considered holy because of its magnetic spirituality and links with places where St Francis lived and preached (Porcal, 2006). The Way is also a cultural itinerary. It encompasses a significant cultural and scenic heritage, which adds to its value as a meeting place where the people who are journeying along it

Fig. 3.1. Natural environment. (Consortium Umbria and Francesco's Ways data.)

can learn and exchange information while contributing to the conservation and development of the heritage itself. Besides being a pilgrim route and an aid to development of the surrounding cultural and scenic heritage, the Way of St Francis also attracts tourists because of the highly symbolic value of the area through which it passes. Consequently, it possesses the minimum standards that benefit tourists such as adequate information, presence on internet sites and other social media, layout and maintenance of dedicated trails and paths, appropriate vertical and horizontal signage, but, above all, the itinerary and its related services conform with the religious, touristic and cultural motivations that drive its potential users.

The Way of St Francis thus becomes a tourist product that should be promoted and marketed by public institutions and private businesses. Indeed, in 2011, a new consortium 'Umbria and the Way of St Francis' was co-funded by the Umbria Region. Its only mission is to develop, promote and market the Way. The consortium develops specific packages for the diverse types of pilgrims/tourists who are interested in following in the footsteps of St Francis. These include: devout, pious pilgrims who are interested only in

the religious and spiritual dimension of the Way, hikers, cyclists, horse-riders, groups of tourists and so on. A well-differentiated offer of many different types of accommodation and restaurants along the Way ensures the travellers' multiple, different demands can be satisfied. All the necessary services are available to support tourists in their search for spirituality, knowledge and discovery of the area, or even just their desire to rest and relax and enjoy authentic relationships and experiences. The consortium's ultimate aim in its activity is to propose and encourage genuine relationships with residents and the area that is visited and satisfy purely tourist demands for, for example, accommodation, restaurants, transport and so forth. Recent marketing and merchandising initiatives that were designed to benefit tourism along the itinerary include a branded waterbottle and lunchbox to be sold where tourists are accommodated and a special pilgrim's menu based on excellent local produce.

Like all major pilgrim routes, the Way of St Francis provides ritual symbols that are conferred on pilgrims/tourists. It has its own official Credential, a religious travel document that all pilgrims carry on their journey, which testifies as to their identity and intentions and

Fig. 3.2. The Way of St Francis: The path of the faith. (From http://www.viadifrancesco.it/)

is stamped in the resting places or sights that are visited along the Way. Upon presentation of the Credential in Assisi, pilgrims/tourists obtain a certificate called the Testimonial to the Way of St Francis (*Testimonium Viae Francisci*), which officially certifies that they reached the end of the Way and proves they arrived at the tomb of St Francis. Testimonials originated in penance- and punishment-associated pilgrimages that civil courts inflicted on whoever sinned against the Church and had to atone for their sin. The Testimonial provided proof sinners had reached their goal and could receive absolution and remission of the punishment. The modern Testimonial to the Way of St Francis is of personal value only, like the souvenir of an experience the individual has enjoyed. Its issue is, however, linked to precise conditions. The pilgrim/tourist must have walked the last 75 km or cycled the last 150 km to the Tomb of St Francis in Assisi.

The Way of St Francis is an itinerary that encourages systemic regional development. By means of its distinctive scenery and works of art it brings a multitude of individuals, activites, resources and skills into contact with each other. It highlights the differences and particular features of the areas it passes through but gathers them together under the one common theme of St Francis. The Way of St Francis may become an innovative, complex, multidimensional tool for the development of tourism in the area. New business opportunities may be found in the need to supply ancillary services and products, thus ensuring equal distribution of the income from tourism across various local businesses. The itinerary is thus a cultural and economic product and a tool for strategic marketing of the area. It draws in diverse representatives of public and private interests who are committed to establishing inter-relationships with pilgrims/tourists.

The former want to help the latter achieve and live an experience that they are interested in, that involves them emotionally and that encourages them to establish a strong bond with the place they visited.

The Pilgrim Station (Statio Peregrinorum): First Monitoring of Pilgrims

The Franciscan pathways are the first religious itineraries in Italy to gather and present data about pilgrims. The census was set out in the Pilgrim Station (Statio peregrinorum) which was inaugurated in April 2015 by the Friars of St Francis Basilica in Assisi in collaboration with the Umbria Region, Develop Umbria, the 'Umbria and the Way of St Francis' consortium and referents of the diverse pathways that are linked to St Francis. Besides the Way of St Francis, Franciscan pathways include: The Assisi Walk (Cammino di Assisi), In the Footsteps of Francis (Di qui passò Francesco), The Way of Assisi (Chemin d'Assise), Via Lauretana, The Franciscan Sign (Cammino Francescano della Marca) and Via Amerina.

The Pilgrim Station provides for the reception of pilgrims who arrive on foot, horseback, bicycles or on three-wheeled handbikes, issues the Testimonial and collects statistics on arriving pilgrims. 2015, the first year of this experiment, saw activation of the first system for monitoring pilgrims in Italy. Data, which are reported below, are derived from the first census covering May–October 2015,[1] and are the outcome of work done by laypeople and religous volunteers. The Pilgrim Station (Statio Peregrinorum) includes pilgrims who travel the Way of St Francis and other Franciscan pathways. Excluded from the data analysis are pilgrims who leave from Assisi for Rome, pilgrims who reach Assisi but have journeyed along the Way for under 100 km, pilgrims who do not reach Assisi and pilgrims who do not request the Credential or accept the Testimonial.

There were 1600 pilgrims included in the study in 2015. According to Credential data the overall flow of pilgrims who completed at least one stage along the Franciscan pathways was estimated to be 10,000 individuals. The sample of

1600 pilgrims was almost equally divided between males (55.15%) and females (43%) (Fig. 3.3).

As regards age distribution, 60% of pilgrims fell within the 30–60 age group, about 22% were over 60 years old, 13% belonged to the young 18–30 age group and only 5% were under 18 years of age. These results showed that prevalently adults and elderly people undertake long journeys along religious itineraries (Fig. 3.4).

The census showed that pilgrims journey prevalently in groups (69%) and only 31% travel alone (Fig. 3.5).

The geographical distribution was as follows: 45% of Italian pilgrims came from the north of the country. The rest were equally

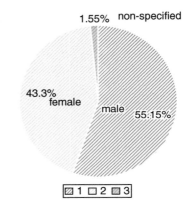

Fig. 3.3. Gender of pilgrims. (From Pilgrim Station (*Statio Peregrinorum*) data.)

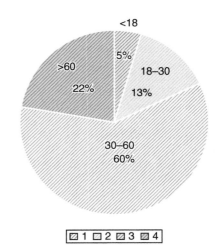

Fig. 3.4. Age distribution of pilgrims. (From Pilgrim Station (*Statio Peregrinorum*) data.)

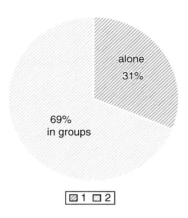

☑ 1 ☐ 2

Fig. 3.5. How pilgrims travel. (From Pilgrim Station (*Statio Peregrinorum*) data.)

distributed between central Italy (25%) and the south (30%). Most European pilgrims came from

Germany (24.6%), followed by France (18.44%), Poland (8.66%) and Austria (7.62%). Non-European pilgrims came mainly from Brazil (6.4%) and the USA (4.8%).

Data showed religious tourism was constituted mainly of active workers, as a total of 23% of pilgrims said they were employed as civil servants or teachers, 13% were freelance professionals, 7% worked for private companies, almost 13% were retired and 9% declared they were students.

The 2015 census, the first attempt to gather data on pilgrims, did not include questions about the pilgrims' reasons for deciding to undertake one of the Franciscan pathways. This question was inserted into the activity-monitoring 2016 questionnaire, and reports from unofficial sources state that religious reasons are prevalent and special devotion to St Francis most probably accounts for them.

Note

[1] Data referring to 2016, the Jubilee Year of Mercy, have not yet been reported. Unofficial sources suggest a positive trend in pilgrims along the Franciscan Pathways as 3180 pilgrims were registered at the Pilgrim Station (*Statio Peregrinorum*).

References

Alderman D.H. (2002) Writing on the Graceland wall, on the importance of authorship in pilgrimage landscapes. *Tourism Recreation Research* 2(72), 27–33.

Andriotis, K. (2011) Genres of heritage authenticity: denotations from a pilgrimage landscape. *Annals of Tourism Research* 38(4), 1613–1633.

Armanski, G. (1978) *Die Kostbarsten Tage des Jahres*. Massentourismus: Uraschen. Formen, Folgen Berlin, Rotbuch Verlag, Germany.

Bremer, T.S. (2005) Tourism and religion. In: Jones, L. (ed.) *Encyclopedia of Religions*. Macmillan Reference USA, Thompson Gale, Detroit, Michigan, USA.

Canestrini, D. (2001) *Andare a quel paese*. Feltrinelli Traveller, Milan, Italy.

Clancy, M. (2014) Slow tourism: ethics, aesthetics and consumptive values. In: Weeden, C. and Boluk, K. (eds) *Managing Ethical Consumption in Tourism*. Routledge, London, pp. 56–69.

Cohen, E. (1979) A phenomenology of tourist experiences. *Sociology* 13(2), 179–201.

Cohen, E. (1992) Pilgrimage centers, concentric and excentric. *Annals of Tourism Research* 19(1), 33–50.

Cohen, E. (1998) Tourism and religion, a comparative perspective. *Pacific Tourism Review* 2. 1–10.

Collins-Kreiner, N. (2010) The geography of pilgrimage and tourism: transformations and implications for applied geography. *Applied Geography* 30, 153–164.

Collins-Kreiner, N. and Kliot, N. (2000) Pilgrimage tourism in the holy land: the behavioral characteristics of Christian pilgrims. *GeoJournal* 50(1), 55–67.

Davie, G. (2000) *Religion in Modern Europe: A Memory Mutates*. Oxford University Press, Oxford, UK.

Digance, J. (2003) Pilgrimage at contested sites. *Annals of Tourism Research*, 30(1), 143–159.

Digance, J. (2006) Religious and secular pilgrimage: journeys redolent with meaning. In: Timothy, D.J. and Olsen, D.H. (eds) *Tourism, Religion and Spiritual Journeys*. Routledge, London, pp. 36–48.

DuPront, A. (1967) Tourisme et Pelerinage: reflexions de psychologie collective. *Communications* 10, 97–121.

Eberhart, H.V. (2005) Pellegrinaggio e ricerca: tendenze e approcci attuali. *Lares* LXXI(1), 73–98.

Gatrell, J.D. and Collins-Kreiner, N. (2006) Negotiated space, tourists, pilgrims and the Baha'i terraced gardens in Haifa. *Geoforum* 37, 765–778.

Giulietti, P. and Bettin, G. (2012) *La via di Francesco*. Edizioni San Paolo, Milan, Italy.

Griffin, K.A. (2007) The globalization of pilgrimage tourism? Some thoughts from Ireland. In: Raj, R. and Morpeth, N.D. (eds) *Religious Tourism and Pilgrimage Management: An International Perspective*. CAB International, Wallingford, UK, pp. 15–34.

Griffiths, M. (2011) Those who come to pray and those who come to look: interactions between visitors and congregations. *Journal of Heritage Tourism* 6(1), 63–72.

Jackowski, A. and Smith, V. (1992) Polish pilgrim-tourists. *Annals of Tourism Research* 19(1), 92–106.

Kong, L. (2001) Mapping 'new' geographies of religion, politics and poetics in modernity. *Progress in Human Geography* 25(2), 211–233.

MacCannell, D. (1973) Staged authenticity, arrangements of social space in tourist settings. *American Journal of Sociology* 79(3), 589–603.

MacCannell, D. (1976) *The Tourist, a New Theory of the Leisure Class*. Shocken, New York.

Mazza, C. (1996) La dimensione culturale del turismo religioso in vista del Giubileo, Convegno BIT Milano. Available at: www.chiesacattolica.it (accessed 1 March 2018).

Mazza, C. (2005) Sulle tracce della fede. Turismo religioso. Available at: www.chiesacattolica.it (accessed 1 March 2018).

Morazzoni, M. and Boiocchi, M. (2013) I Cammini culturali e le nuove vie di turismo religioso. Il progetto di promozione turistica Strada delle Abbazie. Fede, arte e natura nella grande Milano. *AlmaTourism Journal of Tourism, Culture and Territorial Development* 7, 44–58.

Nocifora, E. (2010) Turismo religioso e pellegrinaggio. Il caso romano. *ROTUR/Revista de Ocioy Turismo* 3, 181–194.

Nolan, M.L. and Nolan, S. (1989) *Christian Pilgrimage in Modern Western Europe*. The University of North Carolina Press, Chapel Hill, North Carolina, USA.

Nolan, M.L. and Nolan, S. (1992) Religious sites as tourism attractions in Europe. *Annals of Tourism Research* 19, 68–78.

Nyaupane, G.P. and Budruk, M. (2009) South Asian heritage tourism: conflict, colonialism, and cooperation. In: Timothy, D.J. and Nyaupane, G.P. (eds) *Cultural Heritage and Tourism in the Developing World: A Regional Perspective*. Routledge, London, pp. 127 and 145.

Nyaupane, G.P., Dallen, J.T. and Poudel, S. (2015) Understanding tourists in religious destinations: a social distance perspective. *Tourism Management* 48, 343–353.

Olsen, D.H. (2009) 'The strangers within our gates': managing visitors at Temple Square. *Journal of Management, Spirituality and Religion* 6(2), 121–139.

Palmer, C. (2004) An ethnography of Englishness: experiencing identity through tourism. *Annals of Tourism Research* 32(1), 7–27.

Parkins, W. and Craig, G. (2006) *Slow Living*. Berg, Oxford, UK.

Porcal GonzaLo, M.C. (2006) Turismo cultural, turismo religioso y peregrinaciones en Navarra. Las Javieradas como caso de estudio. *Cuadernos de Turismo* 18, 103–134.

Prahl, H.W. and Steinecke, A. (1979) Der Millionen-Urlaub: Von der Bildungsreise zur totalen Freizeit, Darmstadt.

Ramírez, S.M. (2011) Reseña de 'Cases in Sustainable Tourism. An Experiential Approach to Making Decisions'. In: de Irene M. Herremans (ed.) PASOS. *Revista de Turismo y Patrimonio Cultural* 9(2), 485–486.

Rizzo, L.S., Rizzo, R.G. and Trono, A. (2013) Itinerari Religiosi come Motori di Sviluppo Locale Sostenibile in Veneto? Per una Proposta di Valorizzazione di Heritage non Consueto o spesso 'Inavvertito': i Santuari e le Chiese Minori. *AlmaTourism Journal of Tourism, Culture and Territorial Development* 7, 59–92.

Savoja, L. (2011) Turismo lento e turisti responsabili. Verso una nuova concezione di consumo. In: Nocifora, E., de Salvo, P. and Calzati V. (eds) *Territori lenti e turismo di qualità, prospettive innovative per lo sviluppo di un turismo sostenibile*, Franco Angeli, Milan, Italy.

Sharpley, R. and Sundaram, P. (2005) Tourism: A sacred journey? The case of ashram tourism, India. *International Journal of Tourism Research* 7(3), 161–171.

Shinde, K. (2008) Religious tourism: exploring a new form of sacred journey in North India. In: Cochrane, J. (ed.) *Asian Tourism: Growth and Change*. Elsevier, Oxford, UK, pp. 245–257.

Smith, V.L. (1992) Introduction: the quest in guest. *Annals of Tourism Research* 19, 1–17.

Timothy, D.J. and Olsen, D.H. (2006) *Tourism, Religion and Spiritual Journeys*. Routledge, London.

Turner, V. (1973) The center out there: pilgrim's goal. *History of Religions* 12(3), 191–230.

Turner, L. and Ash, J. (1975) *The Golden Hordes: International Tourism and the Pleasure Periphery*, Constable Limited, London.

Uriely, N. (2005) The tourist experience. Conceptual developments. *Annals of Tourism Research* 32(1), 199–216.

Vázquez De la Torre, M.G., Pérez Naranjo, L.M. and Martínez Cárdenas, R. (2012) Etapas del ciclo de vida en el desarrollo del turismo religioso: una comparación de estudios de caso. *Cuadernos de Turismo* 30, 241–266.

Vukonić, B. (1996) *Tourism and Religion*. Elsevier Science Ltd, London.

Vukonić, B. (2002) Religion, tourism and economics, a convenient symbiosis. *Tourism Recreation Research* 27(2), 59–64.

WTO (2011) Religious Tourism in Asia and Pacific. World Tourism Organization, Spain. Available at: http://asiapacific.unwto.org/publication/religious-tourism-asia-and-pacific (accessed 14 March 2018).

4 Pilgrimage, Religious Tourism and Heritage in Calabria

Alfonsina Bellio*

Institut d'Études Avancées de Nantes – Groupe Sociétés, Religions, Laïcités (GSRL), Paris, France

From Pilgrims to Spiritual Tourists

The Way of St James (or Camino de Santiago) was declared a European Cultural Route by the Council of Europe on 23 October 1987. This started a new season for contemporary tourism based on greater attention given to pilgrimage routes. A number of actions have been undertaken ever since in order to promote this journey and many others which have particular political and economic significance. According to sociological data, what might have appeared as an exclusively Spanish phenomenon has indeed become an international, multicultural and multireligious way (Grossi, 2008, pp. 229–231).

Over the past few decades, religious tourism, also known as spiritual tourism, has expanded to an extent that was unimaginable in the past. An important sector of the economy and international marketing is devoted to the needs of the crowds made up of 'spiritual travellers', and travelling for religious purposes is promoted with the aim of improving the development of both the economy and the community (Iannario, 2004). These tourists and pilgrims together visit the most significant places of worship. Their trips are organized by specific agencies and promoted by parishes or religious organizations for spiritual as well as cultural and recreational purposes. As the

Archbishop of Ravenna declared, religious tourism 'is the pulpit of the new millennium' (Sesana, 2006, p. 92). The Church itself, beginning with the pontificate of Pius XII, has attached great importance to this dimension of Christian practice, which soon became the subject of a specific pastoral ministry.[1] Thus, the anthropology of religion intersects with the anthropology of tourism.

First of all, it is worth highlighting the transformation of the 'traditional' concept of pilgrimage, whose meaning has extended to the point of embracing new forms of travelling and spiritual quests belonging to contemporary worlds, where moving has become increasingly faster, less expensive and, therefore, more accessible to the masses. In the life of a believer, a pilgrimage represents an experience needed to break away from his or her everyday life.

The medieval images of this liminal experience perfectly convey the spiritual meaning of purification and search for proximity to the divine, with an entire range of trials that need to be overcome.[2] Other than being motionless and exiled to a closed universe (Le Goff, 2005), 'every man in the Middle Ages was a potential and symbolic pilgrim' (Le Goff, 1990, p. 7): the great pilgrimages triggered an irreversible turning point in a person's life before and after such an experience. They would depart with the awareness of

---

*E-mail: alfonsina.bellio@gmail.com

adhering to a model of perfection in their faith, but with no certainty of their return or in the outcome of their journey.

The pilgrimage becomes a metaphor for the religious experience in itself and it is linked to a double movement, that is, the attraction to the divine and, at the same time, the strength and inner life needed to go towards it. Within the Judaic–Christian tradition, walking is assumed to be a primordial as well as ultimate deed, as an *exodus*, in the sense of a journey towards a final destination (Piazza, 2004, p. 70). Victor and Edith Turner describe a pilgrimage as externalized mysticism, and mysticism as an inner pilgrimage (Turner and Turner, 1978). In the traditional concept of pilgrimage, the journey, including all its trials and challenges, and the final destination are equally important; the aim of the journey itself lies in the transformation of the participant, who is moulded by this experience. On the other hand, the contemporary tourist, even in the role of spiritual tourist, prefers to seek certainties and a condition of comfort. As a result, the route itself loses all its importance compared to the destination, on which all spiritual attention is placed (Simonicca, 1997). During the Middle Ages, the great sacred routes were reserved for a specific percentage of the population. However, in modern times, the folkloric world has become known for its very popular pilgrimage routes, and its own places of worship linked to a divine election, whose founding legends become symbolic devices establishing beliefs, practices and identity relations marking the community. A shrine is, therefore, the place in which the Virgin appeared, where the power of the divine manifested itself. It is 'that' specific location and no other one, where, starting from the founding moment of the divine epiphany, a process of construction of new places of worship initiates, together with a whole series of religious, sociological and political dynamics, which affect decision-making at different levels and, in the most important cases, promote the location itself on an international and global scale (cf. Claverie, 2003).

Shrines in Calabria

Ever since the ancient Byzantine times, the Calabria region in the southern part of Italy has been a significant location for those seeking proximity to the divine. The caves in that area housed Basilian monks during the exodus that followed the violent persecutions resulting from the iconoclastic edict by Leo III the Isaurian in 726 (Cappelli, 1963, p. 279; Minuto, 2002). These historical events have always been linked to the establishment of new places of worship, such as the foundation of shrines, evoked by legends whose narrative structure explains the origin of the specified devotion, attributing it to miraculous or prodigious events, as well as to the divine intervention in particularly unfortunate, if not desperate, circumstances for a given community. For example, today there is a whole constellation of Marian cults whose founding legends narrate the salvation of entire communities that were constantly exposed to the perils of the Turkish invasions. These cults are still alive today and are linked to shrines whose legends often present the repetition of the same narrative pattern. In short, these are places where the protection of divine figures has manifested itself against invaders, but also against natural disasters, earthquakes, floods and other phenomena that caused devastation in entire areas.

A common pattern often involves the apparition of the Virgin Mary before a young shepherd, that is, a liminal figure linked, in the southern agro-pastoral popular culture, to the notion of simplicity, ambiguity, wildness, fierceness, with connotations referring to the underworld (Spera, 2012).

The foundation of a shrine is often characterized also by the discovery of a statue or a painting in a specific location, thanks to prodigious signs that communicate the precise will of the divine not to move the holy image away from that specific site (Sole, 1998, 2000).

The particular Marian vocation of devotional practices in Calabria is embedded in a wider historical and cultural context, linked to the propagation of apparitions of the Virgin Mary with the consequential revival of pilgrimages that characterized the period going from the second half of the sixteenth century to the end of the seventeenth century (Cajani, 1985, pp. 121–127).

The analysis of the important transformations, which describe the contemporary religious and spiritual panorama in Calabria, must necessarily be rooted in the history of this region, which went through a dramatic change between the 1950s and the 1970s (Bellio, 2014, pp. 149–151). The methods of production, the relations between social and gender groups, the ways of believing and the religious practices of this world seem not to have undergone great changes since the Middle Ages (Cingari, 1982). However, this same world did explode in a span of just three decades, giving rise to new un-imaginable socio-cultural institutions.

The great transformations characterizing the contemporary state of this region have led to alternative interpretations, from an idea of post-modernism (drawing on Lyotard, 1984 [1979]), without modernity on the one hand, to the hypothesis of an ultramodern society or, in any case, the shift towards ultra-modernity of part of the Calabrian society (Willaime, 1995, 2006).

By focusing on a contemporary figure at the origin of a very important cult, an analysis can be made of the forms of contemporary pilgrimage and religious tourism in Calabria from a specific perspective, that is, the perspective of mystic figures in present times. The present chapter, including some results, is part of an ongoing research project addressing a wider picture of the direct relationship with the non-visible in this socio-cultural area. Considering the Catholic context of the Calabria region and the direct intermediaries with the divine therein, focus has been placed on Fratel Cosimo (i.e. Brother Cosimo). His experience gave rise to a community dedicated to the *Madonna dello Scoglio* (literally, Our Lady of the Rock) as well as to new facilities needed to host and manage the enormous flow of pilgrims visiting Santa Domenica, a hamlet near the town of Placanica in the province of Reggio Calabria.

Fratel Cosimo can best be described as a *soul shepherd*: starting off as a humble young shepherd and becoming a shepherd of souls. This contemporary figure has been adopted as a specific methodological and interpretative instrument, that is, an ethnographic paradigm. In fact, he is a real character, whose story and anthropological features, along with his background, assume a paradigmatic function with respect to other figures of prophets, mystics and seers in Calabria.[3] The model of Cosimo Fragomeni must be taken into consideration: the proposed meaning here is a sort of ethnographic inversion of the Weberian notion of ideal type, though it remains equally effective.[4]

The story of Cosimo Fragomeni, known as Fratel Cosimo, seems to emerge directly from the mystic halo surrounding the liminal figures. From 11 to 14 May 1968 this young, little edu-cated shepherd (he was forced to leave his studies in the first year of middle school) witnessed a Marian apparition on a big boulder full of bram-bles, which would then be identified as 'lo Scoglio' (the Rock).

As can be read on the official website of the *Comunità Madonna dello Scoglio* (Our Lady of the Rock Community), the event under consider-ation recalls the pattern of many hagiographic narratives, which emphasize the mild character and spirituality typical of these figures since their early childhood. These traits foretell signs of their future, which is presented with precise terms on a lexical level.[5] Indeed, reference is made to mys-tical figures and to 'epifania di grazia' (epiphany of grace), highlighting the erudite jargon and the theological subtleties that mark the linguistic repertoire of Cosimo, a young boy from a family of humble origin. The production of discourses con-tributing to the process of establishing the mystic figure also includes the prophecies announcing the birth of 'un grande santo' (a great saint) in Placan-ica,[6] following a well-known pattern in classic hagiography. Groups of faithful believers soon gathered around this figure, who was acknow-ledged as having miraculous powers. However, to-wards the end of the 1980s, large crowds started flocking to see him, after his participation in charis-matic movements and, at the same time, cases of healing occurred during his prayer meetings.

On 13 August 1988, Rita Tassone recovered from typhoid osteomyelitis with bone sarcoma, which had paralysed her. Further cases of heal-ing occurred throughout the years and during numerous prayer gatherings before the eyes of the rejoicing crowds. As for many people from Calabria, I had the opportunity to visit the Rock long before I started to develop my interest in this specific research: as is the case in my other ethnographic studies, this too developed from a meeting between the researcher and a direct witnessing of this world and its profound trans-formations over the past few decades. The scien-tific literature regarding these figures range from ethno-psychiatric interpretations to the ana-lyses of the shift from folkloric religious forms to charismatic models that preserve certain cul-tural continuities (Cardamone and Schirripa, 1990, 1997; Schirripa, 2002). This observation is built around the transgressive dimension of the body, which becomes the stage of the battle between the Holy Spirit and the Devil.

The corporeal and public manifestations of such a demonic possession, healed by invoking the Holy Spirit, are classified in terms of 'silent rebellion to a history of subalternity' (Schirripa, 2002, p. 202): the keywords are thus 'subalternity' and 'silent rebellion'. This framework of religious sociology, starting with Durkheim (1995 [1912]), has analysed the dimension of collective excitement that produces the sacred and is evoked by the social dynamics triggered by the prophetic charisma.

On a number of occasions, I had the opportunity to observe the practices characterizing the activity of Fratel Cosimo and his faithful followers, the elements constituting the 'area di credibilità' (believing extent), that is, objective data that make a phenomenon reliable and thus real (Castiglione, 1981, p. 22). I was then able to record the transformations of both the places and the ritual actions.

At the end of the 1980s, just like other young people from my home town, Belvedere Spinello, I too went to Placanica on a coach trip organized by some believers. I was curious to learn more about what I had heard of by word of mouth. We departed in the morning in order to reach the hill where Fratel Cosimo used to hold his prayer gatherings on a weekly basis. At that time, no accommodation facilities were available for visitors. The participants would bring their own folding chairs and place them all around the area, wherever they could find some space to sit. Even then there were street vendors who sold cold drinks and ice cream. In that period, the collective ceremonies were not presided over by any of the members of the official Church, which exercised both caution and assessment.

Some religious figures were already climbing up to the Rock of the apparition, but these were all personal initiatives. Mass was not celebrated, at least that was the case on that hot Saturday afternoon in August 1989. It was the first time I had gone to the Rock together with a group of people from my home town. Once there, we scattered around, knowing only that we had to be back on the coach at the end of the prayers. Many young local people were in charge of broadcasting chants through loudspeakers. I was struck by a repetitive supplication to the Holy Spirit and a refrain that was continuously sung, conveying a feeling of serenity: 'Blood of Jesus

Christ, descend on us'. At that time it could not even have been predicted, but years later I found myself studying the ritual dimension of Catholic charismatic groups during my research activities.

Only later, after the prayers and hymns of praise, did Fratel Cosimo take the floor, in an almost unreal silence among a crowd of flushed faces. In absolute calmness and with a collected voice, he started speaking and at a certain point during his speech he revealed the healings, resulting from divine grace, that were taking place among the crowd. Many people in the crowd fell to the ground and stayed there without moving. Their eyes remained shut and their arms stretched apart. They were assisted by members of the group who were close to the leader and could control any possible gestures or manifestations. In some cases, if people screamed or rambled on, they would bring a cross or a rosary to their mouths and ask them to kiss it. Later I was informed that this was a form of protection against the Devil, while this particular condition is defined as resting in the spirit.[7]

Excruciating cries, interpreted as manifestations of the presence of the Devil, would occasionally break the silence. Upon the announcement of every healing, the beneficiaries, those who had received the grace, would immediately be identified in the crowd. For instance, Fratel Cosimo once announced 'Right now, a man who has long been suffering from a knee condition is healing, he now feels tingling in his legs. He is doubting and wondering whether it is really him.' At that point, a handkerchief was lifted up and waved in the air. Accompanied by applause and words of gratitude to God, the protagonist of this healing stood up, walked through the crowd, which opened up to let him through, and reached the stage where he immediately spoke into the microphone bearing live witness to this experience in an atmosphere of great collective excitement.

Moving on to another date, in 2004 I went to Placanica at the request of an acquaintance who asked me to accompany her to the Rock. Many things had changed since my previous experience. The climax of the ceremony was now during the celebration of the Mass, with a strong presence of religious authorities from all over the region and elsewhere: a long line of white tunics marked the moment of the Eucharistic procession. The choir and the group accompanying the liturgy were still present. Fratel Cosimo would give his speech as before, yet there was an extremely important element that immediately caught my attention: before the prayer gathering started, someone announced that nobody was authorized to walk up to the microphone during the celebration, including those who might feel they were touched by grace. Only after the conclusion of the ceremony could the members of the organization be contacted to give their testimony. This time no handkerchiefs were waved to signal a grace received among the crowd. Shortly before the service ended, a member of the organization invited those who had benefited from a grace during the previous gatherings to step on stage and give their testimony. These prayer meetings were held on a regular basis and with a similar pattern: they were held on Wednesdays and Saturdays, with an even greater attendance on 11 May, the anniversary of the first apparition which Fratel Cosimo had of the Lady of the Rock,[8] and 11 February, the World Day of the Sick for the Catholic Church.

The gatherings started with confessions, which involved an adequate number of priests. Then, Fratel Cosimo held personal meetings with his faithful followers who had made their reservations by phone. The meetings were followed by the recital of the rosary, the Way of the Cross, and a procession with the Blessed Sacrament. After a concelebrated Mass and a prayer of intercession by Fratel Cosimo, a final Marian procession was held. Compared to 15 years earlier, the size of the crowd had increased so much that it was no longer possible to reach the Rock directly by car. A parking lot, large enough to accommodate thousands of vehicles including several coaches, had been built in the valley. It was now necessary to walk up the hill, which required a bit of effort. The transformation of the practices and of the places testify to the actions carried out by the religious authorities on the one hand, but also to the actions of the local authorities in the management of the community. The small town of Placanica had become more and more renowned. Thanks to this constant flow of pilgrims it had turned into one of the most visited venues for religious tourism both in Calabria and in southern Italy, with all the consequences that followed in terms of economy and community management.

Rationalization and Patrimonialization

The last stop on our ethnographic journey around this paradigmatic figure takes us to 2013, more than two decades after the Our Lady of the Rock Community was established by volunteers who ensured that every gathering would run smoothly. The area underwent transformations in order to adjust to the needs of the visitors. The most important project then was the construction of a big shrine to welcome all the pilgrims. The full project is available on the web page, the official communication channel, along with its description and motivations, which allude to a specific indication by the Virgin Mary that a holy place should be built there, as was the case elsewhere. On 15 June 2013, the first stone, blessed by Pope Francis, was laid during a ceremony presided over by Monsignor Giuseppe Fiorini Morosini, Archbishop of the diocese of Reggio Calabria.

The practices of the 1980s changed though. Religious authorities now played a prominent role and the more centralized management of the space and every collective activity were clearly defined. What had been produced in the course of time could especially be appreciated during the procession of the Blessed Sacrament, as if looking at a snapshot: the area, filled with a massive presence of white stoles and chasubles in procession, became the image of approval and appropriation on the part of the official Church.[9]

Fratel Cosimo would still hold his prayer session, but the live announcement of healings was a long lost memory. Everything had changed due to the progressive attempt to set aside the charisma of the seer-prophet in response to ecclesiastic action that progressively shaped and incorporated this figure in the official liturgy. The potentially transgressive extent of the initial healing manifestations, which highlighted this charisma in the Weberian sense of authority legitimized on the basis of individual virtues or extraordinary gifts, had been gradually reduced.

During the services, Fratel Cosimo would no longer announce the ongoing healings as he did in the past, but merely limit himself to a more general invocation of the Holy Spirit. The mechanism of the testimonies, which founded the construction of the discourse on the legitimacy of the prophetic figure, was managed and filtered according to specific indications: there was no longer any possibility of instantly sharing the prodigious event, the enthusiasm of the collective participation, neither was there the direct and immediate communication of the beneficiary with the crowd. Over time, this continuous and extensive remoulding tended to reduce the role of the intermediary as a 'living saint'. Similarly, it limited the search for miracles expressed by the crowds in favour of a religion that attributes the source of every salvation to God while the official Church is the only interpreter and intermediary of the divine will.

I have started to trace the development of other movements in Calabria that started roughly 30 or 40 years ago around a charismatic figure. Today, they are also undergoing a similar subtraction of their leader's authority and charisma. On the one hand, there is a normalization and worshipping of the charismatic leader enacted by the ecclesiastic authorities; on the other hand, there is a form of compliance with official norms on the part of the leader himself. The contemporary forms of mysticism in Calabria have given rise to new places of worship. Over time, the patrimonialization process has concerned the Church and the local authorities, with a gradual transformation of the sites into centres of contemporary religious tourism. At the same time, the phenomenon has taken another direction. The modernization process announced by the Second Vatican Council (O'Malley, 2010; Sevegrand, 2012) seems here to result from the need to limit the popular and 'superstitious' component during the collective expression of faith.

Since the 1970s and 1980s, the Church in Calabria has been enacting an extensive process of normalization of cults, beliefs and practices, with the aim of cancelling or at least reducing the aspects that are less compliant with the official liturgy, that is, the most transgressive manifestations of 'popular religiosity' linked to expressions of 'excitement' and 'pathos'.[10]

Thus, the history of the forms of religion in Calabria over the past few decades is also the history of this activity of transformation. Local authorities have only taken action when the phenomenon extends its area of influence to the point of relating directly to issues involving urban management and public order. In such a case, a measure regarding patrimony and tourism is enacted around the intermediary figure and this is important to understand how the patrimonialization of religious phenomena can unfold.

The case of Fratel Cosimo and the construction of facilities linked to the worship of Our Lady of the Rock is paradigmatic of a whole socioeconomic process. An additional, extremely important element emerges. It provides a specific analytical perspective and contributes to completing the picture of contemporary religious tourism. The transformations of a place and of practices of worship over time reveal the authorities' communication and action strategies, as well as the ways the discourses around faith are constructed. Contemporary religious pilgrimages and tourism become important tools of instruction, a kind of life-long catechesis, whose effects are visible over the years. Therefore, according to the interpretation proposed in the present chapter, they have a pedagogical function while expressing the implementation of official norms. Over time, a whole system of prescriptions and prohibitions appears not only for the pilgrims, but for the seer-prophet as well. The prayer gatherings and the huge crowds, also involving people who may not necessarily be church-goers in their places of origin, become a sort of open-air catechesis.[11] During this process, the prophet's body goes from being the direct instrument of the divine to being, little by little, the instrument of an official ecclesiastic domestication not only of practices but also of collective beliefs. In this sense, it is possible to understand the adhesion of the figure of Cosimo Fragomeni to two different models through time. The image of the young shepherd with little education coming from the agro-pastoral world is characterized by the otherness inherent in his own condition, and this otherness gives him direct access to *sacer*. He eventually becomes the shepherd of souls, who spreads the message of the Gospel regarding inner and later physical purification and healing. The potentially chaotic and subversive element of the agricultural and agro-pastoral context, given its proximity to this ruthless condition, becomes, little by little, the main element of an official and liturgical piety, in which the Weberian prophetic charisma tends to be absorbed by the charisma of office. In the case I am examining in the contemporary overview of Calabria, along with other cases, the prophet proclaims the Word of God, he interprets the Word, yet his role of charismatic leader is gradually toned down by complying with the liturgy and protocol that limit the individual in accordance with the message.

Therefore, in this context, we are far from the prophetic type defined not only by the sociology of religion, starting with Max Weber and Ernst Troeltsch,[12] but also by the history of religion, which questions both the established order and the authority, thus presenting a subversive and political function. Thanks to this particular perspective, the forms of contemporary religious tourism in the Calabria region can be dealt with by looking at the patrimonial policies but also at the contemporary policies regarding the management of collective devotional events.

Notes

[1] After the Second Vatican Council, following the reform of the Roman Curia, a Pastoral Ministry to tourism was established and entrusted to the Congregation for the Clergy. On 30 April 1969 the latter edited the publication *Peregrinans in terra* by the General Directory for the Pastoral Care in Tourism. Magistero Pontificio e documenti della Santa Sede sulla *Pastorale del Turismo*, Libreria Editrice Vaticana, Città del Vaticano, 2009, p. 7 (English edition Congregation for the Clergy, General Directory for the Pastoral Ministry in the Field of Tourism *Peregrinans in terra*, 27 March 1969, *AAS* LXI (1969), 361–384); Mazza, 1992.

[2] Among the vast literature on these subjects we shall here mention just the direct references used in the drafting of this text: Vauchez, 1975; Oursel, 1978; Turner and Turner, 1978; Sartori, 1983; Dupront, 1987; Ohler, 1989; Le Goff, 1990 ; 2005; Cardini, 1996; Stopani, 2010.

[3] Due to space limitations, it is not possible here to provide further details of this research line, which I have embraced since the drafting of my PhD thesis (Bellio, 2006b), also focusing on the semantic scope of the terms defining the forms of direct contact with the non-visible in different cultural contexts and, more generally, on the transformations of the Calabrian religious field, through the specific lens afforded by the figures of intermediaries with the supernatural (Bellio, 2006a, 2008, 2009, 2011).

[4] The concept of ideal type, beginning with the reflections by Max Weber (Weber, 1949 [1904]; 1978 [1921]), besides being a key element of his epistemology, becomes a fully fledged heuristic device within the framework of social sciences in the twentieth century (Vârtejanu-Joubert, 2010, p. 511).

[5] www.madonnadelloscoglio.calabria.it/wordpress/home/fratel-cosimo/, accessed in September 2015.

[6] Many years before he was born, a prophecy used to circulate in the valley: 'In Santa Domenica of Placanica – the people used to murmur – one day a great saint will be born, he shall perform many miracles and these places shall be worshipped by many souls. Large crowds shall come here to worship the Madonna who shall attend to their supplications.' The prophecy is reported by journalist and writer Patrizia Cattaneo in www.patriziacattaneo.com/lang2/fratel_cosimo.html, last accessed in August 2014, and in Cattaneo (2014).

[7] In charismatic cults, this expression is used to define a form of effusion of the Holy Spirit, that is a kind of state that is apparently comparable to fainting: those who have had this experience define it as a sudden weakening of the lower limbs and dizziness, leading the subject to fall to the ground, usually with the support of the persons next to them so that they can lie down, followed by a great sense of inner peace. According to the groups of Charismatic Renewal, during this condition the Spirit performs physical and spiritual healing, whereas from the interpretative perspective it has been described in terms of hysterical, mediumistic, parapsychological or hypnotic phenomenon (Madre and Efraim, 1982, pp. 25–29).

[8] www.madonnadelloscoglio.calabria.it/wordpress/home/informazioni/, accessed in August 2014.

[9] By decree no. 37, 7 December 2008, Gerace Giuseppe Fiorini, Bishop of Locri, signed the official recognition of the worship of the *Madonna dello Scoglio di Placanica* (Our Lady of the Rock in Placanica). The text briefly summarizes the stages of the assessment procedure and establishes the theological and liturgical outline of the religious manifestations occurring at the *Scoglio*, the Rock, appropriately evaluated by the relevant ecclesiastic authorities but also by laypersons 'prepared ad hoc'.

[10] Along these lines, Bible scholar S. Parisi addresses the specific issue of the biblical sense and of authenticity of the religious feast as a liturgical necessity regulating excitement, a sort of 'celebratory essentiality' that 'regulates popular euphoria' (Parisi, 1995, pp. 202, 203).

[11] As can be read in the apostolic exhortation *Catechesi Tradendae* by John Paul II, 'to make disciples' is a central element among the activities of the Church.

[12] Cf. Weber (1964), Weber (1997), Weber (2001 [1905]), Troeltsch (1992 [1912]) and Troeltsch (2005 [1902]).

References

Bellio, A. (2006a) *Les femmes qui vont avec les morts en Calabre*. In: Bonnet, J. (ed.) *Malemorts, revenants et vampires en Europe*. L'Harmattan, Paris.

Bellio, A. (2006b) *Veggenti e Sibille*. *Prospettive etnografiche e riferimenti letterari*, PhD thesis, University of Cosenza, Italy.

Bellio, A. (2008) *Au-delà du silence. La parole des femmes voyantes, petit patrimoine calabrais*. In: Fournier, L.S. (ed.) *Le petit patrimoine des européens: objets et valeurs du quotidien*. L'Harmattan, Paris.

Bellio, A. (2009) *Women who cook with angels in Calabria*. In: Medina, F.X., Àvila, R. and De Garine, I. (ed.) *Food, Imaginaries and Cultural Frontiers. Essays in Honour of Helen Macbeth*, 'Estudios del Hombre', 24, CUSH (Centro Universitario de Ciencias Sociales y Humanidades de la Universidad de Guadalajara), Guadalajara, Mexico, pp. 101–125.

Bellio, A. (2011) *Il pendolo della marginalità. Donne calabresi tra la Sibilla e Maria*. In: Porcellana, V. (ed.) *Il doppio margine. Donne tra esclusione e cambiamento*. Libreria Stampatori, Turin, Italy.

Bellio, A. (2014) *Tradition en Calabre contemporaine: Formes d'invention, réinvention et instrumentalisation*, 'Anthroserbia', Problèmes d'ethnologie et d'anthropologie, Monographies numériques, no. 7, 2014. Kovač, S. and Milenković, M. (eds) Université de Belgrade, Faculté de philosophie, Département d'ethnologie et d'anthropologie, pp. 147–164.

Cajani, L. (1985) *Gli anni santi: dalla Controriforma alla fine del potere temporale*. In: Fagiolo, M. and Madonna, L.M. (eds) *Roma Sancta. La città delle basiliche*. Gangemi, Rome, pp. 121–127.

Cappelli, B. (1963) *Il monachesimo basiliano ai confini calabrolucani*. Fausto Fiorentino Editore, Naples, Italy.

Cardamone, G. and Schirripa, P. (1990) *Lo scoglio e la salvezza: un culto terapeutico in Calabria*, 'Daedalus. Rivista del Laboratorio di Storia', no. 4, pp. 127–145.

Cardamone, G. and Schirripa, P. (1997) *Retorica della terapia, corpo e narrazione della malattia. La terapeutica carismatica nel meridione d'Italia*. In: Beneduce, R. (ed.) *Saperi, linguaggi e tecniche nei sistemi di cura tradizionali*. L'Harmattan, Turin, Italy, pp. 157–182.

Cardini, F. (1996) *Il pellegrinaggio. Una dimensione della vita medievale*. Vecchiarelli, Manziana, Italy.

Castiglione, M. (1981) *I professionisti dei sogni. Visioni e devozioni popolari nella cultura contadina meridionale* Liguori, Naples, Italy.

Cattaneo, P. (2014) *Fratel Cosimo e i miracoli della Madonna dello Scoglio*. Gribaudi, Milan, Italy.

Cingari, G. (1982) *Storia della Calabria dall'Unità ad oggi*. Laterza, Bari, Italy.

Claverie, E. (2003) *Les guerres de la Vierge. Une anthropologie des apparitions*. Gallimard, Paris.

Dupront, A. (1987) *Du sacré. Croisades et pèlerinages. Images et langages*. Gallimard, Paris.

Durkheim, É. (1995 [1912]) *The Elementary Forms of Religious Life*. Trans. Fields, K.E., Free Press, New York.

Grossi, A. (2008) *Le vie dello spirito. Sociologia del pellegrinaggio contemporaneo*. In: Magistrali, G. (dir.) *Turismo sociale*. Maggioli, Rimini, pp. 229–235.

Iannario, M. (2004) *Turismo religioso: da esperienza mistica individuale a prospettiva di sviluppo economico-territoriale. Dinamiche spaziali e input per un nuovo sistema di mercato*. In: Bencardino, F. and Marotta, G. (eds) *Nuovi turismi e politiche di gestione della destinazione. Prospettive di sviluppo per le aree rurali della Campania*, DASES Università degli Studi del Sannio, Franco Angeli, Milan, pp. 165–176.

Le Goff, J. (1990) *Medieval Callings*. Cochrane, L.G. (trans.) The University of Chicago Press, Chicago, Illinois, USA.

Le Goff, J. (2005 [2003]) *The Birth of Europe*. Lloyd, J. (trans.). Blackwell, Malden, Massachusetts, USA.

Lyotard, J.F. (1984 [1979]) *The Postmodern Condition. A Report of Knowledge*. University of Minnesota Press, Minneapolis, Minnesota, USA.

Madre, P. and Efraim, F.R. (1982) *Il riposo nello Spirito*. RnS, Rome.

Mazza, C. (1992) *Il turismo religioso*. Longo, Ravenna, Italy.

Minuto, D. (2002) *Profili di santi nella Calabria bizantina*. Giuseppe Pontari Editore, Reggio Calabria, Italy.

Ohler, N. (1989 [1986]) *The Medieval Traveller*. Hillier, C. (trans.) Boydell & Brewer, Woodbridge, UK.

Oursel, R. (1978) *Pèlerins du Moyen Age*. Fayard, Paris.

O'Malley, J. (2010) *What Happened at Vatican II*. Harvard University Press, Cambridge, Massachusetts, USA.

Parisi, S. (1995) Feste religiose e fede del popolo in YHWH. *Vivarium. Rivista di scienze teologiche*, Nuova serie, III, 2, maggio-agosto, 183–203.

Piazza, O.F. (2004) *Turismo religioso. Il viaggiare tra spiritualità e territorio*. In: Bencardino, F. and Marotta, M. (eds) *Nuovi turismi e politiche di gestione della destinazione. Prospettive di sviluppo per le aree rurali della Campania*. Franco Angeli, Milan, pp. 69–82.

Sartori, L. (1983) *Pellegrinaggio e religiosità popolare*. Il Messaggero, Padova, Italy.

Schirripa, P. (2002) Health, charismatic cults and contemporary folk culture. *AM Rivista della Società italiana di antropologia medica* 13–14, 191–204.

Sesana, G. (2006) *Pellegrini e turisti. L'evoluzione del viaggio religioso.* Hoepli, Milan.

Sevegrand, M. (2012) *Vatican II (1959–1965). Feuilleton d'un Concile en 34 épisodes.* Golias, Villeurbanne.

Simonicca, A. (1997) *Antropologia del turismo. Strategie di ricerca e contesti etnografici.* Carocci, Rome.

Sole, G. (1998) *Il viaggio dei pellegrini. Saggio di antropologia religiosa.* Centro Editoriale e Librario Università della Calabria, Rende, Italy.

Sole, G. (2000) *Il cammino verso la Grande Madre. Il pellegrinaggio in un santuario di montagna.* In: Lombardi Satriani, L.M. (ed.) *Madonne, pellegrini e santi. Itinerari antropologico-religiosi nella Calabria di fine millennio.* Meltemi, Rome.

Spera, V. (2012) *Le berger et l'imaginaire populaire en Italie méridionale. Réalité productive, conflits culturels et dynamiques mythico-rituelles.* In: Bonnet-Carbonell, J. (ed.) *Des bergers en Europe. Pratiques, rites, représentations.* L'Harmattan, Paris, pp. 147–166.

Stopani, R. (2010) *L'altra Francigena. La quotidianità del pellegrinaggio medievale.* Le Lettere, Florence, Italy.

Troeltsch, E. (1992 [1912]) *The Social Teaching of the Christian Churches.* Vol. 1. Wyon, O. (trans.). Westminster John Knox Press, Louisville, Kentucky, USA.

Troeltsch, E. (2005 [1902]) *The Absoluteness of Christianity and the History of Religions.* Reid, D. (trans.) Westminster John Knox Press, Louisville, Kentucky, USA.

Turner, V. and Turner, E. (1978) *Image and Pilgrimage in Christian Culture. Anthropological Perspectives.* Columbia University Press, New York.

Vârtejanu-Joubert, M. (2010) *Idéaltype religieux.* In: Azria, R. and Hervieu-Léger, D. (eds) *Dictionnaire des faits religieux.* Presses Universitaires de France, Paris, pp. 511–514.

Vauchez A. (1993 [1975]) *The Spirituality of the Medieval West from the Eighth to the Twelfth Century.* Friedlander, C. (trans.). Cistercian Publications, Kalamazoo, Michigan.

Weber, M. (1949 [1904]) Objectivity in social sciences and social policy. In: Shils, E.A. and Finch, H.A. (eds and trans) *The Methodology of the Social Sciences.* The Free Press, New York, pp. 50–112.

Weber, M. (1964) *The Sociology of Religion.* Fischoff, E. (trans.). Beacon Press, Boston, Massachusetts, USA.

Weber, M. (1978[1921]) *Economy and Society: An Outline of Interpretive Sociology.* Roth, G. and Wittich, C. (eds) University of California Press, Berkeley, California, USA.

Weber, M. (1997) *L'etica protestante e lo spirito del capitalismo.* Rizzoli, Milan, Italy.

Weber, M. (2001[1905]) *The Protestant Ethic and the Spirit of Capitalism.* Parsons, T. (ed.) Routledge, London/New York.

Willaime, J.P. (1995) *Sociologie des religions.* Presses Universitaires de France, Paris.

Willaime, J.P. (2006) Religion in ultramodernity. In: Beckford, J.A. and Wallis, J. (eds) *Theorising Religion. Classical and Contemporary Debates.* Ashgate, Burlington, Virginia, USA, pp. 77–89.

5 Fighting for the Saint: Ritual Rivalries in Traditional Pilgrimages

Laurent S. Fournier*

IDEMEC UMR 7307 CNRS, Aix-Marseille-University, Aix-en-Provence, France

Introduction

Anthropologists and historians of local pilgrimages often talk about more or less ritualized outbursts of violence expressing customary rivalries among parishes. During local pilgrimages, the pilgrims often settled their quarrels; they often fought for the honour of serving the saint of the day. First, I propose to examine in this chapter some examples of ritual battles happening in local pilgrimages. From the point of view of the touristic valorization of contemporary pilgrimages, such a historical legacy raises many questions. The study of the ways civil and religious authorities accept or do not accept this history will be undertaken in the next part of the chapter. I will show that pilgrimages are not limited to their religious content but are also occasions to express political or social antagonisms.

Ritual Battles in Provence

Many ethnographers and historians report rivalries and ritual battles occurring in local pilgrimages. In Provence, a Catholic region in the south of France, these rivalries seem to have been very common in the past, even if only little evidence remains of them nowadays. The researches of local historians and folklorists enable us to envision the main features of such practices, which are well known in a lot of villages.

Fighting for the honour of the saint

The first example I would like to mention was discovered when I was studying the contemporary changes in local religious festivals in Provence (Fournier, 2005). Between the villages of Saint-Remy-de-Provence and Eyragues, in the north of the Bouches-du-Rhône district, a few kilometres south of Avignon, the chapel Saint Bonnet of Lagoy traditionally hosted, each year, the parishioners of the two villages, who used to make a pilgrimage on 15 January. Today, however, the pilgrimage doesn't exist anymore. The people of Eyragues still honour Saint Bonnet on 15 January but they stay in their village because of, they contend, the too violent quarrels occurring in the past between the two parishes when they met at the chapel. Through fieldwork, it is indeed possible to document the old rivalry between the two villages. This rivalry still exists in narratives, mutual mockeries or derogatory nicknames given to the people of the opposite village. During the twentieth century,

*E-mail: laurent.fournier@univ-amu.fr

the traditional rivalry was revived by political struggles between socialist 'reds' and conservative 'whites', because the people of Saint-Remy-de-Provence are said to be 'red' and the people from Eyragues have a reputation for being 'white'. However, in practice, these political struggles are less powerful than the old customary conflicts between the parishes, which are very often mentioned when the informants recall the atavistic hate between the two neighbouring villages.

According to several informants the origin of the rivalry came from the fact that the boys of the two villages pretended that the saint belonged to them; they threw stones at each other around his chapel and finally fought. Fighting and stone throwing was the tradition. A mayor was even made destitute in the nineteenth century because he encouraged his electors in this violence. The Provencal folklorist Charles Galtier (1990, p. 70) calls the stone fighting 'aqueirado' and speaks about 'a ritual game practised at the end of pilgrimages'. In other cases he indicates that this game could be practised with dried mud or fruits. He considers this game as very old and compares it with the 'lithobolia' stone fighting in ancient Greece. He therefore connects the practice with a specific sort of symbolism. According to anthropologist Jean Servier, quoted by Galtier (1990), the opposition between the two rival factions would enable the pilgrims to 'ask the saint what were his intentions towards them… in order to get an omen. The end of the game would enable to predict the fortune of the next year: wet or dry according to the wining team, representing one of these universal principles.'

Galtier (1990, p. 71) also notes that several pilgrimages in Provence were also the time for a 'bravado' – a special moment in the festivals when armed soldiers would parade with firearms, throw firecrackers and make loud explosions of black powder in the towns of Manosque, Gréoux, Fréjus, etc. In these cases violence is part of the ritual script of the festivals. It can either remain at a symbolical level, or become a ritual feature like the attack of a fortress in the 'Moros y Cristianos' style (Albert-Llorca and Gonzalez Alcantud, 2003). In these examples, however, the ritual is more like a sort of theatrical game within which the violence is figured, represented, but not necessarily real.

The stick-fight pilgrimage

Another ethnohistorical Provencal example concerning real violence is reported by Marie-Hélène Froeschlé-Chopart (2014). This record mentions 'lou roumeiragi deis cops de batoun', the stick-fight pilgrimage in the village of Brenon, near Castellane in the Alpes-de-Haute-Provence district (Froeschlé-Chopart, 2014, p. 56). This pilgrimage was so called because 'the young people of the neighbouring villages came armed with sticks and fought for the honour of stealing the instruments during the ball: this fight often occasioned murders'. Again, in this example, struggles and provocations among youngsters were regularly happening during a local pilgrimage.

Another example in Seillans (near the city of Draguignan) was 'lou roumeiragi deis pesseguis durs', the festival of hard peaches (Froeschlé-Chopart, 2014, p. 64). This pilgrimage traditionally ended with a stone fight around the Saint Arnould chapel. In this case, 'those of Seillans' fight against 'those of Bargemon', a neighbouring village. In the beginning it's all jumps and dances for the ball, as accompanies any festival.

> But soon the spirit changes; a dispute opposes an inhabitant from Seillans and another one from Bargemon. The spirits heated by the dances and often by the wine burst into flames and the theater of pleasure becomes a collective stone-fight with the big heaps of stone laying around. These people run after each other for miles. When the people from Bargemon are not enough to fight, the quarrel begins between the peasants and the artisans of Seillans. They fight against each other and throw stones even in town. […] We are not able to explain the reason of this frenzy […]. The wounds, the procedures, the most severe forbidding, nothing has changed this practice, nothing has abolished it. (C.-F. Achard, quoted by Froeschlé-Chopard, 2014).

According to these historical accounts, there was some sort of necessity to fight on these occasions. The struggle is well organized and concerns the people of Seillans if the people of Bargemon are not enough. In this case, the territorial divisions between the villages are not at the centre of the struggle any more: the social divisions between peasants and craftsmen become central. The pilgrimage, because it happens beyond the boundaries of the village, in an open space, becomes a moment when we meet otherness but also the perils represented by the other. In the context of traditional communities, characteristic for their endogamy and xenophobia, this exceptional situation brings a lot of excitement. In the beginning the people look at each other with defiance, then they fight. Dancing and struggling become a passion, a furore according with the stereotyped image of passionate southerners. At the same time, violence as a transgression of law is conceived as a homage and as a sacrifice for the saint, who is protected from those considered not legitimate enough to honour him.

Because they bring crowds together, festivals always mean danger, excess, outbursts of violence and provocations between rival factions. Historically, this is an explanation for the numerous interdictions of festivals, these interactions answering the requirements of both conservatives and progressives. For the first group, the 'whites', the festive excesses go against public order. For the second group, the 'reds', they divert the people from social progress. Pilgrimages are therefore a time when emotions and frustrations are collectively expressed. This is very different from the idealized vision of a pacific and fraternal pilgrimage answering to the Christian values of sharing and charity.

A Universal Feature?

Interestingly, this situation when local pilgrimages are the time for more or less ritualized fights and conflicts exists far beyond the case of Provence. Indeed, this situation has not only been documented in other French or Christian European regions, it also exists in other continents and in other historical periods in very different religious contexts. It is therefore possible to question the feature of a ritual fight connected with a religious festival as a universal anthropological feature.

The violence of festivals in French Brittany

In French Brittany, Anatole Le Braz (1994 [1894]) gives the example of the Saint-Servais festival and its 'warlike procession': 'Instead of the usual pacific willow stick, the pilgrims waved an oak or a holy penn-baz, with a metal end, seeming an enormous prehistoric club, fixed to the right fist with a leather string' (Le Braz, 1994 [1894], p. 949). The battle mentioned here concerns 'those from Quimper' and 'those from Vannes'. After each verse of the magnificat the clubs would rattle. The people from Quimper shouted 'Shake the frost, oat and wheat for Quimper' and the people from Vannes answered 'Shake the frost, oat and wheat for Vannes'. Like in many traditional rituals the victory of a party is believed to bring abundant crops in the connected country. In a way, the end of the battle is vital because it determines welfare for the coming year.

In the same pilgrimage people also fight to carry the banner and the small statue of the saint: 'The club scrum begins. They get up, crash down, and twirl around in bloody circles. They strike like madmen. The rector and his cantors are hidden in the sacristy. People fight for the banner and the little wooden statuette. The women are not the less involved: they bite, they scratch...' The violence of the procession is incredible, and causes many victims each year. The carts go back home loaded with wounded people. However, one should be cautious when using such sources because Le Braz, a folklorist and a novel-writer, may have embellished the narratives he assigns to a naive peasant supposed to have witnessed all these scenes. But even if this is not a true ethnographic account, it recalls practices described in other places by anthropologists.

Towards a large-scale comparison: From Iran to Korea

This feature of violence happening during pilgrimages or during religious festivals in general is connected by political anthropologists with a social phenomenon known as factionalism. In early modern Iran, violence was always expected for religious festivals. It came from disputes between Shia and Sunni at the beginning, then the factions survived without any other motivation than themselves. The divisions between factions were commonplace in the Safavide cities in the early modern period. According to Perry (1998, p. 110):

> For festivals and other public meetings, one of the two parties attacked the other one in order to have the precedence, and the rest of the time wrestlers and young people from each party

would challenge those from the other side. Sometimes, pitched battles then took place in the old square of the town, with hundreds of people fighting on each side. The participants were always from the working classes, and although they only fought with sticks and stones there was always a few killed and a lot of injured.

Another example from Korea is quite comparable. In Korea there existed a ritual stone fight, at the beginning of the spring. This fight had a sacred and a propitiatory function and was called 'dol palmae ssaum'. The historian Laurent Quisefit (2012) mentions a stone fight described by an English folklorist in the nineteenth century:

> Several hundreds of the best stone shooters from the capital chose their side and armed with stones weighing 400 to 800 grams each gathered for the battle. When I arrived the stones flew in the air [...]. Covered with dust and sweat, each side came the nearer possible and threw rocks in the air in a surprising way. Then came a sudden stop. A shout, just like if a goal had been marked. One of the best shooters had been killed. His body was carried far away from the field and the battle began again. Before dawn another shooter had fallen on the other side, so the score was now even. (Quisefit, 2012, p. 54)

Several fights between guilds or opposed factions, bringing injuries or deaths, are described by anthropologists in connection with religious ceremonies or season changes, in various contexts. This cultural feature seems to be constant. The previous examples should be compared with the ritual wars documented by Max Gluckman (1954) in Africa and by other authors in other cultural areas. The notion of 'feud' so well documented by Evans-Pritchard (1940) among the Nuer in Soudan might be considered as another example of these ritual wars. Historically, it would also be interesting to compare these practices with the 'night battles' studied by Carlo Ginzburg (1966) through the archives of the Catholic inquisition in Italy.

The comparison of all these different examples helps to identify some significant elements: (i) a violent fight opposing two parties or factions; (ii) happening at a precise time of the year, usually in connection with a seasonal change or with a public festival; and (iii) leading to a happy ending for the victorious party. This is a very simple structure, which doesn't fit at all with the contemporary conceptions of pilgrimages as religious and pacific meetings.

Stakes in the Debate

The examples presented in the previous sections connect the important times of religious life and the pilgrimages with a violence based on emulation or on the quest for honour. Brotherhoods or local factions in charge of the festivals take part in this violence. For anthropologists, such practices have often been interpreted as periodical challenges bringing the attention of the saints or of the ancestors or promoting the fertility of the earth. According to other authors, more social or political aspects are put forward. In any case however, the situation is well documented: customary rivalries exist everywhere in the world and are expressed during local festivals and pilgrimages.

What do contemporary debates on pilgrimages say about this old anthropological material? Not much, indeed, because religion first evacuated these practices before they became interesting again for touristic reasons. Pilgrimages today concern a modern conception of religion, totally cut off from older popular practices. Pilgrimages today are limited to their religious and to their official parts, which are emphasized without imagining the emotions and the social stakes of pilgrimages in the past.

The organizer's point of view

Today, 'religious tourism' is first connected with the monuments, the sites and, not so much, with the followers who might have another vision from the organizers. In the Christian world, there has been a strong influence of the 'peaceful' vision of the Church, which promotes pilgrimages as a means of religious education. There is also a politic of the Church concerning pilgrimages, valorizing the bigger ones and trying to pacify the local conflicts connected with the smaller ones. The general secularization of society has also led to the displacement of the honour conflicts from the village or parish scene to more urban and laic settings. Such a change has to be placed in the context of modernization described by Norbert Elias and Eric Dunning (1986). Industrialization and urbanization led the modern individual to stop using violence publicly. New practices like modern sports enable the 'controlled decontrolling of emotions', whereas traditional times of freedom like the village festivals don't play the same role. Moreover, relations to others have become common in a multicultural world. Situations when a big crowd is assembled are more frequent. Honour questions don't need public festivals to be solved anymore.

Furthermore, only the faithful have remained in the pilgrimages. They come to share a faith, not to settle quarrels. Modern pilgrimages assemble more homogeneous crowds, while they were exceptional occasions of meeting in the past, which justified a greater excitement in a context when media and spectacles were totally absent. Today, the pilgrimage organizers tend to present pilgrimages as the possibility to share important religious values; there are no dissentions because only a minority participates. This might be considered as progress because the ritual fights have disappeared from pilgrimages, but this also leads to the loss of anthropological knowledge on pilgrimages. Disconnected from their social and political assets, pilgrimages may have lost a part of their meaning.

How to bring together religion and tourism?

According to another perspective, other people use the very notions of 'tourism' and 'religion'. This perspective appears in specialized publications. For instance, the journal *Tourism Recreation Research* (2014) questions the relationships between tourism and pilgrimage, asking if the tourist is a 'secular pilgrim' or a 'hedonist in quest of pleasure'. The discussion concerns the use of the pilgrim metaphor to speak about the tourists. Is this metaphor a good one? Isn't it an external perspective, very different from the pilgrim's own vision?

The journal I mention gives the examples of the ways heritage tourists pay devotion to artworks, the hedonist practices on some pilgrimages, or pilgrimages to the shrines of rock'n'roll stars (Margry, 2014). Of course there is a risk of emptying the notion of pilgrimage when applying

it to the profane world. But at the same time human activities are always ambiguous: pilgrims also have profane motivations, and for their part tourists also try to reach spirituality and the sacred. Moreover, the two sorts of activity correspond to a 'quest for authentic experience', following the tourism specialist Dean MacCannell (1976). Therefore, tourism could be considered as a form of modern pilgrimage from a Durkheimian perspective. In both cases there would be a spiritual quest, a need for change, economic outcomes for a given territory, etc.

Such a discussion is interesting but what would be moral and normative considerations from the organizer's point of view are replaced by a conceptual or intellectual approach. This perspective doesn't concern itself with empirical questions and might build up a moralistic vision of tourism by understanding it as a 'pilgrimage'. Finally, this perspective is too Eurocentric to take into account larger comparative views. It uses neither the organizer's point of view nor the anthropological material and the examples presented at the beginning of this chapter.

Towards an anthropological approach

Looking at the existing discussions, I would suggest an anthropological perspective, taking into account the diverse conceptions of the audience. Fieldwork needs to be carried out in order not to get stuck in the 'organizer's' or the 'specialist's' points of view. This fieldwork is important to understand how diverse views can be expressed in a given pilgrimage. But at the same time, how is it possible to present the 'dark' part of the pilgrimages without being an awful spoilsport in the eyes of the religious organizers of contemporary pilgrimages? What are the stakes connected with the presentation of the anthropological knowledge concerning the fights happening in older pilgrimages? Is it possible to valorize such aspects in order to promote religious tourism today, or is that beyond political correctness?

These questions show the complexity of a reflection on religious tourism and on the relationships between tourism and pilgrimage. Comparing the different perspectives, it seems impossible to limit pilgrimages to their religious aspects only. But it is not much better to valorize the public disorders identified in a lot of historical and anthropological sources. Anthropologists have to find a way to pay attention both to the ritual fights from the past and to the contemporary will to limit pilgrimages to religious practices. Trying to develop pilgrimages as a tourism destination, they should document the disturbing aspects as well as the more consensual. This is the only way to open pilgrimages to an audience including tourists and even people from other religions.

In this respect, it is important to note that the nature of the risks connected with pilgrimages has changed a lot. In the past, the risks mainly came from travelling afar, out of the community, and through the people met in the pilgrimages, leading to rivalries and fights. Today, the risks connected with the crowd are the more important, if we believe the reports concerning the victims of violence in great pilgrimages like in Mecca or Varanasi. Reflection on religious tourism therefore depends on a changed context. It occurs a long time after a rupture could be observed in the traditional conceptions of pilgrimages. First, secularization emptied pilgrimages of their local social and political meanings. Most of them have only kept a religious meaning. Their transformation into tourist destinations is irrespective of the feelings of the past local communities. It is important then to take care that tourism doesn't transform pilgrimages into a simple religious folklore, ignoring all the conflicts and the dynamics of the past pilgrimages.

References

Albert-Llorca, M. and Gonzalez Alcantud, J.A. (eds) (2003) *Moros y Cristianos. Representaciones del otro en las fiestas del Mediterraneo occidental*. Presses Universitaires du Mirail, Toulouse and Diputacion de Granada, Granada, France.

Elias, N. and Dunning, E. (1986) *Sport et civilisation: la violence maîtrisée*. Fayard, Paris.

Evans-Pritchard, E.E. (1940) *The Nuer. A Description of the Modes of Livelihood and Political Institutions of a Nilotic People*. Clarendon Press, Oxford, UK.

Fournier, L.S. (2005) *La fête en héritage: enjeux patrimoniaux de la sociabilité provençale*. Publications de l'Université de Provence, Aix-en-Provence, France.

Froeschlé-Chopart, M.-H. (2014) La fête au village dans l'ancienne Provence selon Claude-François Achard. In: Bertrand, R. and Fournier, L.S. (eds) *Les fêtes en Provence autrefois et aujourd'hui*. Publications de l'Université de Provence, Aix-en-Provence, France, pp. 51–66.

Galtier, C. (1990) *Les Saints guérisseurs en Provence et dans le Comtat Venaissin*. Horvath, Le Coteau, France.

Ginzburg, C. (1984 [1966]) *Les batailles nocturnes. Sorcellerie et rituels agraires aux XVIe et XVIIe siècles*. Champs Flammarion, Paris (trans. Giorgana Charuty).

Gluckman, M. (1954) *Rituals of Rebellion in South-East Africa*. Manchester University Press, Manchester, UK.

Le Braz, A. (1994 [1894]) Au pays des pardons. In: *Magies de la Bretagne*. Robert Laffont, Paris.

MacCannell, D. (1976) *The Tourist. A New Theory of the Leisure Class*. Schocken Books, New York.

Margry, P.J. (2014) Whiskey and pilgrimage: clearing up commonalities. *Tourism Recreation Research* 39(2), 243–247.

Perry, J. (1998) Artificial antagonism in pre-modern Iran: the Haydari-Ne'mati urban factions. In: Kagay, D.J. and Andrew Villalon, L.J. (eds) *The Final Argument. The Imprint of Violence on Society in Medieval and Modern Europe*. Boydell Press, Woodbridge, UK, pp. 107–118.

Quisefit, L. (2012) La violence lithobolique en Corée: jeu de guerre, simulacre cathartique et rituel agricole. In: Robène, L. (ed.) *Le sport et la guerre. XIXe et XXe siècles*. Presses Universitaires de Rennes, Rennes, France, pp. 53–62.

Tourism Recreation Research (2014) Is Tourist a Secular Pilgrim or a Hedonist in Search of Pleasure? *Tourism Recreation Research* 39(2), 235–267.

6 Chinese Migrations and Pilgrimages around Prato (Italy) and Wenzhou (China)

Daniele Parbuono*

China-Europe Cultural Heritage Centre, Chongqing University of Arts and Sciences, Chongqing, China; Department of Filosofia, Scienze Sociali, Umane e della Formazione, Università degli Studi di Perugia, Perugia, Italy

Introduction

Religions, migrations, places of worship and pilgrimage are the keywords of this chapter, organized into two interconnected sections.[1] In the first section I examine worship in a migration context, focusing attention on the city of Prato (Italy), which – after having doubled its population since the 1950s on the basis of a strong internal migration (workers coming from the South of Italy) – in recent decades has been faced with an exponential increase of population coming from abroad, in particular from the People's Republic of China.

In this complex urban context, the 'Tempio dell'Associazione Buddista della comunità cinese in Italia' (Temple of the Buddhist Association of the Chinese community in Italy) is not only a fundamental meeting place for the Chinese living in the city, but – during the main feast days – welcomes 'migrant pilgrims' who come from neighbouring areas and other regions.

This space, which at the same time is a strong point of reference for the social vitality of migrants, thus assumes a function of 'worship complementarity' in Italy, in relation to religious practices that many Chinese undertake during their travels in their country of origin.

In the second section, I reflect on the fact that for rituals and for the most important practices, they tend to go to religious figures, monks or shamans inside the Chinese temples: in their country of origin many of them take on the characteristics of real pilgrims. The terms *chaosheng* 朝圣, 'pay homage to the holiness', or *chaoshan* 朝山, 'go to the hearing on a mountain', which in English can express the word 'pilgrimage', emphasize the importance of the veneration of the sacred mountains, privileged places of devotion for both Buddhism and Taoism. Starting from these assumptions in this text, I try to think about the places to which they go, the religious figures to whom they address themselves and the rituals used by the Chinese 'return pilgrims'.

Chinese Migration to Prato

The data that immediately caught my attention from the beginning of this ethnographic research in 2012 were definitely demographic. According to the Town of Prato website,[2] mass immigration of Chinese to the area began in the 1990s, composed of people who came directly from the People's Republic of China, from other Italian cities and other European states, and from neighbouring areas (Marsden, 2003). These data are confirmed by the fact that, in the late 1980s and early 1990s, the first large

*E-mail: daniele.parbuono@hotmail.com

migration flows from the coastal province of Fujian 福建 came to Italy, and also Prato; as recalled by Antonella Ceccagno (2003, p. 46):

> Le principali aree di origine dei fujianesi approdati in Europa sono due, l'una sulla costa – l'area intorno alla città di Fuzhou nel Fujian centrale, e Fuqing, una zona costiera della prefettura di Fuzhou – l'altra nell'entroterra del Fujian centrale – la prefettura di Sanming e in particolare Mingxi[3]

The first Chinese immigrants – present in Italy since the 1960s, then growing in number in the 1980s – however, came mostly from the adjacent province of Zhejiang 浙江 (Campani *et al.*, 1992); this group, among the Chinese in Italy (also in Prato), has historically been the most significant from a numerical point of view. In the late 1990s and early twenty-first century, then, the migration of Chinese from the northeast area began, from the Manchurian region (Liaoning, Jilin, Heilongjiang); 'Il primo cinese originario delle province del nord-est ha ottenuto la residenza a Prato nel 2001' (Tolu, 2003, p. 139).[4]

Compared to other immigrant groups, since the 1990s, the Chinese have been mainly engaged in their own economic activities, with a particular inclination for creating manufacturing laboratories in the dressmaking industry or 'ready-to-wear fashion', '[…] not in direct competition with Prato's textile industry, which produces textiles' (Baldassar *et al.*, 2015, p. 11). In general, reflecting on the new dynamics and new trends in Chinese international migration since the twenty-first century, Kevin Latham and Bin Wu (2013, p. 19) explain the strong flow acceleration as a result of some 'critical' factors:

> They include a combination of 'push' and 'pull' factors that encourage migrants to leave China while attracting them to Europe. Those factors are as follows: State-owned enterprise (SOE) reform; The rapid growth of international trade between China and Europe; The strong growth of the Chinese people's income and consumption; The unequal distribution of wealth and the benefits of economic reform in China; The establishment of key niche economic sectors; The development of illegal immigration routes; The relaxation of immigration policies in key European countries; Extensive family networks, often reaching across several European countries; and the internationalisation of higher education.

Several causes have also determined the conditions that confirm Prato as an attractive Italian destination for the Chinese work migration (Bressan and Krause, 2014): the crisis of companies; relative ease of use of large urban spaces that have been in disuse since textile production activities moved into the industrial area (Bressan and Tosi Cambini, 2011); the wide margins of manoeuvre in a national production market that in recent decades has looked more to productive delocalization than to domestic investment (economics, reorganization, implementation of knowhow and development of production systems, etc.) as a solution to sectoral difficulties (Gambino and Sacchetto, 2007; Redini, 2008); and '[…] le caratteristiche del lavoro svolto nelle ditte cinesi (estrema flessibilità, impiego massiccio del cottimo, lavoro familiare, sistemi particolari di organizzazione del lavoro per ridurre i costi e regolare i rapporti fra datori di lavoro e dipendenti) […]' (Rastrelli, 2003, p. 84).[5]

But it would be short-sighted to believe, or to give the impression, that the conditions of Chinese business, which are closely related to the dynamics of migration, are relegated to a kind of self-referentiality or commercial-productive self-sufficient isolation. Over the past three decades, professional potentialities expressed by the large number of Chinese immigrants have represented a primary resource that many Italian companies have leveraged in order to remain competitive in comparison to the market dynamics that have determined increasingly narrow profit margins for the manufacturing component of commercial-productive chains. At the same time, the huge financial resources that are available to Chinese entrepreneurs (and their families) have played an important role in guaranteeing the stability of the luxury market in Prato: it is mostly wealthy Chinese who buy expensive cars, precious jewels and fine homes (Brandi and Iacopini, 2013).

As often happens, the search for work in an area that – for a complex series of reasons – needs 'migratory manpower' was only the initial reason for the massive Chinese presence in Prato. During the first phase, the peculiarities of Chinese immigration corresponded to what Abdelmalek Sayad (1999) writes about Algerian immigration in France, but that could apply to many other arrival and provenance contexts. A first phase of 'working migration' soon became a 'family migration' that led to reunions of various

Table 6.1. Official record of foreign residents in Prato (2016).

	Foreign residents as of 30 September 2016[6]								
	M	F	M+F	%		M	F	M+F	%
People's Republic of China	9,333	9,138	18,471	51.23	Japan	4	16	20	0.06
Albania	2,392	2,180	4,572	12.68	Czech Republic	–	20	20	0.06
Romania	1,308	2,135	3,443	9.55	Iran	11	8	19	0.05
Pakistan	1,248	764	2,012	5.58	Greece	10	9	19	0.05
Morocco	851	643	1,494	4.14	Cape Verde	10	9	19	0.05
Nigeria	494	451	945	2.62	Croatia	8	11	19	0.05
Bangladesh	303	166	469	1.30	Ethiopia	9	9	18	0.05
Philippines	190	274	464	1.29	Portugal	6	11	17	0.05
Poland	45	292	337	0.93	Hungary	3	14	17	0.05
Ukraine	50	281	331	0.92	Argentina	6	10	16	0.04
Georgia	23	287	310	0.86	Austria	3	13	16	0.04
Senegal	228	65	293	0.81	Yugoslavia (Serbia-Montenegro)	6	9	15	0.04
Peru	116	176	292	0.81	Estonia	2	13	15	0.04
India	82	120	202	0.56	Mexico	6	8	14	0.04
Ivory Coast	84	88	172	0.48	Republic of Congo	7	6	13	0.04
Brazil	35	122	157	0.44	Cameroon	6	7	13	0.04
Tunisia	79	52	131	0.36	Venezuela	4	8	12	0.03
Sri Lanka (formerly Ceylon)	63	67	130	0.36	Slovakia	2	9	11	0.03
Honduras	36	80	116	0.32	Syria	9	1	10	0.03
Moldova	27	76	103	0.29	Maurizio	2	7	9	0.02
Russia	13	81	94	0.26	Finland	1	8	9	0.02
Egypt	55	29	84	0.23	Lithuania	–	9	9	0.02
Germany	23	49	72	0.20	Guinea	4	4	8	0.02
France	32	38	70	0.19	Belgium	3	5	8	0.02
Spain	17	47	64	0.18	Sweden	1	7	8	0.02
Cuba	13	51	64	0.18	Togo	2	5	7	0.02
Ecuador	25	30	55	0.15	Indonesia	2	4	6	0.02
El Salvador	26	27	53	0.15	Iraq	2	4	6	0.02
Bulgaria	16	37	53	0.15	Ireland	2	4	6	0.02

Continued

Table 6.1. Continued.

Foreign residents as of 30 September 2016[6]

	M	F	M+F	%		M	F	M+F	%
Ghana	31	17	48	0.13	Guatemala	1	5	6	0.02
Algeria	34	13	47	0.13	Gambia	5	–	5	0.01
Dominican Republic	11	30	41	0.11	Democratic Republic of the Congo (formerly Zaire)	4	1	5	0.01
Eritrea	14	19	33	0.09	Mali	4	1	5	0.01
United States of America	4	29	33	0.09	Palestine	3	2	5	0.01
United Kingdom	12	20	32	0.09	Serbia	3	2	5	0.01
Kosovo	13	17	30	0.08	Vietnam	3	2	5	0.01
Somalia	9	21	30	0.08	Bolivia	2	3	5	0.01
Thailand	4	24	28	0.08	Chile	2	3	5	0.01
Bosnia-Herzegovina	11	16	27	0.07	South Korea	1	4	5	0.01
Netherlands	14	12	26	0.07	Kazakhstan	–	5	5	0.01
Colombia	8	16	24	0.07	Uzbekistan	–	5	5	0.01
Macedonia	13	8	21	0.06					
Turkey	13	8	21	0.06	Others	39	43	82	0.23
Belarus	2	19	21	0.06					
Switzerland	7	13	20	0.06	Total	17,605	18,452	36,057	100.00

kinds, not only with new migrants arriving directly from China, but also with Chinese who had previously emigrated to other European states: 'Manual labour migrants are accompanied by students, entrepreneurs, traders, highly skilled professionals and political refugees of both sexes' (Thunø, 2007, p. 2).

In 1985 there were 163,287 recorded residents in Prato, of whom 591 were foreigners, while in 1995 the same ratio was 167,991/3019; and in 2005 183,823/19,771, up to the current situation, which has increased to 191,150/34,794. Within these already significant numbers, a large proportion of foreigners is represented by the Chinese, who currently, according to official estimates, number 18,471 (residents), but according to the common feeling between 30,000 and 40,000; assumptions that have also been confirmed by Kevin Latham and Bin Wu (2013) and even justified in light of the explanation offered to me by Simone Faggi, deputy mayor of Prato (interview of 24 June 2016): 'There are from 15,000 to 17,000 residents, to which must be added at least 10,000 legally resident… they reach 27,000 or 28,000 […]. The illegal immigrants, at this moment I think that […] are not more than 10% of the regular ones; then they raise the Chinese attendance to 32,000 or 35,000' (my translation).

A Place of Worship for a Buddhist Association

In 2007, 15 years after the beginning of the massive Chinese migrant flows – the official surveys report about 10,000 attendances but, following in proportion the gap between the official estimate and the figures appraised, there may have been more than 20,000 – the construction of the Temple of the Buddhist Association of the Chinese community in Prato was started and it was finished in 2009.

It should, however, be noted that the definition of 'temple' is semantically restrictive in comparison to the current conditions of use and to the future expectations that the community express towards the structure; as Antonio, a qualified interpreter and one of the leaders of the Association-Temple (deceased in 2016), and the President of the Association, Mr Huang Shulin, have repeatedly told me. First of all, it should be noted that the Temple consists of a

series of temples in a unique complex structure organized into five distinct overarching sections. The first section is designed for activities that we could define as associative: a first room, at the end of which there is a large TV, where there are almost always some men and, sometimes, a few women (usually elderly) watching Chinese channels together; the presidency and Association secretariat (where interviews and official meetings usually take place); and a small room with several beds where monk guests usually sleep; and a lounge room with a big study table and a TV connected to an electronic console that kids sometimes use for videogames (in the past 2 years, I have often seen this room used as an additional prayer and meditation space).

The second section consists of a small room-temple that opens the space devoted to the Buddhist religion (Celli, 2006; Masson and Istituto Ricci di Parigi e Taipei, 2008). The third section is composed of a larger room, the main one, also dedicated to Buddhist worship, but if needed it is also used for associated activities such as shared lunches organized on the occasion of important religious celebrations for 'pure land' Buddhism, including the 'spring festival' (Chinese New Year) and the 'lanterns festival' (Chunjie 春节 and Dengjie 灯节), on the first and 15th days of the first moon (Parbuono, 2016). In this room most of the rites, ceremonies and practices are carried out to ensure the good fate of believers and to commemorate the dead; for example, the anniversaries of the Bodhisattva Guanshiyin 观世音 on the 15th day of the second, third and the ninth moons, when the community devotes itself to the 'practice of the seven days' in honour of Guanyin (from da Guanyin qi 打观音七), the Buddhist deity more venerated in China; and the 'feast for the liberation of the souls of the deceased', which overlaps with the worship of ancestors of Confucian origin, observed on the 15th day of the seventh moon, which is observed by both Buddhists, who define that festival as yulanpen hui 盂兰盆会, and Taoists, who define it as zhongyuan jie 中元节 (or wangren jie 亡人节, or even guijie 鬼节). The prominence of the rites relating to death among the practices of the return pilgrims (and pilgrims in general) in China is connected to the central place of ancestor worship particularly found in the Confucian tradition and the virtues of filial piety, but that has found ample space in Buddhism and Taoism also (Fig. 6.1).

Fig. 6.1. Tempio dell'Associazione Buddista della comunità cinese in Italia (Temple of the Buddhist Association of the Chinese community in Italy). Prato, 2016. (Picture by Daniele Parbuono.)

The fourth section consists of an additional small room-temple with an altar dedicated to popular religion, often associated with Taoist worship (Masson and Istituto Ricci di Parigi e Taipei, 2008; Bianchi, 2009), where we find the god of wealth, Caishen 财神 and the lord of the ground, Tudi gong 土地公.

The fifth section is made up of a large dining hall, with an adjacent kitchen, whose tables if necessary are also used for educational purposes, for Chinese grammar and language lessons – given to the children of immigrants born in Italy – or lessons on sacred texts involving small groups of people, mainly female.

So, this social space is set up as a temple that is not only a temple, but a series of temples: a series of temples that are not only a series of temples, but rather aspire to become a monastery. At the time of research, in fact, the community that revolves around the 'centre' has no longer the 'part-time monk', Xizhen 西真 (interviewed on 8 October 2014), shared with the monastery Xiuliangsi 休凉寺, on Daluoshan Mount 大罗山 in Wenzhou 温州, who covered the needs of worship for the first years of activity,

and can only rely on the help of temporary 'guests monks' sent alternatively from China. But for years the Association-Temple yearned to obtain one or more monks to be present in Prato throughout the year, then, possibly, to expand the physical space of the Temple, building a series of bedrooms and worship spaces, transforming the building into a fully fledged monastery.

This project, following a long gestation period due primarily to bureaucratic difficulties, is now nearing completion: after having repaved a large portion of the square outside the kitchen area, the Association has purchased a significant portion of the buildings adjacent to the Temple and – having completed the restoration started in the summer of 2016 – during 2017 will inaugurate the new spaces with a 'monastic' purpose. In the meantime, however, the present condition of the Temple has led to several consequences on the worship level that are closely related to the overall migration context. Until today, the people attending the Temple in everyday life and during important festivals have mainly relied on self-directed management of the cult, subjective or collective, due to the prolonged absence of a 'mediator' or 'professional operator'. From the religious point of view, in a context in which, as Sayad asserts, the immigrant lives in a 'durable provisional' condition (Sayad, 1999); this involves a form of obvious reorganization of 'sense' and 'practice'. This 'reorganization' that the subject, alone or in groups, is led to self-practice – and to self-define from the symbolic and spiritual points of view – facilitates the occurrence of temporary 'separations', temporary 'surrender' to the context felt as 'other' (Italy, Tuscany, Prato). Consequently, it encourages temporary forms of 'aggregation' to the 'sacred' dimension (the Chinese one) that is also set up as a place of affection, a space of possible returns; a moment for encounters that give spiritual and human reassurance. In this sense, when the Chinese migrant goes to the Association-Temple, although resident in Prato, they are making a sort of symbolic pilgrimage that connects them spiritually, 'intangibly' to the worship of the homeland.

The Temple, not only physically, but equally (and especially) from a symbolic point of view, is felt as a controlled space, as an 'exceptional place' (Giampaoli, 2010; Toscano, 2012) in which the migrant is able to hold together the 'here' and 'there', the 'inside' and 'outside', the 'self' and the complex context that surrounds them.

Just by starting from the Temple, it is possible to activate or redefine a series of social ties that, as explained by Zai Liang (2001, p. 694) talking about 'migration networks', 'connect migrants, former migrants, and nonmigrants in origin and destination areas through ties of kinship and shared community origin [. . .]. The availability of migrant networks increases the probability of migration by lowering the costs and raising the benefits of migration. Migration networks constitute a valuable social capital [. . .].'

The Temple space becomes the vehicle through which the aggregation of new affective dimensions, new groups of sharing and, we might say, new family forms – that regardless of blood ties (Giorda and Sbardella, 2012) are structured by socio-cultural contiguity, by contingency sharing and by necessity due to migration 'insecurity' – is pushed.

At the same time, the religious experience in the Temple serves as a connecting point between the migrant and their family of origin or that part of their family of origin that remains in China.

Return Pilgrimages

'My research has confirmed that certain Chinese festivals, such as annual New Year, Mid-Autumn, Ching Ming and Chung Yeung Festival and special events such as weddings and funerals are important reasons for overseas Chinese to pay home visits', Maggi W.H. Leung (2007, p. 218) reminds us. In China, the migrant – together with the part of his family left in the homeland and in many cases during these important festivities – returns to attend those monasteries and those temples for which the Prato solution can only evoke a partial spiritual significance. Right there the migrant participates in the rites and worship dimension in an 'orthodox' way (Fig. 6.2).

In this regard, Ester Bianchi (2014, p. 77) writes:

> [. . .] una consuetudine comune tra gli immigrati cinesi vuole che, per le proprie esigenze di carattere religioso, essi continuino a rivolgersi a istituzioni e figure rimaste in patria, benché si stia progressivamente ampliando il numero dei frequentatori dei nuovi templi cinesi fondati sul suolo italiano a partire dagli anni 2000.[7]

Frank N. Pieke and Mette Thunø (2005, pp. 503–504), as a result of research on European migration of people from two rural villages in Fujian, confirm this thesis linking the dimension of the religious and cultic 'return' to the possibilities offered by the economic welfare gained abroad:

> Similarly, when business is slow in Italy, migrants return to the village on holidays for periods of several months. A dozen investments from overseas migrants have also been made in hotels and entertainment centers, reinforcing the link between migration, leisure and entertainment as aspects of a newly found modernity. Simultaneously, overseas migrants have started to give donations to more traditional cultural activities such as abandoned Buddhist temples and neglected ancestral halls in the village. [. . .] In both villages, consumerism, popular religion and ancestor worship are crucial in cementing transnational ties between the village and the migrant populations abroad.

We could define these special trips, in which human needs for reconnection are blended with the worship needs, as full-fledged 'return pilgrimages'.

Fig. 6.2. Pilgrimages in China. Taishan, 2007. (Picture by Ester Bianchi.)

Through interviews with Chinese migrants that we undertook in Prato and through the information obtained by Ester Bianchi during previous research in the province of Zhejiang, useful information emerges to better define the places and methods of these 'returns'. Most of the migrants with religious involvement – who are returning to China to go at least once to visit some temple – often choose the one closest to the family residence (whether it is simply to pray/worship the deity or to observe rites or specific practices). They can be called 'pilgrims', given that a part of their journey has religious purposes. In fact, the more generic Chinese term for the pilgrimage is jinxiang 进香 ('offer/burn incense'), a term that emphasizes the purpose of the pilgrimage, namely the incense offer – a fundamental practice of Chinese worship (Lagerwey, 1987) – more than the path taken in order to make the offer itself. Although the most frequent destination of return pilgrimages is temples near to the cities of residence – local temples – it is not uncommon that the migrant, once in China, devotes their

time to the visiting of one or more distant sacred places – temples and monasteries built to commemorate important events (the birth of a master, the appearance of a deity or prodigious facts) or the most significant residences of the Taoist or Buddhist clergy, in particular buildings or sacred spaces located in the hills or in mountains.[8] Effectively:

> Per il carattere silenzioso, tremendo e affascinante dello spazio che esse racchiudono, le montagne costituiscono, da sempre e in molte civiltà, un luogo privilegiato per sperimentare fisicamente il sacro. Così in Cina, le montagne sono considerate come luoghi dove la potenza delle divinità, buone o cattive, è particolarmente manifesta ed efficace [...]. Questo è talmente vero che in Cina tutte le montagne sono suscettibili di essere 'sacre'. (De Bruyn, 2008, p. 61)[9]

Symbolically, hills and mountains occupy a prominent place in Chinese religions: the mountains, rising from the ground, are a space close to the sky, places of retirement, peace and meditation – 'L'esercizio della meditazione è divenuto uno dei metodi essenziali della ricerca del sacro in Cina

[…]' (Despeux, 2008, p. 139)[10] – therefore, of spiritual practice. In the most general sense, in Chinese religion, the mountain is a metaphor for the relationship with the sacred, the divine, which is why '[…] è del tutto normale che i Cinesi abbiano spontaneamente immaginato i loro altari cultuali a forma di montagna […]' (De Bruyn, 2008, p. 74),[11] as well as the cultural parallelism between the mountain and the human body not being surprising:

> […] la montagna attira, da sempre, i Cinesi anche grazie ai labirinti e alle sinuosità che nasconde nelle sue valli e nelle sue profondità. Queste sinuosità montagnose sono state molto presto recepite come tanti visceri segreti che testimoniano la vitalità intrinseca delle montagne. E questa percezione della montagna ha profondamente influenzato la visione che i Cinesi avevano del loro corpo. Sono persino arrivati a rappresentare il corpo umano sotto forma di montagna. […] questa identità corpo-montagna influenzerà profondamente la comprensione cinese di ciò che può rappresentare un itinerario interiore. (De Bruyn, 2008, p. 75).[12]

In Chinese, as already specified, 'pilgrimage' is also referred to as chaosheng, that is 'to pay homage to the sacred', or chaoshan, which means 'to go to the hearing on a mountain'; so, then, we could summarize the concept by saying that in China to make a pilgrimage means, frequently, to make a pilgrimage to the mountains (Magnin, 1987).

Many of the Chinese migrants in Prato come from Wenzhou (Latham and Wu, 2013), a city that lies on the banks of the river Oujiang 瓯江, south of Zhejiang, a province rich in important places of pilgrimage. Just to give some examples we could mention Putuo shan 普陀山 (Yü, 1992), one of the four sacred mountains of Chinese Buddhism; Tiantai shan 天台山, the birthplace of the Tiantai 天台 tradition; and the monastery of Ashoka, where there is a relic of Sakyamuni Buddha (Chochini, 2008). Regarding Taoism it should be remembered in particular that three of the ten 'Grotto-heavens', considered as the most powerful Taoist mountains, are located in this province. The ten 'Grotto-heavens' are traditionally considered as the 'assistants' of the 'Five Sacred Mountains of Taoism', powerful deities' dwelling places:

> Le grotte sono porte di accesso al mondo spirituale, vere e proprie 'camere di meditazione' archetipiche, universi in miniatura dotati di

luminarie […]. Nello Dongtian fudi yuedu mingshan ji ('Memorie su Cieli Grotta, territori benedetti, picchi e montagne'), Du Guangting (850–933) menziona inoltre l'esistenza di dieci Cieli Grotta: Wangwu Shan (Henan), Weiyu Shan (Zhejiang), Xicheng Shan (Shanxi), Qingcheng Shan (Sichuan), Xixuan Shan (parte dello Huashan, Shaanxi), Luofu Shan (Guangdong), Chicheng Shan (Zhejiang), Linwu Shan Uiangsu), Gouqu Shan o Maoshan (Jiangsu) e Kuocang Shan (Zhejiang). (Bianchi, 2009, pp. 302–306).[13]

In general, the whole of Zhejiang is rich in sites sacred to Taoism as well as to the popular religion (Dean, 1993, 2003; Dell'Orto, 2008; Goossaert, 2013); even the Maoshan 茅山 (Jiangsu 江苏) and Longhu shan 龙虎山 (Jiangxi 江西), Taoist mountains that are among the most venerated, are located not far from Wenzhou. In this regard, many migrants report having visited one of these places at least once in their life, but most of them – for religious purposes – do not leave Wenzhou, which offers many possibilities including, for example, a very important Buddhist monastery, Jiangxinsi 江心寺 ('The Temple in the Heart of the River'), dating back to the Song dynasty and affiliated to the Chan School (Cochini, 2008).

As for Taoism, however, we should mention the Dongyue 东嶽 ('Eastern Peak'), in Pingyang, and, for the popular cult, Tianxian gong 天仙宫 ('Square of the Heaven Immortal') – 'This temple is devoted to a goddess of the Song dynasty known as Sacred Mother Lu (Lu shengmu), who is worshipped only in the Wenzhou area' (Yang, 2004, p. 740). Outside the centre, but always near to Wenzhou, the pilgrims (both resident and return pilgrims) can visit dozens of temples or monasteries, Buddhist, Taoist or dedicated to popular religion: Pingshan si 屏山寺, Yuanfutang simiao 永福堂寺庙, Puguang simiao 普光寺庙, Shangfang si 上方寺, Ziyun guan 紫云观, Daxiongbao dian 大雄宝殿 and Xiangshan si 香山寺 (Buddhist temples); Huanglong daoguan 黄龙道观, Yuanbi daoguan 元弼道观, Sanguan tang 三官堂, Taiyang gong 太阴宫, Yangfu miao 杨府庙, Chenfu miao 陈府庙 and Mazu gong 妈祖宫 (Taoist temples or related to the popular religion). The closest mountain to the city is Daluo 大罗, where there are 36 monasteries, temples or places for women's retirement (antang 庵堂) and 72 for men, among which we should mention Shengshou chansi 圣寿禅寺, Fuhu si 伏虎寺, Xiuliang si 休涼寺, Wumei yuan 五美园 (Shiji si 实际寺), Xiangshan si 香山寺, Baoyan si 宝严寺, Guoan si 国安寺, Qianyuan si 乾元寺 and Tianzhu si 天柱寺, which is currently in a phase of overall 'religious revival', to the point of being commonly called 'Buddhist Country' (Daluoshan Foguo 大罗山佛国). In this case, as explained by the monk Xizhen, it often happens that the return pilgrims who attend the Temple of Prato move away from the places of worship closer to their homes, to go to meet him at his habitual residence, the Xiuliang si 休涼寺, indeed, one of the Daluoshan monasteries.

Conclusions

From the functional point of view, return pilgrimages are made primarily to fill all these gaps in terms of the 'need for the sacred' accumulated in the migration context, which is only slightly filled by the 'temporary sacredness' of places of worship built abroad. Most Chinese believers, also returning pilgrims, address themselves to the monks, clergy, mediums and shamans first of all for rituals involving the deceased (called 'Yin' rites), with the aim of alleviating the suffering of the missing people supporting them in their afterlife and promoting their positive rebirth rather than the elevation to the highest Taoist Heavens or to the Buddhist 'pure land'. As already mentioned, the most important ritual is celebrated on the 15th day of the seventh moon in favour of the 'hungry spirits' and generally in favour of all of the deceased. When on this occasion – in 2012, 2013, 2014 and 2016 – we observed attendant migrants at the Temple of Prato active in the rituals of chaodu 超度, some of them explained to us that they have relatives in China simultaneously celebrating the same rituals in favour of the common deceased. In other words, the rite performed in Italy can only be considered fully effective if it is observed in the presence of a monk, but it is definitely more effective if it is observed in a homeland monastery, to which almost all migrants aspire to return at the end of their life.

The return pilgrims also seek monks, clergy, shamans or mediums for the 'Yang rites', that is, rites concerning the living people; such rituals are directed to obtaining the intervention and help of the deity in the most different areas of the faithful's life: good luck and success in business, good results in study, health or recovery from illness and protection for the conception of a child.

In summary, only through the 'return' – then sporadically if we consider that some people are unable to return to China for years – does the migrant have the perception of re-joining, also through the various forms of pilgrimage described, the land–place–history–blood link.

In these complex relationships among subject, migratory group, host environment, worship, meeting places and connections with the original realities – relying on 'potentials' provided by the aggregation spaces that offer a resource in terms of the redefinition of human relationships 'here' (in Italy), and relying on the symbolic 'power' of the objects of worship that reconnect the migrants with the spiritual and interior dimension shared with the reality left 'there' (in China) – the Temple of Prato acts for the migrant as a thin connecting line to their complicated dimensions of the 'precarious' migratory life. It is perhaps worth thinking about the Temple of Prato, its public spaces and the evocative power of its religious objects, borrowing the concept of 'heterotopia' from Michel Foucault (Foucault, 1966; 2006; 2010); thinking of the Temple as a place of real utopia, as a window to 'spazi differenti [...], una specie di contestazione al contempo mitica e reale dello spazio in cui viviamo'[14] (Foucault, 2010, p.13), as a real space open to other spaces, a place that puts 'other places' and 'places-other' into communication.

To observe the Temple – keeping in mind the concept of heterotopia – as a symbolic connection for spaces not just physical, but also spiritual, helps us to understand why during the calendrical festivals, in addition to the Chinese living in the area, Prato becomes the destination of daily micro-pilgrimages for Chinese migrants residing in other Italian cities, more or less close. As Anna – secretary (now former secretary) of the Association-Temple – explained to me in August 2014, people arrive from other Tuscan cities, such as Viareggio, Empoli, Florence, Lucca, Pisa, Pistoia and Arezzo, but believers can also arrive from Naples, Milan, Bologna and Rome.

Carolyn V. Prorok (2003, p. 283) reminds us that 'Transplanting pilgrimage traditions, or the process of remaking the collective self in sacred places, requires new sacred places as worthy destinations' and, indeed, the 'Temple of the Buddhist Chinese community in Italy', within the complex dynamics of existence typical of the migratory condition, performs this function in a supplementary but also complete way: it meets the need for physical proximity in the relationship with the sacred, it joins migrant networks around new social and familiar ties, and it connects the symbolic power of distant spaces in new transnational worship channels (Hannerz, 1996).

Notes

[1] This chapter examines and updates some matters already discussed in previous essays (Parbuono, 2015). The research – concerning the Prin (Progetto di Rilevante Interesse Nazionale – Project of Relevant National Interest) 'Migrazioni, legami familiari e appartenenze religiose: interrelazioni, negoziazioni e confini' of which Cristina Papa is Scientific Project Head, triennium 2014–2017 – is currently underway but, for what has emerged up until now, I must thank Ester Bianchi, with whom I work constantly and to whom I owe a great part of the information on the 'return pilgrimages'.

[2] www.comune.prato.it/immigra/cinesi/anagrafe/annuali/htm/cpmig.htm, accessed on 29 December 2016.

[3] My translation: 'There are two main areas of origin of Fujianese landing in Europe, one on the coast – the area around the city of Fuzhou in central Fujian and Fuqing, a coastal area of Fuzhou's prefecture – and the other in the hinterland of central Fujian – Sanming prefecture and in particular Mingxi'.

[4] My translation: 'The first Chinese hailing from the northeastern provinces obtained permanent residence in Prato in 2001'.

[5] My translation: '[...] The characteristics of work in Chinese firms (extreme flexibility, high use of piecework, family work, special work organization systems to reduce costs and regulate business relations between employers and employees) [...]'.

[6] http://statistica.comune.prato.it; consulted on 27 November 2016.

[7] My translation: '[...] among Chinese immigrants it is a common practice that, for their religious needs, they continue to address themselves to institutions and figures that remain at home, although the number of attendances at the new Chinese temples founded in Italy since the 2000s is gradually rising'.

[8] For an in-depth study of Buddhist pilgrimages in China, see Magnin (1987); on Taoist pilgrimages, Lagerwey (1987). In general, for the Buddhist pilgrimages, see Aitken (1995) and Celli (2011).

[9] My translation: 'For their silent character, tremendous and fascinating space they encompass, the mountains have always, and in many cultures, been a privileged place to physically experience the sacred. So in China, the mountains are seen as places where the power of the gods, whether good or bad, is especially evident and effective [...]. This is so true that in China all mountains are likely to be "sacred".'

[10] My translation: 'The exercise of meditation has become one of the essential methods for the sacred search in China [...].'

[11] My translation: '[...] it is totally normal for the Chinese to have spontaneously imagined their worship altars in the shapes of mountains [...]'.

[12] My translation: '[...] the mountain has always attracted Chinese thanks to the labyrinths and windings hidden in its valleys and in its depths. These sinuous mountains were soon perceived as having many secrets inside that testify to the inherent vitality of the mountains. And this perception of the mountain has deeply influenced the vision that the Chinese have of their body. They even represented the human body in the form of a mountain. [...] This body-mountain identity deeply influenced the Chinese understanding of what an inner journey might be.'

[13] My translation: 'The caves are gates to the spiritual world, full-fledged archetypical "meditation rooms", miniature universes equipped with illuminations [...]. In *Dongtian fudi yuedu mingshan ji* (Memoirs of Grotto-heavens blessed lands, peaks and mountains), Du Guangting (850–933) also mentions the existence of ten Grotto-heavens: Wangwu Shan (Henan), Weiyu Shan (Zhejiang), Xicheng Shan (Shanxi), Qingcheng Shan (Sichuan), Xixuan Shan (part of Huashan, Shaanxi), Luofu Shan (Guangdong), Chicheng Shan (Zhejiang), Linwu Shan (Jiangsu), Gouqu Shan or Maoshan (Jiangsu) and Kuocang Shan (Zhejiang).'

[14] My translation: '[...] different spaces [...], a sort of simultaneously mythic and real contestation of the space in which we live'.

References

Aitken, M.E. (ed.) (1995) *Meeting the Buddha: On Pilgrimage in Buddhist India*. Riverhead Books, New York.

Baldassar, L., Johanson, G., McAuliffe, N. and Bressan, M. (eds) (2015) *Chinese Migration to Europe. Prato, Italy, and Beyond*. Palgrave Macmillan, Basingstoke, UK.

Bianchi, E. (2009) *Taoismo*. Electa, Milan, Italy.

Bianchi, E. (2014) Alcune riflessione sugli immigrati cinesi e il loro rapporto con il Buddismo. In: Barbarella, C. (ed.) *Identità e pluralità nel dialogo interreligioso*. AliseiCoop Pubblicazioni, Perugia, Italy, pp. 77–86.

Brandi, E. and Iacopini, S. (2013) Dal cocomero al Suv. I consumatori cinesi a Prato. In: Berti, F., Pedone, V. and Valzania, A. (eds) *Vendere e comprare. Processi di mobilità sociale dei cinesi a Prato*. Pacini, Pisa, Italy, pp. 135–220.

Bressan, M. and Krause, E.L. (2014) 'Ho un luogo dove lavoro e un luogo dove abito'. Diversità e separazione in un distretto industriale in transizione. In: Cancellieri, A. and Ostanel, E. (eds) *Immigrazione e giustizia spaziale. Pratiche, politiche e immaginari, Mondi Migranti. Rivista di studi e ricerche sulle migrazioni internazionali*, 1, pp. 59–81.

Bressan, M. and Tosi Cambini, S. (eds) (2011) *Zone di transizione. Etnografia urbana nei quartieri e nello spazio pubblico*. Il Mulino, Bologna, Italy.

Campani, G., Carchedi, F. and Tassinari, A. (eds) (1992) *L'immigrazione silenziosa. Le comunità cinesi in Italia*. Edizioni della Fondazione Giovanni Agnelli, Turin, Italy.

Ceccagno, A. (2003) Le migrazioni dalla Cina verso l'Italia e l'Europa nell'epoca della globalizzazione. In: Ceccagno, A. (ed.) *Migranti a Prato. Il distretto tessile multietnico*. Franco Angeli, Milan, Italy, pp. 25–68.

Celli, N. (2006) *Buddhismo*. Electa, Milan, Italy.

Celli, N. (2011) Pellegrinaggi: Buddhismo. In: Celli, N., Pelissero, F, Vecoli, G. and Mandel, K. (eds) *Pellegrinaggi*. Electa, Milan, Italy, pp. 73–169.

Cochini, C. (2008) *Guide des temples bouddhistes de Chine*. Les Indes Savantes, Paris.

Dean, K. (1993) *Taoist Ritual and Popular Cults of Southeast China*. Princeton University Press, Princeton, New Jersey, USA.

Dean, K. (2003) Local Communal Religion in Contemporary south-east China. *The China Quarterly* 174 (Religion in China Today), 338–358.

De Bruyn, P.H. (2008) Le montagne sacre in Cina: zone erogene di un corpo cosmico. In: Masson, M. and Istituto Ricci di Parigi e Taipei (eds) *Grandi religioni e culture nell'Estremo Oriente. Cina*. Jaca Book, Massimo, Milan, Italy, pp. 61–82.

Dell'Orto, A. (2008) Cosmologia, Territorio e religione popolare cinese. In: Masson, M. and Istituto Ricci di Parigi e Taipei (eds) *Grandi religioni e culture nell'Estremo Oriente. Cina*. Jaca Book, Massimo, Milan, Italy, pp. 43–60.

Despeux, C. (2008) L'accesso al sacro tramite la meditazione. Tecniche buddhiste e taoiste. In: Masson, M. and Istituto Ricci di Parigi e Taipei (eds) *Grandi religioni e culture nell'Estremo Oriente. Cina*. Jaca Book, Massimo, Milan, Italy, pp. 139–155.

Foucault, M. (1966) *Les mots et les choses: une archéologie des sciences humaines*. Gallimard, Paris.

Foucault, M. (2006) *Utopie eterotopie*, Moscati, A. (ed.). Cronopio, Naples, Italy.

Foucault, M. (2010) *Eterotopia*, Vaccaro S., Villani, T. and Tripodi, P. (eds), Mimesis, Milan, Italy.

Gambino, F. and Sacchetto, D. (eds) (2007) *Un arcipelago produttivo. Migranti e imprenditori tra Italia e Romania*. Carocci, Rome.

Giampaoli, M. (2010) *Al di là dei limiti: Vita e trasgressione quotidiana al Père-Lachaise a Parigi*. Phd thesis (tutors, Papa, C. and Jamous, R.), Dottorato Internazionale in Etnologia e Antropologia (AEDE), University of Perugia, Perugia, Italy.

Giorda, M.C. and Sbardella, F. (eds) (2012), *Famiglia monastica. Prassi aggregative di isolamento*. Pàtron, Bologna, Italy.

Goossaert, V. (2013) A question of control: licensing local ritual specialists in Jiangnan, 1850–1950. In: Lin, S. and Katz, P.R. (eds) *Xinyang, shijian yu wenhua tiaoshi* 信仰、實踐與文化調適. *Proceeding of the Fourth International Sinology Conference*. Academia Sinica, Taipei, pp. 569–604.

Hannerz, U. (1996) *Transnational Connections. Culture, People, Places*. Routledge, London.

Lagerwey, J. (1987) Le pèlerinage taoïque en Chine. In: Chélini, J. and Branthomme, C. (eds) *Histoire des pèlerinages non chrétiens. Entre magique et sacré*. Hachette, Paris, pp. 311–327.

Latham, K. and Wu, B. (2013) *Chinese Immigration into the EU: New Trends, Dynamics and Implications*. Europe China Research and Advice Network, London.

Leung, M.W.H. (2007) Rethinking 'home' in diaspora. A family transnationalized? A place of nostalgia? A commodity for sale? In: Thunø, M. (ed.) *Beyond Chinatown. New Chinese Migration and the Global Expansion of China.* NIAS Press, Copenhagen, Denmark, pp. 210–233.

Liang, Z. (2001) Demography of Illicit Emigration from China: A Sending Country's Perspective. *Sociological Forum* 16(4), 677–701.

Magnin, P. (1987) Le pèlerinage dans la tradition bouddhique chinoise. In: Chélini, J. and Branthomme, C. (eds) *Histoire des pèlerinages non chrétiens. Entre magique et sacré.* Hachette, Paris, pp. 279–310.

Marsden, A. (2003) L'analisi dei dati sull'immigrazione. In: Ceccagno, A. (ed.) *Migranti a Prato. Il distretto tessile multietnico.* Franco Angeli, Milan, pp. 105–133.

Masson, M. and Istituto Ricci di Parigi e Taipei (eds) (2008) *Grandi religioni e culture nell'Estremo Oriente. Cina.* Jaca Book – Massimo, Milan, Italy.

Parbuono, D. (2015) Da Prato a Wenzhou: i pellegrinaggi dei migranti cinesi. In: Giacalone, F. (ed.) *Pellegrinaggi e itinerari turistico-religiosi in Europa. Identità locali e dinamiche transnazionali,* Morlacchi University Press, Perugia, Italy, pp. 409–424, 457–459.

Parbuono, D. (2016) Il centro del centro. Il Tempio buddhista e il capodanno cinese nello spazio urbano di Prato. *Anuac. Rivista dell'Associazione Nazionale Universitaria Antropologi Culturali* 5(1), 171–203.

Pieke, F.N. and Thunø, M. (2005) Institutionalizing Recent Rural Emigration from China to Europe: New Transnational Villages in Fujian. *International Migration Review* 39(2), 485–514.

Prorok, C.V. (2003) Transplanting Pilgrimage Traditions in the Americas. *Geographical Review,* 93(3), 283–307.

Rastrelli, R. (2003) L'immigrazione a Prato fra società, istituzioni ed economia. In: Ceccagno, A. (ed.) *Migranti a Prato. Il distretto tessile multietnico.* Franco Angeli, Milan, Italy, pp. 69–104.

Redini, V. (2008) *Frontiere del "made in Italy". Delocalizzazione produttiva e identità delle merci.* Ombre corte, Verona, Italy.

Sayad, A. (1999) *La double absence.* Éditions du Seuil, Paris.

Thunø, M. (2007) Introduction. Beyond 'Chinatown': Contemporary Chinese Migration. In: Thunø, M. (ed.) *Beyond Chinatown. New Chinese Migration and the Global Expansion of China.* NIAS Press, Copenhagen, Denmark, pp. 1–31.

Tolu, C. (2003) Diversificazione nei luoghi di origine dei migranti cinesi. In: Ceccagno, A. (ed.) *Migranti a Prato. Il distretto tessile multietnico.* Franco Angeli, Milan, pp. 137–166.

Toscano, B. (2012) Sketch del paesaggio eccettuato. In: Papa, C. (ed.) *Letture di paesaggi.* Guerini, Milan, Italy, pp. 99–108.

Yang, M.H.M. (2004) Spatial Struggles: Postcolonial Complex, State Disenchantment, and Popular Reappropriation of Space in Rural Southeast China. *The Journal of Asian Studies* 63(3), 719–755.

Yü, C. (1992) P'u-t'o Shan: Pilgrimage and the Creation of the Chinese Potalaka. In: Naquin, S. and Yü, C. (eds) *Pilgrims and Sacred Sites in China.* University of California Press, Berkeley, Los Angeles, California, USA, pp. 190–245.

7 Globalizing Romani Culture: The Pilgrimage to the Sea in Les-Saintes-Maries-de-la-Mer (France)

Gaëlla Loiseau*

UMR6266 IDEES-LH, ED556 HSRT (Homme, Sociétés, Risques, Territoires), Université du Havre, Le Havre, France

Introduction

Since the mid-twentieth century, the Camargue statue of 'Sarah', the black virgin, swathed in layer upon layer of brightly coloured lengths of material, has been an official symbol of identification and affiliation for the gypsy. It is in the light of her potential for commodification and globalization that I have chosen to examine the character of Sarah. In the manner of Kopytoff (2006), I have undertaken a biographical approach to this symbolic object, which, in the course of her journey as far as Brazil, appears to have passed through different 'value regimes' (Roitman and Warnier, 2006, p. 208). Throughout our study, we shall see that it is not the value that gypsies attribute to this object today that determines its introduction into and movement within a globalized system. On the contrary, it is the attribution of values that seem exclusively reserved for gypsies by non-gypsies that moulds Sarah's plasticity. Sarah's mobility is symbolic, therefore, of a globalized imagery of the gypsy (Aubrée, 2013).

Regionalist and Catholic Influence

The history of the pilgrimage of the gypsies, who return each year to pay homage to Sarah at Saintes-Maries-de-la-Mer, is to be found in the interstices of the Catholic Church's interests and Provençal regionalism (Bordigoni, 2002, 2004). At the beginning of the twentieth century, Manadier, the Marquis Folco de Baroncelli-Javon, was eminently involved in developing 'Camargue authenticity', not only through his professional activities, which aimed to 'restore the purity of the Camargue bull and horse breeds' (Bordigoni, 2002, p. 491), but also in the implications this would have for local economic development.

The steps that Baroncelli undertook to showcase the figure of the 'Camargue Gypsy' fall into a context where the 'exoticizing' display of real characters, notably those from the colonies, generated a great deal of interest (Blanchard, 2011). His pronounced penchant for gypsy exotica is symptomatic of the artistic tastes and popular social delights experienced by some sections of European aristocracy at the beginning of the twentieth century (Asséo, 2010; 2011), even if the period was marked by the spread of racist attacks in the media whose aim was to 'denationalize' them (Asséo, 2007; Filhol, 2013).

The appeal to gypsies of the Saintes-Marie-de-la-Mer pilgrimage developed around a symbolic object of affiliation: the 'Saint Sarah' statue, the sanctification of which was not endorsed by the Church and is of unknown origin (Bordigoni,

*E-mail: gaellaloiseau@gmail.com

2004, p. 13). Baroncelli used his status of town councillor in 1935 to get the Catholic Church to authorize the procession of Sarah's statue, which up till then had remained confined to the church crypt, to the sea; Salome and Jacobe, on the other hand, were already figures of veneration (with processions to the sea) recognized by the Catholic Church.

What captures attention is the fact that regionalists and representatives of the Catholic Church interfered consistently in their respective domains (often concomitantly) with a view to maintaining the gypsy presence in Saintes-Maries-de-la-Mer. Both sides featured well-identified leading figures (Folco de Baroncelli and Henri Aubanel for the regionalists and Fathers Barthélémy and Causse for the Catholics), who strove tirelessly to fashion or adapt this 'gypsy' mark in their respective 'terrains'. There were no gypsy personalities involved in influencing recognition of the gypsy pilgrimage. While in the 1950s the Catholic Church had obtained the backing of the Nacioun Gardiano to add national significance to the pilgrimage and counter the gypsies' conversion to the evangelical movement (Bordigoni, 2004), it had not always been in a position of power with regard to the direction given to this key moment in local Camargue life. An important, determining fact illustrates this two-fold regionalist and Catholic influence on the fate of the statue of Sarah's procession, and *in fine*, of the 'gypsy' pilgrimage of Saintes-Maries-de-la-Mer. In the 1960s, the Catholic Church wished to replace the bothersome Sarah procession to the sea by a Way of the Cross. Father Causse, who found himself leading the inauguration of the said Way of the Cross, recorded:

> So we stopped at the first station, I climbed onto the podium, I had the megaphone and began a short address to give a clear signal and at that very instance Aubanal was at the head with the gardians, and Sarah was beside us so when we started, Aubanel cried out: 'hey, don't stop here, come on, let's move on' and then the Gypsies followed. I'd started to talk but the procession carried on leaving and I ended up making my comments with only the priests there! [...] it was Aubanel who had ... he was against it, I knew he was against it from the start we'd decided that Sarah shouldn't be transformed into a Way of the Cross. That was in 66 [1966] and since then the priests have joined in.[1]

This reaction on the part of the regionalists, which emphasizes the desire to maintain an incarnation of the celebration of Sarah by means of a cyclical human gathering, in lieu of a topographical institutionalization, is indicative of its fitting in with the pilgrimage in a 'ritualized' temporality, which brings it up to date with the present and in its various forms of 'presences', rather than in a 'memory-based' form (Halbwachs, 1941).

The massive turnout of gypsies in Camargue has been understood as an opportunity to showcase local folklore, which itself appeals explicitly to visitors. Therefore, to use a concept put forward by Arjun Appaduraï (2005), gypsies, and more specifically devout gypsies, form part of the Camargue ethnoscape, as does the gardian, together with the Arlesian woman, and very probably the tourists themselves. On 24 and 25 May each year, these three figures, independently and by their simple presence, participate in adding visibility to the pilgrimage. It must be noted that other exogenous figures such as journalists, photographers, but also members of the clergy or street artists, participate via their respective roles in setting the scene and atmosphere of the pilgrimage. In this staging, the figure of the gypsy (which can be played by non-gypsy tourists) is eagerly awaited in the dual position of visitor (to Sarah) and of extras (in the street). This ethnoscape thus gives a certain consistency in the collective imagination to the populations considered as 'elusive'. Yet it is precisely through their ability to allow themselves to be 'captivated' in a fragmentary manner (Williams, 1988) that the process of including the figure of the gypsy in the Camargue ethnoscape can function, not only for the construction of the regionalists' identity but also that of the gypsies themselves. The Saintes-Maries-de-la-Mer pilgrimage highlights the fact that the image of the gypsy might be produced and circulated by non-gypsies.

A form of cultural 'transaction' is therefore at play and we shall explore to what extent it operates and continues today at a global level through the agency of the symbolic object represented by the statue of Saint Sarah. In order for this phenomenon to be understood, one must consider the hybrid and polymorphous dimension of gypsy identities (including the Calé identity) that represents a disruptive element for global society.[2] The tendency of gypsy populations of enabling non-gypsies to 'take possession of them' plays a determining role in the process of identity building. The space 'given up' by the gypsies becomes a space of control in interethnic relations. It allows them to be involved in the relationship with others and be able to 'play around with' the way in which what they have given up 'circulates' and 'fashions' what has produced them from a non-gypsy alterity according to their own registers of interpretation.

A System of Values Deployed around Sarah

Few commentators really focus on describing what gypsies 'get up to' in Saintes-Maries-de-la-Mer, although they form the nerve centre of the event. A clue to understanding the value that gypsies attribute to Sarah's statue is in the 'coats' or 'capes' that they make to drape over the saint they consider as their patron, their protector. Their relationship to Sarah's statue is enacted by means of a strip of cloth,[3] which is usually life-size and rather gaudy, said to contain a part of 'oneself' and one's kin. A traveller explained that her daughter had embroidered as many flowers as the members of her family on the coat she had made for Sarah. In putting on the coat, the family could 'be one' with Sarah by adorning her with uniform finery charged with personal history. It must be noted that women, through their sewing, play a decisive role in achieving this connection with Sarah. The private sphere (family, intimate) is 'embodied' in the cloak (it could have been made from a length of fabric having previously served as a curtain or garment), which materializes the relationship with Sarah. She is ultimately reduced to a face without any real corporality, or more exactly to a 'figure' towering over an allegorical multiplicity of bodies, struggling to extricate itself from an accumulation of cloaks reaching right up to the neck. Sarah then enters a cathartic process, taking her from her status as sacred object to one of 'semi-human figure', vitalized by the crowd touching her, supporting her with words and songs all the way to the sea where the people at the head of the procession throw themselves into the water to bathe. The procession to the sea bestows its blessing on the gypsy people in all their diversity, taking away the sorrows, confidences, pains, and granting the requests of all individuals presenting themselves to Sarah, who

drape a coat over her, give her a piece of jewellery, a crown, a photo or a little note. Thus, the traveller cited above reports:

> The more coats there are means the more people come and the more people that find her beautiful, the more well-known she becomes, you see? [...] Because if there aren't a lot of coats, well, you know, it's just another statue. Because if you take the coats off, underneath it's a statue all the same.

The superposition of the 'emotional charges' contained in each of the coats represents the 'gypsy' value of Sarah. It is worth noting straight away that this 'value' does not exclude non-gypsy contributions. In this respect, Sarah appears to belong to the public domain and more precisely 'to be common property' and can assume no form of exclusivity. The Catholic Church, which orchestrates the liturgical proceedings of the pilgrimage, often uses monopolistic strategies of the belief linked to Sarah and is therefore exposed to controversy on the part of gypsies. During Mass on 24 May preceding the beginning of Sarah's procession to the sea, the moment when the reliquary caskets of Mary Jacobe and Mary-Salome are taken down (when the imbroglio is at its height[4]), the priests put great effort, not without some heavy-handedness, into 'unravelling' fact from fiction concerning the worship of Sarah, by evoking the place she occupies within the Catholic Church. The 24 May 2014 was no exception to this custom since one of the officiants succeeded in spawning confusion among gypsy families, as the rachaï[5] Gilbert Tenailleau recounts:

> Earlier, at the end of the Mass, a priest said 'I'll tell you who Sarah is'. It would have been better if he hadn't said anything because nobody understood a thing. [...] He meant to say 'St Sarah is the heart of the Gypsies'. People really hadn't understood very much at all so there were people down below who I know that said to me 'did you hear what the priest said? Well, he shouldn't be allowed to talk like that! And so we cried "Long live St Sarah! Long live St Sarah",' because they'd understood in their heads, in their ears (...) that the priest was saying that St Sarah didn't exist. For them, that was just too hard to take.

Offending Sarah is a sacrilege not only from a religious dimension (where Sarah constitutes *de facto* dissent) but rather in that it sullies the massive, heterogeneous, cosmopolitan, official assembly of one voice in its devotion to the gypsy presence, which is a rare scene, an exception in the political context of contempt for travellers. Whatever the religious leaders might think, the coats alone seem able to say 'who is' Saint Sarah, as a concrete and contemporary manifestation of an accumulation of 'living proofs' of 'gypsy' veneration. Indeed, the underlying misunderstanding seems to be based on the propensity of non-gypsies for wishing to forge the identity of Sarah – as well as gypsy identity itself – by means of history lessons, which the latter are not particularly passionate about and, which, because of an absence of 'traces', risks undermining the precious balance on which this popular gathering rests.

On the political front, there are illustrations of attempts to break up this gypsy consecration by instrumentalizing the pilgrimage. Thus, the choice made by the mayor, Roland Chassain, and his acolyte, the deputy (member of parliament) Christian Estrosi (both members of the right-wing Union for a Popular Movement (UMP) party, who radiate an excess of malevolence towards gypsies[6]) to pose in front of Sarah[7] rather than the 'historical' and Provençal saints Mary-Salome and Mary Jacobe, was seen as an offensive act aimed at delegitimizing and humiliating the figure of Sarah (and the gypsies she represents) at the same time restoring the regional image, as if to signify that Sarah remains a Provençal construct. In any case, through their presence, they contribute to embodying a 'mixture of styles' that the gypsies appear to lay claim to by means of this pilgrimage. While explaining that the parish priest of Saintes-Maries-de-la-Mer had had the intention this year of asking the tourist information officers of Saintes-Maries-de-la-Mer to 'manage the procession and to ensure it wasn't a meeting place but a place of prayer', the rachaï Gilbert Tenailleau exclaimed:

> Well, we all laughed, didn't we! Because, hmm … because it isn't … Travellers: it's mayhem! It's a shambles. There are so many people, there are other ones who join in and if it isn't a shambles, it's no good. [...] He's got a lot of experience in chaplaincy. But this morning, in my view, he really got it wrong.

It would appear, therefore, that the gypsies manage to inspire their 'mediators' (which is what

they call 'rachaï') into using a form of intervention that not only refutes any form of dogmatic expression, but furthermore endorses the hybridity of the pilgrimage. The proper way of 'grasping the situation' evoked by the rachaï seems to be strongly infused with loyalty towards those who, as we have seen, seem eager to be 'taken over', without however losing control of what non-gypsies do through them.

Sarah's not being endowed with sainthood in the eyes of the Catholic Church does not make her less of a devotional medium, making it possible to establish the popularity of the clerical institution. The value that it attributes to the pilgrimage, therefore, is to be found at a peripheral level of the object venerated by the pilgrims. However, the fact that the statue is located in the church crypt makes the Catholic chaplaincy the authorized custodian of the prerogatives that consist of manipulating Sarah and administering her coats, which are periodically removed to make way for new 'creations'. Yet the distribution of the coats, or at least having access to them, is of vital importance to the pilgrims. Some families return for the pilgrimage each year and want to retrieve the coat they made and gave the previous year so as to redistribute, display and recycle once more the value it contains through its prolonged contact with Sarah:

> They have a rather saintly value. It's a little like if you got back the candles, you know? Except that it's a coat made by each family. Each family or each person, depending on how it works. As for me, I know that I always make one and I always try and get it back the next year and I often cut it up and give it to people who didn't come or who have sick people.(...) They took part in the procession. They were on Sarah for a while, in the church in the crypt they're given a more sentimental value, a religious one as well.

The value the gypsies attribute to these pieces of cloth is ephemeral according to what this traveller, who comes to the pilgrimage every year, tells us. The Church has no prerogative to fix any 'validity' or obsolescence to the vitality of the 'link' to the sacred nature of the coats.

This year, the rachaï seems to have abandoned the 'administrative' role of redistributing the finery offered up to Sarah and upon which the gypsies' whole system of belief is based.

Until now as they were removed the coats were put into cardboard boxes with their year which enabled people to retrieve the coats they had made, to retrieve it and take it home, either to keep them intact or to cut them up into little pieces to give them to people, give them to the family. (…) The rachaï who is at Saintes at the moment decided that, well, he was fed up with all these boxes of coats and apparently he threw them all away. Which means that this year I haven't been able to retrieve my last year's coat because it doesn't exist anymore! After a while, until now, after a little while the old coats that hadn't been taken, served, were taken to retirement homes, to small associations to make little things. After a while, they'd lost their value, you see. They kept one or two years' worth and then the rest, afterwards, people came to get them throughout the year, any old one, you know? If they hadn't made one they could go and take somebody else's who didn't want to get it back. You see? Then the rachaï, this winter, he must have thrown a fit, we don't know and he chucked everything out. The coats, the rosaries, this and that… So that means the person I know very well, I see him every year, whose job it was to look after Sarah, told me 'I don't know if I'll get your coat back'. So he looked for it and told me 'It's not there anymore, there aren't any boxes left. Even the rosaries, everything that'd been put on Sarah.' Well, I went and complained. And p'raps others went and complained too. […] He must've had a dressing down from those at the top as well and some other people as well.

This incident related by our interlocutor reflects the fact that the priest granted himself the right of alienation for something that belongs to a pilgrim's private and community dimension. Yet the measures of exchange set up for the distribution of Sarah's robes are akin to a 'total service' in that 'the thing circulating has kept within itself the trace of the persons between whom it has circulated' (Mauss, 2012, p. 84) and that possessing a piece of cape is inalienable (Weiner, 1992). The Church's involvement in the pilgrimage, therefore, hinges on diplomacy, whereby it must hold onto the gypsies' affection on the one hand, and annex their religion on the other. This 'proper way' of 'grasping' mentioned above by the rachaï Tenailleau is enacted by being able to stick to a public service of storing, recycling (in the framework of associative activities) and maintaining accessibility to the coats, with the

added vocation of being able to 'return' them to the gypsies' private sphere, as previously mentioned, where they can continue to 'take action':

> Well me, I've got one … a santon. I mean, you saw in my thingummy there, my Saint Sarah in my cupboard. What I often do is I cut up the piece of fabric I got back and make another coat in my own way. Then afterwards, well, the rest if nobody asks for it back I keep it and cut it up a bit more.

Through the distribution of material and personal pieces of fabric: no mix-up. Everyone seems to 'recognize' him/herself, to find their bearings in spite of the heaping and piling up of layer upon layer of coats. The profusion of colours, materials and shapes of Sarah's finery constitutes a cosmology (Prévost, 2012) whose particularity hinges on the perpetual renewal[8] in which the tourists participate.

Sarah Transferred to a Global System

The gypsy pilgrimage of Saintes-Maries-de-la-Mer turns the order of interethnic relationships on its head in that it ushers in the possibility of contacts where it is the non-gypsies who advance towards the gypsies and not the reverse.

> There's a group of Brazilians this year. And the one who can speak French the best said to me: 'we put on nine capes' and of course they want to get them back. Bah, does that surprise you? What a surprise! To take them back to Brazil, eh?

adds a nun from the Saintes-Maries-de-la-Mer chaplaincy. She adopts a tone that seems to signify that she hasn't dismissed the idea that these capes will 'increase in value' with the especially long journey on the one hand, but also through the relationship they will materialize with the 'gypsy culture' for which the pilgrimage has become a truly worldwide showcase. 'Movement and exchange confer value on currencies just as on objects in general – this is common knowledge since studies on certain systems like the Kula exchange – but, moreover, "transfigures" them' (Dupuy 2009, p. 133). Indeed, the 'traces' left on the internet by these Brazilian tourists confirm that their 'pilgrimage' fits into an economy of identity and culture transcending the religious and touristic sphere. A video posted by

Nathy_Sche on Youtube[9] retraces the steps of nine women aged between 30 and 50 years. They all appear with their long hair down, dressed in colourful frocks and accessories denoting 'gypsy' costumes (scarves, gold ring earrings, bracelets, shawls, belts encrusted with golden coins, fans, etc.). The captions on the images containing brief, sometimes erroneous or essential commentaries navigate between the various musical attractions on offer in the streets during the pilgrimage, which incidentally Nathy and her friends contribute to, as do many other tourists. The main protagonist can therefore be seen dancing – or 'playing the gypsy' – in a restaurant and among the crowd in the centre of the village. This is another particularity of the Saintes-Maries-de-la-Mer pilgrimage, which offers a setting where a 'xenophile' game (Guerreiro de Faria, 2012) can play itself out by commingling in the varied 'gypsy scene', which thinks nothing of tipping over into caricature (gypsy women telling fortunes, whereas in fact this practice has completely died out in France). If one views all the videos posted by Nathy Schellin since 2009, one discovers that she has devoted herself entirely to what seems to be 'a Brazilian invention' of exoticization of the gypsy, more specifically the 'dança cigana' (Bomfim, 2002). This term includes a type of dance that is essentially individual and feminine consisting of highlighting the 'gypsy' costume by means of sweeping perambulations in a performance area. These dances take their inspiration from the cinematographic register, which feeds the international fantasy image of the 'gypsy'.[10] The garment, here used as a vector for a fantasized identity, is inspired by two narrative archetypes: the 'gypsy' temptress with regard to women and the 'bandido' or 'bandolero' for men. In these women's get-up, therefore, there is a form of dressing-up that I believe worth addressing from the perspective of a transaction of culture and identity. Borrowing from 'gypsy-ness' with its origins in nineteenth-century European romanticism spurs a need to represent 'whites' in a context of national construction focused on the concept of multiculturalism.

For some years now, Brazil seems to have developed a passion for 'el povo cigano' (the gypsy people), which has not benefited from any notable recognition regarding national minorities. The umbanda religion, created in the late 1920s by middle class Brazilians, has played an essential role in this process by recently incorporating Sarah into the 'oriental' pantheon of umbanda spirits, alongside the 'Brazilian-ness' of the 'caboclos' and 'preto velhos', spirits respectively, representative of indigenous Americans and blacks (Dianteill, 2008). If the gypsy woman has always featured in umbanda, she was situated on the side of the transgressing spirits acting in the twilight, in contrast to the 'enlightened' entities (orixa), who, historically,[11] were identified with Catholic saints (Guillot, 2010, p. 60). The recovery of the linguistic Romani name of 'Sara kali'[12] in umbanda is a response to an acknowledged desire on the part of the elites of this religious movement to 'de-Africanize' Brazilian religious practices by no longer positioning Africa as the land of origin of the divinities but as a 'simple area of transition' (Dianteill, 2008, p. 28). In order to consolidate their intentions, during a spiritualism congress in 1941, they mentioned umbanda as originating in Lemuria, ancient Egypt and ancient India, and attributed a Sanskrit origin to the term of 'umbanda' itself (Dianteill, 2008). The transfer of Sarah into this new religion, therefore, would seem to appertain to strategies and confrontations regarding a globalized portrayal of Brazilian identity. The way in which she is 'incorporated' and depicted by women identifying with this 'mythological' corpus is a reflection of a hybrid interpretation somewhere between 'saint'[13] and 'pomba gira'.[14] Imported by bold, strategy-making personalities in 2007, Sarah was drawn into the heart of the Brazilian ceremonial and political apparatus, and the date of the Camargue pilgrimage (24 May) was retained as the annual celebration of 'national Romani day' (Mello and Veiga, 2012), flouting international conventions concerning celebrations of gypsy culture.[15]

Situated in a touristic and exclusive area of Rio de Janeiro, the reproduction of Sarah has found refuge in a cave fitted out by Mirian Stanescon, the instigator of this new religion, who gave herself the name of 'queen of the gypsies' in Brazil (Mello and Veiga, 2012) and was recently awarded a medal of merit by the city of Rio de Janeiro.[16] The oriental-style aesthetic[17] adopted by this woman (in her 60s) has been scrupulously respected in each one of her public appearances. While navigating on social media, one can notice a substantial number of

Brazilian women assuming and asserting an identification with the exoticized figure of the gypsy in the public (and digital) space. Compelled by a series of artifices (aesthetic, biographical, rituals, etc.) centred upon the religious dialectic of the 'revelation' (spiritual, of the identity) and the 'appearance' (choreographic, media-related or indeed political), these women, through performance (Garrabé, 2008), hope to remove themselves from the secular world. The involvement of the body in this process, in the Brazilian context, bears witness to a form of enhanced expression consistent with 'giving substance to an invented event, vouched for or renewed in time' (Garrabé, 2008, p. 183). The middle and upper classes are the ones that take part in the veneration of Sarah as this 'entity' reveals to them a spiritual affinity more than an original identity. This 'Brazilianization' of Sarah is based on a globalizing process of the myth of the Bohemian woman (Sarga, 2008) portrayed as savage and self-sufficient, and elevated to an evocation of freedom running counter to the values today imposed on the Calon women of Brazil (Ferrari, 2012). Lastly, it should be noted that these women knew nothing of the figure of Sarah before her recent mediatization (Mello and Veiga, 2012).

The worship of Sarah in Brazil has this in common with the one in Camargue in that ethnic hybridization and religious syncretism seem to have been established as a prerequisite in order to enable the transfer of a 'capital gain' – socially codified and 'borne' by the women – into the political and economic spheres (Appaduraï, 2013). In Camargue as well as Brazil, we can witness the development of an exogenous 'expertise' that uses the object of 'Sarah' to convey a discourse on 'gypsy authenticity'. Sarah and the gypsies she symbolizes are, therefore, affiliated with the strategies of regional, national or religious postulations that prevail when devising the 'criteria of authenticity'. 'The issue of value and exchange is intrinsically political because it also involves (…) disagreements relating to the very intelligibility of the frameworks and regimes of truth or veracity, which are dynamic, transformative forces of economic life' (Roitman and Warnier, 2006, pp. 213–214). Brazilian tourists, therefore, build up 'knowledge' concerning their experiences of the pilgrimage, which they pass on as cultural and economic capital on their

return to Brazil. Indeed, since the end of the 2000s, a certain number of social intervention initiatives have been developed that offer arguments connected with 'authenticity' (genealogical, cultural, religious, etc.), which legitimize their actions. Nicolas and Ingrid Ramanush, the Brazilian couple who put on a little performance of 'dança cigana' at the Saintes-Maries-de-la-Mer cultural centre during the pilgrimage of 2011, are emblematic of this trend. Their association's website[18] called 'Ambaixada cigana' (Tzigane Embassy) presents works by Nicolas Ramanush as well as various projects combining the world of showbusiness and culture with that of the social sector. Their trip to the Camargue pilgrimage is narrated through a series of photos with commentaries and reinterpreted in keeping with an emphasis on 'gypsyfication'. For example, the gardians are presented as 'Manouche' gypsies representing the order of St George[19] (choosing to see a reference to the gypsy spring festival during which the Balkan Roma pay homage to their patron saint). In Brazil, their association receives public money to take action in Calon camps by using a form of 'awareness' object-lesson of what the gypsy culture is, thus positioning its members as 'ethics emissaries' (Becker, 1985).

For both tourists and non-believing gypsies, attending the Saintes-Maries-de-la-Mer pilgrimage fulfils the desire to be at the heart of the process of constructing 'gypsy-ness'. While in Brazil the pilgrimage provides an added value of culture to those who nevertheless seem to be part of a spiritual 'quest', in France, it is worth noting the presence of 'travelling' personalities presenting themselves as non-religious or non-believers. It is clear today that the Saintes-Maries-de-la-Mer pilgrimage has acquired a value that has gone beyond a strict religious context for travellers. Nonetheless, the message posted on the social media platform Facebook by Nara Naoned during the 2014 pilgrimage seems indicative of a quest that taps into the emotional register:

> I went back to Saintes this year. As impatient as ever like a kid waiting for Christmas! […] I'm non-religious, but the Saintes is important for me. Anyway, no need to be a believer to share a moment of such strong spirituality in this magnificent place. […] Going into the crypt to see Sarah. It's difficult to hold back the tears on contact. Tears, not of sadness, no no, nor of joy. An indescribable feeling – a mixture of fragility

and strength at one and the same time that penetrates my soul. She's the sensitive one. Full of meaning and indistinct at the same time. Timeless. Times in the square where our camps all intermingle, where we can laugh and party, enjoy the sunshine (when there is any), relax, where the children can play and shout without having to worry … all these moments when you can just be yourself without being afraid of people who don't like you.

In the eyes of these people representing non-religious travellers, the pilgrimage is intimately associated with the pleasures provided by the community gathering, while at the same time offset by the sentiment of not being respected as a gypsy. He continues his remarks by denouncing the council's policy and the abusive behaviour of the tourists who are:

> disrespectful, who sometimes seemed to forget that they were dealing with humans [...] Going as far as sticking his camera 30 centimetres from a cousin's face to take 'the shot'. Being rudely jostled around during the Mass for Sarah. [...] 'Forced' to come to blows and threats to stop the 'human safari'.

In this game of smoke and mirrors between 'real' and 'fake' gypsies, the essential image in the eyes of certain community leaders is a form of subversion with regard to this arrogated cohesion.

Conclusion

If Brazil is a country that excels in the art of spreading cultural objects such as the Batucada (Vaillant, 2013) it knows equally well how to 'cannibalize' (Viveiros de Castro, 2009) exogenous cultural registers likely to 'give substance' to Brazilian-ness. As a 'transnational' figure, the gypsy would seem to be an appropriate one to take a place in this transaction of global values, at the risk of 'bearing the consequences' (Mello and Veiga, 2012). In Brazil, it would seem that Sarah is enshrined in a celebration of femininity through an emergent, thus modern, figure of alterity. The contrast between the two cultural contexts of Camargue at the start of the twentieth century and contemporary Rio de Janeiro in Brazil should not hide a globalizing dynamic that the pilgrimage has initialized, integrating regionalism with the nationalist project. The crucial role played by the pieces of fabric in this cultural transfer is striking. Both Sarah's coats and the Brazilian dancers' dresses, in their different ways, raise the issue of the relationship (through the display of these lengths of cloth and their movement between the private and public spheres), and the role played by women in the processes of this cultural transaction needs to be addressed. The pieces of fabric are the agents (Akrich, Callon, Latour) capable of hybridizing identities. The way in which they make it possible to show themselves and be accepted through a process of inclusion of the other seems an interesting path to follow to improve understanding of forms of identification and renewal of identities. Brazilian women's donning the attributes of the gypsy woman comes down to describing themselves in 'another' way, which can be meaningful in a global space, that is, through an emblematic aesthetic of universal exoticism that 'contains' their process of individuation.

Notes

[1] Citation from Father Causse in Bordigoni (2004, pp. 30–31).
[2] Moreover, all the gypsy denominations of identity are most often systematically articulated one with the other so as to constitute a 'homogenous' set systematically contradicted by the diversities of this 'set'.
[3] The evocation of St Martin the Merciful never appears in accounts, but there would be no harm in delving deeper into the subject in order to understand the symbolism of the cape offered by the gypsies to St Sarah. It is worth remembering that very large numbers of gypsies were followers of the Catholic religion until the 1950s.
[4] The congregation gathered in the church to cheer Sarah as well as Saints Mary Jacobe and Mary Salome, whose relics are 'brought down' from the high chapel during Mass.
[5] 'Traveller' name designating a Catholic chaplain.
[6] In July 2013, Christian Estrosi asserted that he wanted to 'put a check on' travellers and published a 'practical guide for the mayors of France in order to prevent illegal occupation of public areas by

non-sedentary populations', which he circulated to mayors in France. Cf. Christian Estrosi propose aux maires un 2guide pratique" contre les occupations illegales, *La Gazette des Communes*, 16 July 2013 updated on 30 July 2013: www.lagazettedescommunes.com/?p=179016.. Furthermore, remarks from travellers about the mayor Roland Chassain all coincide with the observation that they have a repressive policy towards gypsies, who are tolerated only over a few days during the pilgrimages, but in conditions that drastically temper the purported conviviality of such a gathering (no public toilets, pharmacy closed, businesses closed upon municipal order – except in the centre of the village – from 18:00, which leads many into taking their leave during the pilgrimage, fines for caravans parking illegally, increase in monitoring devices, etc.).

[7] On the Saintes-Maries-de-la-Mer tourist office website: www.saintesmaries.com/fr/# (from 1'36 to 1'40) and on the website of the village mayor, Roland Chassain: www.rolandchassain.net/article-le-pelerinage-des-saintes-retour-en-images-sur-3-jours-exceptionnels-118166601.html.

[8] Our traveller interviewee tells us: 'there's a turnover with the coats of … 1 month. I mean that every month there's someone who has to remove the oldest coats because all the same there's people who come all year round bringing more coats.'

[9] The video entitled '#Santa Sara ~ Saintes Maries de la Mer/FRANCA/2014#' posted on 8 June 2014, is a montage of photos and short videos lasting a total of 16 min 48 s. On 23 February 2015, it had had 989 hits and eight 'likes'.

[10] Therefore, the 'Mensagens ciganas' community (which had been 'liked' 12,246 times by 3 March 2015) has published five videos since it was set up in 2012 including extracts of dances taken from the films *Carmen* (Francesco Rosi, 1984, 152 min), *The loves of Carmen* (Charles Vidor, 1948, 99 min), which include figures of the gypsy woman and the bandolero.

[11] The 'orixa' are the Yoruba divinities incorporated in the Candomblé religion that developed in Brazil in the nineteenth century.

[12] 'Sara kali' signifies 'Sara the black' in Romani. We can observe that Sarah is variably represented as 'black-skinned' or 'white-skinned' in the Umbanda religion (cf. Mello and Veiga, 2012, p. 59, photo 6 or http:// bresils.revues.org/556, photo no. 4).

[13] The Brazilian statuette represents Sarah dressed in a white and blue-painted stole, that is, a Marian figure.

[14] Stefania Capone and Maïa Guillot define the 'pomba giras' entities as 'spirits of provocative women, incarnations of female sexual power, manipulating magical forces and rebelling against masculine domination' (www.ird.fr/relitrans/?Umbanda,315).

[15] In effect, on 8 April 1971, the first World Romani Congress opened in London, organized by the International Rom Committee (IRC) attended by gypsy representatives from 14 European countries. The congress adopted several symbols of political affiliation: the green and blue flag with a red wheel, the anthem taken from the traditional song 'gelem, gelem', and 8 April (the date of the opening of the congress) was established as the international Romani day (Liégeois, 1975).

[16] Mirian Stanesco, a Carioca, is a lawyer by profession. She introduces herself also as a consultant, writer, lecturer and defender of the rights of the Rom. From 2008 to 2012, she held the position of representative of the Rom people in the federal government as a member of the CNPIR (Conselho Nacional de Promoção da Igualdade Racial – National Council for the Promotion of Racial Equality). On 21 September 2014, she was awarded the medal of merit (medalha Pedro Ernesto) by the city of Rio de Janeiro as president of the Foundation of Santa Sara Kali and for her actions developed since 1998 said to be in favour of 'the Roma people', whose ancestral customs and beliefs she claims to reveal in one of her books (justifying the absence of a bibliography in her work by the fact that this people has an oral tradition). The document putting forward Mirian Stanescon's candidacy for the prize states that the aspirant underlines her status as a woman to highlight her 'meritorious' action, having no qualms about taking the parody to its limits so as to allow the stigmatizing mechanisms to work by means of a game of contrasts that she employs: 'Sendo a primeira cigana formada no Brasil ou talvez no mundo, vem tentando resgatar a dignidade e a autoestima, não só da mulher cigana, mas, principalmente, de um povo que muitas vezes sente-se sem patria' (In my capacity as the first educated gypsy in Brazil and probably the world, I have assisted in re-establishing the dignity and self-esteem not only of the gypsy woman but of all stateless persons). Cf. Requerimento n°665/2014, 'requer a concessao da medalha pedro ernesto a Mirian Stanescon Batuli de Siqueira' por Vereadora Laura Carneiro, publicacao 25 August 2014.

[17] She always appears heavily made-up, her hair covered in a scarf adorned with golden beads and a brightly coloured yet uniform dress with a very low neckline, wearing gold jewellery as well as accessories like those on tarot playing cards or fans (even the snake around the neck).

[18] www.embaixadacigana.com.br/index.htm.

[19] The following annotation describes a scene with gardians on horseback: 'sobre os cavalos camarguenses, alguns ciganos Manushes (antigamente Ordem de Sao Jorge) que na procissao escoltam a imagem de Sarah la Kali' (on Camargue horses, some gypsy Manouches (formerly of the Order of Saint George) escort the image of Sarah Kali).

References

Appaduraï, A. (2013) *Condition de l'homme global*. Payot, Paris.

Appaduraï, A. (2005) *Après le colonialisme. Les conséquences culturelles de la globalisation*. Payot, Paris (first edition: 1996).

Asséo, H. (2007) «L'invention des «nomades» en Eurpop au XXème siècle et la nationalisation impossible des Tsiganes». In: Noiriel, G. (dir.) *L'identification. Genèse d'un travail d'Etat*, Belin, Paris, pp. 161–180.

Asséo, H. (2010) Figures bohémiennes et fiction, l'âge des possibles 1770–1920. *Le temps des Médias* 1, 12–27.

Asséo, H. (2011) L'inclusion exotique. Des Roms de la Galicie polonaise traversent l'Europe 1900 – années 1920. *Colloque international Migrations et dynamiques urbaines, 'exotisation' des populations et 'folklorisation' des espaces*. CRBC-EHESS, Paris, 8–9 December 2011.

Aubrée M. (2013) Figures mondialisées de l'umbanda brésilienne, communication in the Congress of SISR (Société Internationale de Sociologie des Religions) at Turku University (Finland).

Becker, O. (1985) *Études de sociologie de la déviance*. Métailié, Paris (first edition: 1973).

Blanchard, P., Bancel, N., Boetsch, G. and Lemaire, S. (2011) *Zoos humains et exhibitions coloniales. 150 ans d'inventions de l'Autre*. La Découverte, Paris.

Bomfim, C. (2002) A construçao de uma identidade cigana em um grupo de camadas médias no Rio de Janeiro. Dissertation de mestrado, Rio de Janeiro, Université fédérale de Rio de Janeiro.

Bordigoni, M. (2002) Le 'pèlerinage des Gitans', entre foi, tradition et tourisme. *Ethnologie française* 32(3), 489–501.

Bordigoni, M. (2004) Sara aux Saintes-Maries-de-la-Mer. Métaphore de la présence gitane dans le 'monde des Gadjé'. *Etudes Tsiganes* 20, 12–34.

De Faria, A.G. (2012) Fausse identité gitane: un cas brésilien. *Etudes Tsiganes* 51, 48–63.

Dianteill, E. (2008) Le caboclo surmoderne. Globalisation, possession et théâtre dans un temple d'umbanda à Fortaleza (Brésil). *Gradhiva* 7, 25–37.

Dupuy, F. (2009) Les 'monnaies primitives'. Nouvelles considérations. *L'Homme* 190, 129–152.

Ferrari F. (2012) La 'bonne aventure' par les Calon de Sao Paulo. Entre tromperie, syncrétisme et effiacité. *Brésils* 2, 83–106.

Filhol, E. (2013) De la couleur des Tsiganes en France. In: Laurent, S. and Leclère, T. (eds) *De quelle couleur sont les blancs?* La Découverte, Paris, pp. 269–277.

Garrabé, L. (2008) Ethnographie des jeux du corps dans le maracatu rural (Pernambuco, Brésil). *Journal des Anthropologues* 112–113, 183–203.

Guillot, M. (2010) 'Axé ilê Portugal': Parcours migratoires et religions afro-brésiliennes au Portugal. *Autrepart* 56, 57–74.

Halbwachs, M. (2008) *La topographie légendaire des évangiles en Terre Sainte*. Puf, Paris. (first edition 1941).

Kopytoff, I. (2006) La biographie culturelle des choses. *Journal des Africanistes* 76, 217–248.

Liégeois, J.-P. (1975) Naissance du pouvoir tsigane. *Revue Française de Sociologie* 16, 295–316.

Mauss, M. and Essai don, S.L. (2012) *Forme et raison de l'échange dans les sociétés archaïques*. Quadrige/Puf, Paris (first edition: 1924).

Prévost, B. (2012) Cosmique cosmétique. Pour une cosmologie de la parure, Images Revues (en ligne), 10-2012, 25 October 2012. Available at: http://imagesrevues.revues.org/2181 (accessed 16 November 2017).

Roitman, J. and Warnier, J.-P. (2006) La politique de la valeur: une introduction. *Journal des Africanistes* Tome 76, 205–216.

Sarga, M. (ed.) (2008) *Le Mythe des Bohémiens dans la littérature et les arts en Europe*. L'Harmattan, Paris.

Mello, M.A. da S. and Veiga, F.B. (2012) Le 'Jour national du Tsigane', au Brésil. Espaces symboliques, stéréotypes et conflits autour d'un nouveau rite du calendrier officiel. *Brésil(s)* 2, 41–78.

Vaillant, A. (2013) 'La batucada des gringos'. Appropriations européennes de pratiques musicales brésil-
iennes, Thèse de doctorat, Université d'Aix-Marseille.

Viveiros de Castro, E. (2009) *Métaphysiques cannibales*. Lignes d'anthropologie poststructurale. Puf,
Paris.

Weiner, A.B. (1992) *Inalienable Possession. The Paradox of Keeping-While-Giving*, University of California
Press, Berkeley, Los Angeles, USA.

Williams, P. (1988) Langue tsigane: le jeu romanes. In: Vermès, G. (ed.) *Vingt-cinq communautés linguis-
tiques de la France, tome1: langues régionales et langues non-territorialisées*. L'Harmattan, Paris,
pp. 381–413.

8 The Cult of Señor de los Milagros of Peruvians in Italy

Riccardo Cruzzolin*

Dipartimento di Scienze Politiche, Perugia University, Perugia, Italy

Introduction

The migration phenomenon, regarded as a social event capable of generating practices and discourses, is also the product of a specific regime of visibility (Brighenti, 2010). The migrant is not only a moving body, he or she is also a person who has (often) crossed political boundaries, filled out forms, exhibited documents, and expressed intentions and motivations (especially regarding the nature of his or her stay in a country of which he or she is not a national). His or her trajectory is traced and made intentional due to numerous administrative practices and sociological investigations. In this way, the cognitive and epistemic foundations of a vast scientific literature and its most common concepts (project migration, migration chain, assimilation and many others) are laid. These concepts are actually manifestations of a state thought (Bourdieu, 2013) that gives shape to a hegemonic and pervasive rhetoric, often at the base of the same self-description (and self-construction) of the stranger, the subject that is mostly affected by its discursive functioning. In addition, any regime of visibility, giving salience only to some aspects of reality, relegates others to invisibility. Many foreigners are objectified, that is, 'illuminated' by a disciplinary mechanism that at the same time fails to recognize and refuses to acknowledge their agency (Dal Lago, 2004).

The aim of this chapter is to illustrate the way in which the members of the Peruvian diaspora have been able to realize and use a counter-hegemonic discourse capable of redefining the boundary between visibility and invisibility. The reflections that I will propose here are the result of fieldwork conducted between 2010 and 2014 in an Umbrian city, Perugia, where more than 1000 Peruvians are living. The research was an exploration, through participant observation and the collection of life stories, into the devotional world of the Peruvian migrants.

In particular, here we will refer to the worship of the Señor de los Milagros (or Moreno Christ), an image of the crucified Christ that was painted in Lima by an African in the seventeenth century, or so the legend goes. Revered, especially at the beginning, by the black population, El Señor would soon win new devotees, especially for the high number of miracles He performed. The portentous nature of the painting became eminent during some devastating earthquakes that hit Lima. The telluric power destroyed most parts of the city, but the wall on which the painting was remained standing.

The worship of the Señor de los Milagros has become one of the most impressive devotional

---

*E-mail: riccardo.cruzzolin@unipg.it

phenomena of South America and it is practised by many Peruvian migrants, who, whenever possible, carry in procession a copy of the original painting in their new places of residence (Paerregaard, 2001, 2008).

Inside the Peruvian diaspora, devotional devices are aimed primarily at making present the deity, which, as we shall see, has protected the journey of several migrants; second, at strengthening the cohesion of Peruvians in the local contexts in which they emigrated – in this case, Perugia; and, third, at obtaining the recognition of their communities by the Catholic Church of Rome.

In this chapter, however, I will discuss only two of the crucial moments in the lives of many migrants: the irregular crossing of a political border, and the religious procession in which the Peruvians publicly demonstrate their faith and their moral view.

The devotional devices (prayers, gestures, pledges) make it possible to structure a rhetorical counter-hegemonic discourse that is able to redefine the relationship between what is visible and what is not visible. They can hide the migrant from the eyes of the custodians of political boundaries, but they can also reveal him or her, as an ethical subject, to the religious and civil institutions and citizens of the country in which they have decided to live. Against the visibility imposed by the authorities of a country, the emigrant obtains an invisibility made possible by Divine intervention. But when he or she is a regular resident and the risk is to become socially hypervisible yet politically invisible, religious practice can help the migrant to pursue visibility, showing himself or herself as the bearer of an ethical conception of life.

The Crossing of the Border

The concept of border is inevitably elusive; to treat it properly one should consult a vast scientific literature. In this work the border must be understood as a device, or *dispositif* (Foucault, 1971) that gives a physiognomy, that is, visibility, especially to those who cross it coming from outside. As already highlighted by Barth (1969), the border is not only a line that separates two social groups; rather, it helps to produce these same groups, making them culturally and politically different, and the very ones that pass through it contribute most to its reinforcement.

Yet, the political boundaries remain artifices. Nation-states have tried to make them coincide with natural, geographical boundaries. But, in reality, human societies fade into one another seamlessly (Amselle, 2008). The governments are able to delimit their territories only through concrete acts of force. Once created, then, the borders must be patrolled by monitoring devices and custodians. The migrants intending to enter illegally a country must therefore make themselves invisible.

In 1997, Pierina and one of her sisters, both in Italy, decided to travel to see their brother who was living in Switzerland. He had been able to get Pierina's children from Peru to Switzerland. The family reunited on 29 December, and, after seeing her children, on 1 January, Pierina decided to take a risk:

> To pass the border on foot, like I'm going to buy something, at the border, and then I pretend to return but, instead to return, I ran away with the children. [...] At some point my brother took the wrong way, he was wrong; when he realized to have made a mistake, he tells me: 'oh, the police, the police!' And there was the police, there was customs to go through, then the police stopped us from afar, we saw these policemen who stopped the car, my brother stopped the car, and I told him: 'look, if I return to Peru you, you must help me again!' and my brother says: 'yes, yes, I help you'; he too was really nervous and the children, it was for them the first time and they did not realize what was going on, and the little girl was crying; at one point I gave the girl a small toothbrush and I prayed: 'Señor de los Milagros', praying: 'the powerful hand of Christ, help me, help me', because there is a prayer that says: 'powerful hand of Christ, lead me in the right path, our enemies have eyes but don't let them see us, they have hands but don't let them touch us, make sure they have eyes but become blind, don't let them see us'; and I was praying this prayer ... at some point the policeman says: 'halt!' [...], and I gave to the girl the toothbrush, and the girl was lying on the back of the car (between front seats and back seats) [...]; she was lying down, she began to play with the toothbrush, silent, and I prayed, behind with my nephew and a son, and my other son was ahead. [The officer] said: 'passport', and my brother says: 'yes, yes'; 'anything to declare?' 'No'; 'you bring clothing?' 'No, no, I don't bring anything, here I go to the grocery store', he said, and that's fine, and my son, I remember, he put his hand into his pocket to take out his passport, and, he don't know why, he stayed with his hand inside,

locked, and hasn't take out his passport, he got stuck, not because he was afraid, [...] he too has no explanation for why he remained stuck with his hand inside his jacket pocket. [At the end] we passed, and the police said: 'please, please, go ahead, come on, go, go, go'; for us it was a relief, right away, without knowing, without anything. Chiasso, we arrived at the train station, in the train station we went down, we took the train to ... like ... it was all of God, the train was waiting, [...] it was waiting for us, we hopped on the train, we only had the time to buy a ticket, and to get on the train.

Of all the persons who were in the car only Pierina's brother, the driver, had a valid passport allowing him to cross the border. If Pierina's son had taken out his own travel document, the situation would be immediately apparent to the policeman. A higher power provided that nothing went wrong and pleased Pierina, favouring his intentions.

The story of Sally is even richer, and she still has the small cross that she kept with her during the trip to our country: 'I found it on the floor, this crucifix of wood and metal, and I have always carried it with me'. The reason that pushed her to leave her native land is similar to that of many others: 'In a hurry I have found that, if I had a small savings in a bank account, I found that those little savings were not enough for a week of shopping; I had five children, all little, to maintain, to grow'. Initially, she didn't think of Italy as a possible destination; it was a friend of hers, whose daughter had already reached the Mediterranean country, who made her decide to cross the ocean. Her friend also told her of a priest who was doing a lot for the Peruvian migrants in Italy. Sally decided to leave and to travel with a friend's relative. They reached Prague without incident. Unfortunately, in the Czech town, there was an unexpected problem:

> There was an agency that told you everything you had to do to arrive here, it also gave the telephone numbers of some persons who would put you in contact with these famous pasadores, and we got there; however, the agency told us that from Prague to Austria we could pass without problems, but it was not true, because from Prague, by taking the train to get to Austria, you could have problems [...]. As fate would have it, when we arrived in Prague, we found a group of 13 Peruvians who had been cheated by those famous pasadores. They had been left with nothing. Someone had taken

them, using two, three taxis, to a point. Then it was said to them: 'you have to get out of the taxi and to let all your small luggage' ... because it wasn't possible to bring large suitcases; 'let all and we will expect you on the other side [of the border]'; there was this person in front of them, but along the path they have lost this person, they have lost everything. Someone was smart enough to put his money in his pockets but someone else had left everything in the luggage [...]. We were together with these, and from there we passed to Austria, always paying a person, always illegal [...]. Walking through the fields, we arrived in Austria. In Austria a person was waiting for us; thanks to him we got a hotel where we could clean ourselves off because we were really dirty, but, then, we realized that the real problem was to come here from Austria.

They were told that the last border crossing would not cause problems. But, unfortunately, the first attempt failed. She and her travelling companion took a train. During the trip, while she was absorbed in reading the Bible, right at that moment, came a patrolman who began to request the documents, 'but he did not ask me anything'. Her friend, instead, was checked, and she was sent down. Seeing how the situation was evolving, Sally decided to abandon her intentions and to stay close to her companion. They were checked again during other attempts to cross the border. The third time they were put in prison, 'there were concrete walls with only some mattresses'. Sally saw many soldiers; for this reason she thought they had ended up in a barracks, but they remained there for only one night. Then they were taken to another prison, where they managed to stay together. Sally was afflicted and she cried often because of all the humiliations she was suffering, 'we have not done a crime; however, they treated us in the same way, the same humiliation'. Then she tried to react. In Austria, before ending up in prison, she and her partner had found refuge in the loft of a car repair shop run by an Egyptian. She decided to write to him to make him aware of the situation she was facing and asked a guard to be her messenger. After a short time she and her friend were brought before a tribunal. From this moment forward, the presence of the Señor again became detectable.

> That night, it might be chance, maybe it was my mind, that night there, I woke up after dreaming of two [religious] processions; in our country

there is a saint, San Martin, who is black, and I dreamed [that I was] in the main street of my cities, that I was in a balcony and I could not get out. But from afar I saw these processions, and I could see the image of the Señor de los Milagros that [was turning his gaze towards me]. I said [to my friend]: 'be quiet because we are going to pass and arrive in Italy'.

The religious processions that Sally dreamed about were going on simultaneously, in parallel: 'But the one of the Lord of Miracles was nearer to me'. The next morning, they were provided an interpreter, a Bolivian woman, who could help them during the trial. The judge immediately showed himself to be kindly disposed towards them: 'he was a very young person [...] tall, blue eyes, I'll always remember, even very compassionate'. He asked them why they were in Austria. Sally didn't want to lie and spoke frankly of her economic difficulties, of her daughters, and the need to get a job to maintain them, a wish that had become impossible to fulfil in Peru. According to Sally's memories, the words pronounced by the judge, some of which were deliberately playful to ease the tension of the moment, seemed to invoke a sense of justice that could transcend the law practised in a courtroom, a law created to protect the borders of the state.

The judge said to Sally:

I understand you and I would also help you, because I've got my mother widowed, and with four children, who raised us on her own, and even my mother was a primary school teacher [...] and it seems to me that you are like my mother, but, unfortunately, the law ... [joking] if I was single I could marry you, but I cannot because I'm already married...

Thanks also to the Egyptian who guaranteed for them, they were released under the condition that they would return to Peru as soon as possible. But there was another unexpected event that struck them. At the exit, all the things they had to hand over when they were arrested were returned to them; everything, except the money Sally was carrying: US$1500. Even if they wanted to, they could not return to Peru. Sally was not discouraged and decided to ask for a little financial help from the Egyptian. She also phoned Rose, the daughter of a Peruvian friend of Sally, the same friend who talked to her about Italy. Rose asked her cousin, who was residing in Italy, to reach Sally and her partner in Austria.

The cousin went on the road with the phone number of a very famous pasador (human smuggler), whom she contacted. The pasador told them all to come to Salzburg. Sally and her friend left Vienna and, without any problems, arrived by train at the famous tourist city. They were the first to arrive. Rose's cousin joined them the next morning. Then, in the evening, the pasador led them to a field, where they passed through a simple barbed wire fence. 'On the other side [there was] one that [was making] signals with a lamp' and a small minibus was waiting for them. The next stop was Milan and then, finally, Perugia.

How should we interpret the tales of these migrants? In the first story, the Divine, making Pierina and her family invisible, subverts the political order, legitimizing the illegal crossing of a border. Also in the second tale, despite some initial difficulties, in the end, a dream in which Sally is visited by San Martin and the Lord of Miracles gives Sally and her friend confidence in the success of their daring enterprise.

Some studies on the world system and the 'spatialization' of social injustice (Cancellieri, 2014) show how spatial planning creates inequities in the distribution of resources: since political boundaries hinder the mobility of human beings, the national legal systems inevitably create injustice. As one migrant interviewed by us said: 'one has the right to go to look for work outside his own country if there are no other opportunities'. At the individual level, the paradoxical and sometimes unsolvable state of suspension – between the past and the future, between the country of departure and the country of arrival – can be interpreted, understood and finally resolved thanks to devotional practices: Christ is seen as the invisible force that allows the overcoming of inequity inscribed in space (Hondagneu-Sotelo, 2008).

However, though a condition of invisibility is useful in the irregular crossing of a border, it has to be abandoned when it is finally possible to rebuild a normal life.

The Cult in Italy

In Italy, the need of the Peruvian devotees to thank the Lord of Miracles for the graces

He granted them and to obtain his supernatural protection, in addition to their desire to recover some form of importance and centrality, underlies the organization of the religious cult.

The devotion arose and grew thanks to a painting of the Moreno Christ, a copy of a mural located in Lima and considered miraculous, that arrived in Perugia from Peru around 2000 (see Fig. 8.1).

The picture is full of Catholic symbols. In its lower part, in addition to the crucified Christ, appear the Virgin and Mary Magdalene; in the upper part we can see a bearded God the Father and a dove, symbol of the Holy Spirit. On the right of the cross there shines a sun, while on its left can be discerned a moon, and the background is in darkness. As we have said before, and according to legend, the mural was painted by an African in the seventeenth century, and was originally revered especially by people of low social class. The portentous nature of the painting became apparent during some earthquakes that hit Lima. Although the

strong tremors destroyed large parts of the city and caused numerous crashes, they could not bring down the wall on which was painted the sacred image. At first, the Church viewed the cult inspired by the image with suspicion, but eventually the Lord of Miracles was accepted by the ecclesiastical hierarchies. In the same century the decision was taken to make a copy of the mural to carry in procession through the streets of Lima (Rostworowski de Diez Canseco, 1992). Since then, the image parades every year in October, the month in which some of the devastating earthquakes that made manifest the supernatural nature of the image (20 October 1687 and 28 October 1746) occurred. Even today, there are devotees who regard October as the month of earthquakes.

In Perugia the first procession was organized in the second half of the 1990s, using a small image that was then replaced. It took place in a suburban church that had become known in the city for having given shelter and help to

Fig. 8.1. El Señor de los Milagros in Corso Vannucci, Perugia (Picture by Fiorella Giacalone.)

many South American migrants. In subsequent years, the desire to attribute grandeur and importance to the religious festival has pushed the devotees to enrich the processional litter and the altar where the sacred image was located during the year with precious ornaments, and to extend the processional path.

A key year was 2007. The painting, previously housed in different places, found its final location in the chapel of a church on the outskirts of Perugia. Later that same year, by the will of the bishop, the Moreno Christ paraded for the first time along the main avenue of the historical centre of the Umbrian city, Corso Vannucci. Finally, there was a final procession through the streets of the neighbourhood where the revered painting had been housed, named San Sisto, a well-known and densely populated neighbourhood in which many immigrants reside.

Since then and until now, every year the devotees have organized two processions in Perugia, both on Sundays and during the month of October: the first in the historical centre and the second in the urban periphery, in San Sisto.

The procession that takes place in the centre is the one with the most noble path, because it goes through the public space in which the town hall and the cathedral are located, and thanks to it the Peruvian faithful are able to gain a great visibility within the urban community and to obtain recognition from the civil and religious authorities of the city. Plus, the painting can be admired by many locals and tourists, who almost every Sunday flock to the city's acropolis.

But it is the second procession, the one that brings the holy image through the outskirts, that must be considered as more important. At the end of this procession a communal lunch (almuerzo) takes place in honour of the Christ; the faithful reach a building where it is possible to eat, drink and dance, and where some Peruvian cultural associations will probably offer various traditional dances.

Every religious procession lasts a few hours. Normally a procession ends on the parvis of a church and when it is finished the devotees, many of whom have carried the heavy image on their shoulders, go to the Mass. During the procession several 'characters' make their appearance (Ricoeur, 1993). The Sahumadoras lead the procession spreading incense. They walk backwards, with their eyes towards the Christ, while Cargadores, organized into teams (cuadrillas) of between 24 and 30 men, proceed slowly, in stages, carrying and 'cradling' the religious litter.

The purple clothes that both figures wear emphasize their proximity to the sacred. Purple is the colour of waiting and of penitence. The route of the procession evokes a material and spiritual journey at the same time. When possible, the religious ritual involves the presence of a priest, who, especially during breaks, when the procession stops to allow some brothers in faith to replace the Cargadores who have just carried the image, provides some reflections to the faithful, also quoting some passages from the Holy Bible.

At times, in migration contexts, the devotional practice becomes bifocal (Vertovec, 2009) since, according to occasion, it can underline the community's dimension of the cult or it can strengthen the desire of the Peruvian migrants to be more respected; it can allow the migrants to experience the 'mythical-ritual', or it can stimulate reflections on migrants' social and cultural inclusion in the host society. This double register (the language of nostalgia and that of integration) became clear in the course of the last processions held in the historical centre (in 2011 and 2012), during which the image bowed (ha fatto l'inchino)[1] in front of the town hall, the headquarters of the civil administration, finally entering into the cathedral, the most important church of the city.

The proximity to the ecclesiastical authority gives stability to the cult and offers a horizon of meaning to migration, making the community of the Peruvian faithful a strong and visible political body. The procession expresses both the desire of every single devotee to make him- or herself existentially present (presentificazione) (De Martino, 1958) and the need to be politically and socially recognized as a community. Furthermore, the religious lexicon allows a 'sublimation' and a shaping of migration experience. The ethics of self-sacrifice, especially the readiness to sacrifice oneself in order to secure better living conditions for one's loved ones, ennobles the choice of those Peruvians who have decided to flee from their country of origin in search of a better future. In this way, the migratory journey coincides with a spiritual path, interpreted according to Christian-Catholic values and to the figure of the pilgrim. This journey, full of existential and experiential implications, is annually renewed through the processions dedicated to the Señor.

Conclusions

The veneration to the Moreno Christ has become a global phenomenon. There are many European cities that are home to Peruvian migrants, and their main streets, in the month of October, become tinged with purple. But in Italy, the presence of the Vatican State, which is the centre of the Catholic Church, implies for the faithful of the Señor the possibility of gaining a strong position within the Peruvian diaspora. Actually, it is thanks to the 'Italian' devotees that the Moreno Christ went into San Pietro. In 2010 a delegation of devotees from Perugia, composed of Cargadores and Sahumadoras, reached the confreres of the capital city and, together with them, took on their shoulders the sacred image through the streets of Rome, until Saint Peter's Square was packed with the faithful. Once there, they were greeted by the Pope. The words of our informant, for many years president of the religious association that bounds together the Perugian devotees, clearly express the significance of this event:

> As Señor de los Milagros [...], even if He is in Japan, America, Italy, He is the Señor de los Milagros [...]. I think that el Señor de los Milagros, just that of Lima, entered into the Vatican, [this is] what I think. [...] As if He, He came here, [and] entered into the Basilica [...] of the first pope, the first apostle [...] such a historical thing! Awesome! Because this never happened before; as a result, [each painting] of the Señor de los Milagros is worshipped, is raised, is in the sky.

Each image, each painting of the Christ, is simultaneously a copy and the original one, which re-proposes itself to the faithful (Spera, 2010); it is inserted in a very complex dialectic between the parts (the individual images) and the whole (all the images). Entering St Peter's, the Roman image 'raises' the other images of the Christ too. For the faithful, Nuestro Señor de los Milagros is at once unique and 'divisible'. It is embodied in the history of all its representation, but it also enjoys an absolute ubiquity, a uniqueness, which

confuses. There is a metonymic link between each 'presentation' of the Señor and the set of them, since every time it is displayed as a single, concrete, representation of the Christ, the other images are also commemorated.

The existence of the internet has made this phenomenon even more complex. The cult of the Moreno Christ has produced an impressive and multifaceted 'virtual' landscape (Appadurai, 2001). Many processions are photographed and filmed. The videos produced by the faithful are uploaded on Facebook and Youtube, and they document the efforts and enthusiasm of the devotees intent on celebrating the image by carrying it on their shoulders.

Although the body's involvement remains a basic element in many devotional practices (Giacalone, 2012), the 'virtualization' of the sacred is expanding the 'habitat of meaning' (Hannerz, 2001) accessible to the faithful, that is, the sphere in which the presence of the Moreno Christ is felt, a sphere that comes to coincide with the Peruvian diasporic space. So, thanks to the power of the sacred, many migrants may pick up the threads of their lives, broken by the experience of migration (see Fig. 8.2).

Oración al Señor de los Milagros Patrón de los migrantes peruanos

Oh Cristo Moreno!
Peregrino antes de nacer, hicistes de tu vida
una caminata al encuentro de la humanidad.

Acercate Señor y acompáñanos en nuestro peregrinaje
como migrantes en busca de una vida digna.
Conducenos a una tierra que nos alimente
sin sacarnos la identidad y el corazón.

Haznos un pueblo que viva en la justicia,
la solidaridad y la paz, danos la gracia de ser
acogidos como personas
hechas a Tu imagen y semejanza. Cuida a nuestros
familiares y no permitas que nos alejemos de la
Comunidad Cristiana y de los hermanos que mas
necesitan de nuestra ayuda solidaria.

Que no caminemos mas de lo necesario,
y cuando nos detengamos,
sintamos que no hemos caminado en vano.
Que sea bendecida toda la tierra donde vayamos,
todas la culturas, pueblos y sus descendientes.
Amén.

Fig. 8.2. Prayer to the Lord of the Miracles.

In the past, the status of the pilgrim was a liminal one (Turner and Turner, 1978). Today, the figure of the pilgrim overlaps with that of the migrant. On the official Facebook page of the Perugia association, I found a prayer to the Lord of the Miracles, declared in 2005 as protector of the Peruvian migrants, in which this overlapping is clearly stated.

Globalization and transnationalism are redefining the religious geography of many countries. As a consequence, the complex relationship between sedentism and nomadism is being shaped anew. In particular, holy images carried by the faithful migrants are delineating new political spaces that are waiting to be studied.

Note

[1] Along the route of the procession, when the devotees arrive in the vicinity of an important building that houses a civil or religious authority, they may decide to put the image in front of it, with the face of Christ turned towards it, and to perform three small bows, bending the Holy Painting forward three times. The Cargadores in the front rows stoop to make possible the operation, which serves to pay homage to the authority by presenting to it the Señor.

References

Amselle, J.-L. (2008) Etnie e spazi: per un'antropologia topologica. In: Amselle, J.-L. and M'Bokolo, E. (eds) L'invenzione dell'etnia. Meltemi, Rome.

Appadurai, A. (2001) Modernità in polvere. Meltemi, Rome.

Barth, F. (ed.) (1969) Ethnic Groups and Boundaries. Little, Brown and Company, Boston, Massachusetts, USA.

Bourdieu, P. (2013) Sullo Stato. Corso al Collège de France. Feltrinelli, Milan, Italy.

Brighenti, A.M. (2010) Visibility in Social Theory and Social Research. Palgrave Macmillan, Basingstoke, UK.

Cancellieri, A. (2014) Giustizia spaziale: una nuova prospettiva per gli studi sull'immigrazione? Mondi migranti 1(2014), 121–136.

Dal Lago, A. (2004) Non-persone. L'esclusione dei migranti in una società globale. Feltrinelli, Milan, Italy.

De Martino, E. (1958) Morte e pianto rituale nel mondo antico: dal lamento pagano al pianto di Maria. Einaudi, Turin, Italy.

Foucault, M. (1971) L'Ordre du discours. Gallimard, Paris.

Giacalone, F. (2012) Impronte Divine. Carocci, Rome.

Hannerz, U. (2001) La diversità culturale. il Mulino, Bologna, Italy.

Hondagneu-Sotelo, P. (2008) God's Heart Has No Borders. University of California Press, Berkeley and Los Angeles, California, USA.

Paerregaard, K. (2001) In the Footsteps of the Lord of Miracles: the Expatriation of Religious Icons in the Peruvian Diaspora, Working paper series, WPTC-01-02, ESRC, Research programme on Transnational Communities 1–26. University of Oxford, Oxford, UK.

Paerregaard, K. (2008) Peruvians Dispersed. Lexington Books, Lanham, Maryland, USA.

Ricoeur, P. (1993) Sé come un altro. Jaca Book, Milan, Italy.

Rostworowski de Diez Canseco, M. (1992) Pachacamac y el Señor de los Milagros. Una traiettoria millenaria. Istituto de estudios peruanos, Lima, Peru.

Spera, E. (2010) Ex voto tra figura e parola. Il potere del racconto esemplare. Gramma, Perugia, Italy.

Turner, V. and Turner, E. (1978) Image and Pilgrimage in Christian Culture. Columbia University Press, New York.

Vertovec, S. (2009) Transnationalism. Routledge, London and New York.

9 Cultural Diversity in a Local French Pilgrimage

Guillaume Etienne*

Department of Sociology, Citeres Laboratory, University of Tours, Tours, France

Introduction

Pilgrimages bring together people who are motivated by a range of factors, not only religious. On the one hand, individuals may have multiple motives: celebrating, sociability and even politics can play an important role in the decision to take part in this type of event. On the other hand, one cannot speak of religion in the singular, as there may be a wide range of religious sympathies among the participants. Indeed, behind the apparent homogeneousness that the organizers seek to show, the pilgrims are not 'timorously obedient and uniformly "under the belief"' (Claverie and Fedele, 2014, p. 488). In fact, the various reasons for participating in these events are not just the reflection of a belief (Catholic in our study), and this belief may relate to different objects or practices: 'adherence does not necessarily depend on the certification of beliefs, but can depend on other motives (social or emotional motives, commitment to a form of knowledge, techniques of self-transformation) and highlights the indeterminacy of the objects to which the adherence relates, even within the same circle of beliefs and practices' (Claverie and Fedele, 2014, p. 489).

The pilgrimage I describe here, held in the village of Sainte-Solange in the Berry region of France, celebrates a local saint, and it drew my attention in 2009 because it is described as Portuguese or Franco-Portuguese. The Portuguese have played a key role in the event for 50 years; a large number of people come dressed in traditional Portuguese costumes or colours, and hymns are sung and Mass is celebrated in both French and Portuguese. Moreover, the afternoon is devoted entirely to displays of Portuguese folklore.

While the event is a Catholic pilgrimage, I would like to show that it goes beyond the religious domain, incorporating other aspects and local issues, notably because the participants endow it with different meanings that are not all religious. Participants come for a variety of reasons, and it is therefore not possible to see the event as single-faceted. As we shall see, diversity (either ethnocultural or in the motives of the participants) has not always been accepted, but it is now encouraged, notably because it is a way of boosting the number of participants.

I will first describe the pilgrimage, focusing particularly on specifically Portuguese-related practices in order to understand their role. Second, I will describe how the participants have become more diverse, and particularly how the local clergy see the presence of 'tourists' and 'sightseers' ('*promeneurs*'), as the unwanted

*E-mail: guillaume.etienne@univ-tours.fr

participants are negatively referred to. Finally, I will analyse how the various pilgrims perceive the event today. I will thus show that, over and above its religious character, the pilgrimage has acquired a variety of meanings, which are now either accepted or deliberately left unspoken, thanks notably to the Portuguese, who are acknowledged by the local clergy and organizers to have saved the event.

An Intercultural Pilgrimage

About 500 people join the Sainte-Solange pilgrimage every Whit Monday. While the procession dates back centuries, its particularity is that since the 1960s it has attracted a large number of Portuguese settled in the area and their descendants. Up to the Second World War, thus before the arrival of the Portuguese, the pilgrimage attracted many more people than today: between the late nineteenth century and the Second World War there were between 10,000 and 15,000 people a year. Numbers then dropped significantly, stabilizing at about 500 people during the 1980s. In this situation, the involvement of the Portuguese was seen as life-saving for the event, and it is still accepted today that without them the pilgrimage would probably no longer exist. The presence of the Portuguese is now seen as an integral part of the Sainte-Solange celebration. Not only do they attend the pilgrimage in large numbers, they also work alongside the local organizers and clergy to organize the event and participate in the upkeep and renovation of the site. All the participants, not only the Portuguese, agree that over the past 50 years they have played the main role, both numerically and symbolically.

The pilgrimage starts in the morning with a procession through the village, from the church where Mass is celebrated to the chapel (a 2-km walk). Many of the participants wear traditional Portuguese dress or simply the Portuguese colours. The children wear traditional local costumes or are dressed up as shepherds and shepherdesses. Other people come as more 'ordinary' pilgrims. At Mass, the hymns are alternately French and Portuguese. Throughout the procession, there are songs and prayers, again in both Portuguese and French.

The procession is organized in groups based on a mix of religious and cultural or ethnic criteria. Leading the procession are religious and local elements: local guilds and the banners of Sainte-Solange. Next come the Portuguese,[1] who carry the statues and an effigy of the saint. Most of the people in this group are dressed in traditional Portuguese folklore costumes. Since 2010, the 'Portuguese group' has been followed by the 'African group', which is still fairly small but which the organizers hope will increase in the coming years. In fact, it comprises a few people, a dozen at the most, originating from the Democratic Republic of Congo and Madagascar, but also other countries that are not necessarily in Africa. Nevertheless, the clergy and organizers refer to them under the umbrella term 'African'. Then come the little shepherds and shepherdesses in local traditional dress, the clergy and the relics (Fig. 9.1). The crowd of pilgrims bring up the rear. After an hour's walk, and with several stops in the village, the procession arrives at the chapel at the end of the morning. A stage is set up in front of this chapel where about ten priests celebrate the final Mass, finishing at about midday. Lay people are again involved in the Mass, notably Portuguese who speak in Portuguese, which is not translated.

After Mass, there is a picnic; the atmosphere is relaxed, groups of Portuguese musicians warm up, and small groups form. The stage where Mass was celebrated is used by a succession of Portuguese music and dance groups from 2 o'clock until the evening. The atmosphere is clearly Portuguese, the groups announce their songs in Portuguese, the drinks stands sell Portuguese soft drinks and beer, and Portuguese becomes the main language (Fig. 9.2). We can thus observe a variety of groups of participants, and hence potentially as many reasons for taking part in the pilgrimage and as many representations of it. While this diversity creates the international nature of the event described by journalists today, it raises the question of how the local Church viewed the arrival of new pilgrims at the end of the nineteenth century: were they as ready to accept the cultural difference and festive mood, the dances and music?

Distinguishing the True Pilgrim from the Tourist

Until just after the Second World War, the local Church considered that the only legitimate motivation for coming on a pilgrimage was devotion.

Fig. 9.1. The little shepherds and shepherdesses in local traditional dress, the clergy and the relics (Picture by G. Etienne, Sainte-Solange, 2017).

Fig. 9.2. Folklore in the afternoon, front of the chapel (Picture by G. Etienne, Sainte-Solange, 2015).

Hence, anything that came between the pilgrim and his or her faith was considered as a threat and thus rejected. For the clergy in those days, there was a frontier, reminiscent of the one de-scribed by Durkheim (1960), between the sacred and the profane that could not be crossed. However, like all pilgrimages, the one in Sainte-Solange included many activities alongside the procession (Nolan and Nolan, 1989). These activities, festive or commercial, blurred the religious motives, giving rise to the figure of the suspect pilgrim. Chélini and Branthomme observed that at the end of the Middle Ages, a distinction was made between true and false piety in pilgrimages (Chélini and Branthomme, 1982). When the railway arrived at the village of Sainte-Solange at the end of the nineteenth century, there was a rise in the number of participants, as well as pedlars, beggars and more broadly people defined as tourists.

An inconvenient popularity

The opening of the railway through the village in 1893 led to a considerable growth in the popularity of the pilgrimage. By making access easier, greater numbers of pilgrims were able to come. Nevertheless, this did not entirely please the local clergy, who were unhappy about the arrival of participants not motivated only by religious feeling. During the First World War, the difficulty of access and the absence of special trains for the pilgrims were therefore seen as beneficial filters, as only the most devout believers made the effort to attend. In 1919, although the war had ended, it was still not possible to organize special trains for the pilgrims: 'We have not yet returned to the days when vast crowds of pilgrims gathered in the village, the church, the outskirts of Sainte-Solange or the fields and shady lanes around the Chapel of the Martyr, from 8 or 9 o'clock in the morning', reported *Le Petit Berrichon*, a local Catholic newspaper. And yet, the local Church still did not seem to be entirely happy with the people on the pilgrimage, and the same article continued: 'That does not mean that there were only true pilgrims! With the fine weather … and Peace, the sightseers and tourists have made an unwelcome return…' (*Le Petit Berrichon*, 1919).[2] The following year, the pilgrimage was hindered by a railway workers' strike, which made it very difficult for many pilgrims to travel to Sainte-Solange. Again, this was seen as a way of putting off the less pious: 'this railway crisis would undoubtedly have stopped many sightseers and onlookers, and for the sake of the good conduct and piety of the Pilgrimage, we have no regrets about it' (*La Semaine Religieuse*, 1920, p. 287).

Today, only two stands, next to the church and the chapel, sell religious objects under the aegis of the Association Sainte-Solange. Purchases are thus limited and controlled, the profits going to this Association. Other types of goods are sold, notably drinks in the afternoon from a stand run by members of the Franco-Portuguese Association, part of the proceeds going to the Association Sainte-Solange. In the 1980s, it seems that the pilgrimage took on the appearance of a market, with stands offering not only religious items, but all sorts of other goods. The local clergy disapproved of this new commercial aspect, because it could mask the basic purpose of the event, namely devotion. Moreover, the sales, even of religious objects, were suspected of opportunism, with stallholders displaying falsely holy items. In the eyes of the Church, the increasing popularity of the pilgrimage thus seemed to diminish it, by attracting not only pilgrims but also salesmen and pedlars of all sorts, who seemed to be motivated less by devotion than by commercial interest.

Like the false salesmen, the 'professional beggars, blind men, cripples, people with only one arm, beings with repulsive deformities, display on the roadside the lucrative miseries found on all pilgrimages, imploring charity from the passers-by with imperious entreaties' (*La Semaine Religieuse*, 1895, pp. 473–474). In 1897, a Catholic paper again reported that 'the professional beggars – the blind, the lame, the limbless – are in the street, calling out to passers-by for charity. It is true that infirmity in itself, and particularly from the Christian point of view, has the virtue of arousing mercy, compassion and interest, but when it is exhibited without restraint, with the sole object of making money, it fails to move people who are enlightened, in spite of a generous heart' (*La Semaine Religieuse*, 1897, pp. 341–342). For the local Church, the pilgrimage and religious mood was harmed by the presence of imposters who were only there to make the pilgrims pity them and give them money.

Tourists and sightseers

The eventual acceptance of the pilgrimage as a folk festival is apparent in newspaper reports and minutes of Church meetings, where it is described as part secular, part religious. The 'tourist' is described as a person who attends the pilgrimage purely for enjoyment and with no concern for piety:

> We could say that the event is part secular and part religious, and it's true. Gone are the days when people came on foot or by stagecoach from far afield, sleeping in fields and barns; a pilgrimage of penitence and profound faith for which one made sacrifices in order to be closer to God and to put day-to-day concerns out of one's mind. The railways have contributed to changing all that; the picturesque character has gone, and faith plays a less active role. (*La Semaine Religieuse*, 1911, p. 382)

In spite of this mood of resignation, some visitors were still not welcome; for example, silly people (*la gent bébête*) (*La Semaine Religieuse*, 1914, p. 369), inquisitive people (*les curieux*), unwelcome people (*les mal venus*) and 'this breed of idle people without faith in the soul, nor ideal in the heart, bohemians wearing gloves who sometimes risk turning the pilgrimage into events for sceptical and blasé tourists' (*La Semaine Religieuse*, 1913, p. 342). Inclement weather that put them off was even a source of rejoicing. Sometimes the tourists joined in the activities of the pilgrims, creating confusion about what a good pilgrimage should be. Thus, when the afternoon was organized by the Catholic youth movements in the 1930s, some people were surprised and sorry that the true pilgrims were diverted from their faith and merely watched the procession go by: 'It's enough for the tourists and sightseers to come and watch the procession go by! But shouldn't the true pilgrims take part in the procession and participate actively in the pilgrimage ceremonies?' (*Le Semeur du Berry*, 1937).

Images of a pilgrimage overrun by a crowd of entertainment-seeking non-believers were constantly conjured up more or less vehemently. The presence of 'tourists' was often lamented, but sometimes they were praised for the respect they showed the pilgrims:

> It is clear that there are mere tourists and sightseers in this immense crowd, but it is fair to say that most of them show respect and goodwill towards the religious ceremonies. For the others, the true pilgrims, they filled the church at 8 o'clock, piously attending mass [...], while outside the church, in the village streets and squares, a crowd of people, swelling by the hour,

swarmed around the various stalls offering food, drinks, games and entertainment. (*Le Semeur du Berry*, 1938)

The 'profanations' of the tourists

In 1921, an event – which today would be seen as insignificant – had a profound effect on the pilgrimage. In fact, it nearly resulted in the cancellation of the pilgrimage the following year, only overruled by the clergy at the last minute. That Whit Monday,

> The Archbishop learnt in the morning that the Mayor of Sainte-Solange had authorised dancing on the ground sanctified by the holy relics of our martyred saint [the site of the Saint's tomb]. This was worse than an error, it was a case of filial impiety. Would the Mayor allow people to dance on his mother's tomb? (*La Semaine Religieuse*, 1921, p. 313)

This was seen not just as a real profanation, but as a further sign of the disintegration of the pilgrimage. There were an estimated 10,000 people at the pilgrimage in 1921, and according to a local newspaper, 'among that number, there were evidently many people – far too many we should say – who see in this solemnity merely an opportunity for merrymaking, festivity, pleasure, and not for piety' (*Le Petit Berrichon*, 1921). The Archbishop also spoke of this profanation of the celebration. His words were reported in the same newspaper:

> It was with great distress, said His Excellency, that I learnt when I arrived here that people would be dancing on the tomb of Saint Solange. [...] If people enjoy themselves in cafés or private houses, that's not my concern, but as long as I am Archbishop of Bourges, I solemnly declare that I will not tolerate any such profanation. (*Le Petit Berrichon*, 1921)

The Archbishop of Bourges, the Most Reverend Izart, thus expressed his intention to cancel the pilgrimage the following year if this situation continued or was not rectified. The reporter continued: 'This year, unusually, permission has been granted to install a dance floor next to the monument, and it is the establishment of this place of pleasure and debauchery that has aroused this vehement protest from the Archbishop' (*Le Petit Berrichon*, 1921).

Considering thus that 'the pilgrimage of Sainte-Solange will remain a religious celebration or it will not exist' (*La Semaine Religieuse*, 1921, p. 313), it was decided to cancel the pilgrimage the following year. This announcement was highly unusual, because apart from 1907 following the Law separating Church and State, the pilgrimage had never been cancelled, even during the hardest times when it was very difficult for the pilgrims to get there. One month before the pilgrimage, it was announced that 'as the events that occurred during the pilgrimage last year have not been rectified, the pilgrimage is still cancelled' (*La Semaine Religieuse*, 1922a, p. 242). Finally, 1 week before the celebration, as 'the municipal council of Sainte-Solange gave its firm undertaking on 21st May that the annual pilgrimage would uphold its strictly religious nature' (*La Semaine Religieuse*, 1922b, p. 287), the local clergy organized the procession, with the aim of 'making up for the profanation of last year' (*La Semaine Religieuse*, 1922c, p. 324).

Views and Representations of the Pilgrimage Today

In view of the past refusal to mix profiles, as described above, how did the diversity of pilgrims develop? Since the involvement of the Portuguese in the 1960s, the local clergy and the organizers have moderated their views regarding the festivities. Indeed, in the context of the perceived disintegration of the pilgrimage, the Portuguese presence has been described as a blessing, because on the one hand it has helped maintain the number of worshippers, and on the other hand, by appealing to 'Portuguese religiosity', which does not differentiate between the festive and the sacred, it has been possible to reconcile these two previously opposing aspects (Etienne, 2013).

A space with a range of meanings

Nowadays, all the participants are attached to the pilgrimage, but it does not have the same meaning for all of them. Saint Solange provides the background to the celebration, but is she the main object for everyone? The reasons given for coming on the pilgrimage highlight the religious aspect, but also include the relationships that develop between the participants, the importance of upholding a local tradition and of being part of a group with shared values (be they religious or cultural). We are thus confronted by a variety of approaches, revealed in interviews and from observations.

Some specialists on religious gatherings, such as John Eade and Michael Sallnow, in contrast to Turner's theory of *communitas*, consider pilgrimages as places and times that bring together people with contrasting or even conflicting views. The effectiveness of the cult is based on these 'mutual *mis*understandings', because each group tends to interpret the presence of the others on the basis of their own view.

> The power of a shrine, therefore, derives in large part from its character almost as a religious void, a ritual space capable of accommodating diverse meanings and practices – though of course the shrine staff might attempt, with varying degrees of success, to impose a single, official discourse. (Eade and Sallnow, 2013, p. 15)

I would not go so far as to say that the Sainte-Solange pilgrimage functions only as a religious void. However, this view is interesting in that it shows the polysemous nature of the pilgrimage, as well as the desire of the Church to oversee the event and hence to fill this void. In spite of the attempt of the local Church to foster the religious importance of the pilgrimage, this discourse does not reflect all the meanings given to the event. Each participant clearly identifies a heritage aspect, but on a variety of bases: religious, traditional, territorial or ethnocultural. It is precisely this polysemy that enables the encounter between different groups. While the event has not always been described in terms of heritage, it has always been an opportunity for bringing together different groups of people and hence meanings. As mentioned above, the presence of a large gathering of people at the event is not new from the point of view of the local Church, which took exception to participants who were not motivated by piety.

While the pilgrimage is clearly a Catholic event, it also includes the local people of the Berry region ('Berrichons') and Portuguese people, as well as a small number of 'Africans'. For convenience, it is described as a Catholic

Berrichon event that includes Portuguese people, but not all the participants are believers, they are not all from the Berry, and they are not all Portuguese. The categorizations used are different in kind and seem to be mutually exclusive, although in fact they frequently overlap. The 500 or so participants thus come for different reasons but share a common attachment to the event. According to the descriptions provided by the organizers, there are three main stereotyped groups in the procession, based on belief or group membership; namely, Catholics, Berrichons and Portuguese. While there are clearly representatives of each category, interviews and observations show that this division is restrictive and a more nuanced pattern emerges.

Diversity of participants, multiplicity of attachments

Some participants highlight the religious motive and mention above all the Christian character of the pilgrimage. For these people, the pilgrimage is a way of putting belief into practice. This is typically the stance of the priests who see the event as first and foremost Christian, and above all universal. In the words of a priest speaking during an organizational meeting: 'A pilgrimage is always a pilgrimage. People come to walk and not to speak' (December 2011). And a nun stressed that 'it is not a national holiday, it's a celebration' (March 2013). The pilgrimage here is above all Christian and should not be appropriated by a specific group if it is to the detriment of the religious nature of the celebration.

Do those motivated by their Christian faith come only for that reason? Clearly not, and some try to explain their view of the event by mentioning both the Christian tradition and the tradition of celebrating Saint Solange. These are local people engaged in community or Church activities, or who belong to one of the old village families (Elias and Scotson, 1965; Zonabend, 1977; Etienne, 2015). They stress the importance of the hymns that refer to Solange rather than to Catholicism in general. One of the interviewees described these people as 'les petites mamies de Sainte-Solange' (the grannies of Sainte-Solange), who make sure that it is always the villagers who go into the church first.

Others see the event as a purely Berrichon tradition. It is above all a local event promoting village sociability. These are mainly people who are not religious and who take part in the pilgrimage and its organization because it is a local event celebrating local life (Lautman, 1985). For them, it is place that is important – the pilgrimage is above all a Berrichon event in the village of Sainte-Solange. A non-religious woman explained that she participated in the pilgrimage and its organization because for her it is a village fete where she can use her sewing skills to mend the costumes and banners.

For those who put forward the importance of being Portuguese, the celebration provides an opportunity to maintain certain customs. The most devout and the oldest only attend the morning ceremonies, foregoing the folklore displays in the afternoon. A former immigrant explained that

> Almost every Sunday there's a celebration. That's the way it is in Portugal. That's why in Sainte-Solange there's a procession. First there's Mass, and then the Portuguese meet to dance, sing, eat… Ah, yes, eating is very important, conviviality. I think that's why the Portuguese were very drawn to Sainte-Solange.

The pilgrimage is thus also experienced as an opportunity to celebrate together, sometimes putting the religious aspect into second place. This is seen among the youngest people, who play football while Mass is being celebrated, or the people who only come for the festivities in the afternoon. All these attitudes centre on the idea that the event is a celebration of Portuguese sociability, between friends or in the family.

Finally, there are attempts to shift the focus of group membership by highlighting the intercultural nature of the celebration. The organizers, participants and journalists frequently describe the event as international, intercultural or Franco-Portuguese. Nevertheless, this does not do away with the notion of group membership, far from it. Some people, who I call 'Luso-Berrichons', express their attachment both to the Berry region where they were born and to Portugal, thus combining the two connections. Their local roots are demonstrated by the attachment they describe to the Sainte-Solange celebration, and more generally to the locality and its heritage. French, Portuguese and European flags fly side by side. Passing references are made to specific features of the event without eradicating them. Attachment to Sainte-Solange is a way of saying that one belongs both here and there, constantly stressing the links between the two. The pilgrimage organizers have thoroughly incorporated this aspect. Representations of Fatima and Solange are displayed side by side on the stalls selling religious artefacts. In this way, the Portuguese who have settled here become Berrichon, and the Berrichons sometimes become Portuguese, as described by the President of the local Portuguese Association: 'We have young French people in the group too and who are integrated in the group. And when they are in costume, there's no difference.' In this way, the Portuguese group in the procession includes both people who are 'concerned' (Bertheleu *et al.*, 2014) through family alliances, and the 'wise' (Goffman, 1963) who have been initiated later. The groups and sense of belonging are thus not based on actual geographical or genealogical origin, but on how each person sees the importance of one or other aspect of the celebration.

Discourse and representations of the Portuguese regarding themselves and others

As mentioned above, Eade and Sallnow saw pilgrimages as having multiple meanings. They observed that not only do several discourses about the pilgrimage exist side by side, but also that the groups tend to interpret the motivations of the others on the basis of their own discourse. Thus, the idea that the pilgrimage is closely linked to the Portuguese leads to considering the participants as Portuguese, particularly in the afternoon. When I interviewed people in the afternoon, in French, some replied in Portuguese, as if it was evident that everybody understood Portuguese. Some people told me that they identified with the Portuguese, even when not at the pilgrimage, merely because they had been seen at Sainte-Solange. This idea sometimes goes even further; some local Catholics think that the pilgrimage is a Portuguese event and for that reason do not take part in it. Finally, some people who did not know about the pilgrimage before the arrival of the Portuguese, and who know little or nothing of its history, tend to think that

the event is a Portuguese cult that some French people now go to.

In this way, the Portuguese have thoroughly accepted the idea that it is thanks to them that the tradition has survived. A retired couple from Portugal observed that '[The pilgrimage] would still have existed, but not in the same way'. Similarly, as explained by another former immigrant: 'Fortunately, we kept going [...]. The fact that we held on saved the pilgrimage. Because otherwise, it wouldn't exist any more.' He added: 'It's us who hold things together a bit'. In spite of some reactions by the Church, which objects to the excessive importance of the Portuguese, everyone observes, or perhaps concedes, that the Portuguese now play a major role, not only in the pilgrimage but increasingly in the area.

In fact, what we are witnessing is a shift of the frontiers of the other, which no longer designates the Portuguese. Three factors seem to have been involved. First, the extension of the referent 'Portuguese': previously Portuguese referred to a foreigner. Today, the word describes the children, grandchildren or spouse, in other words many people born in France. Being Portuguese is thus an indication of membership of a group that is completely adapted to local society. Second, the small involvement of the 'Africans' and other immigrants has also been influential; it is they who are now the 'immigrants' and 'foreigners'. This is shown in the songs, the organizational meetings, and in the way people are referred to: when people talk about the immigrants or foreigners, they are referring to the Africans. Finally, another element that has influenced this shift of frontiers for the Portuguese is European membership. The festivities are sometimes described as being European; for example, one of the people interviewed observed that Sainte-Solange had become a bit like Europe.

Conclusion: From Rejection to Compromise

The changes that have occurred in the cult of Saint Solange have regularly placed the participants and organizers in a double bind, to borrow the term used by the Palo Alto Group (Bateson *et al.*, 1956). From the late nineteenth to the mid-twentieth century, a period when huge numbers of pilgrims came to Sainte-Solange, tourists and sightseers were frowned on, because while they helped ensure the survival of the pilgrimage, the clergy did not consider them as having the right motivation. In the 1960s, the presence of the Portuguese raised the issue again, but this time, the Church got round the problem by considering them as bringing new life to a declining cult by celebrating a religious festival 'in their own way', in other words festively. Moreover, this revitalization was part of a more general European process of renewal or reconstruction of rituals (Boissevain, 1992), in this case on a religious basis, in other cases in the form of games (Fournier, 2013). Within a century, there has thus been a shift in the image of the pilgrimage and the way the different participants are viewed.

In spite of the range of meanings given to the pilgrimage, the practices and discourses related to what is now seen as a heritage event are helping reconcile the different viewpoints. All agree that the pilgrimage sites should be promoted during the Heritage Days, because of the symbolic and economic benefits that they yield. In this situation, the Portuguese play a leading role, not only in view of their number and the perception that it is thanks to them that the festival has survived, but also because of the work they regularly organize to renovate the sites. This 'balance of power' thus gives them a decisive say within the pilgrimage organization, raising the status of being Portuguese, which is not the case in other events attended by Portuguese people.

Notes

[1] The word is used both by the people concerned and by the organizers, and refers to the immigrants and also to their children or grandchildren born in France, and sometimes to their relatives by marriage. Thus, the 'Portuguese' do not form a group defined by objective criteria such as nationality, but by the sense of belonging as defined in the work of F. Barth (1969).

[2] Although this paper was not published by the Church, it made its Catholic leaning clear by displaying an image of Christ on the cross on the first page of each issue, subtitled 'Dieu protège la France' (God protect France).

References

Bateson, G., Jackson, D.D., Haley, J. and Weakland, J. (1956) Toward a theory of schizophrenia. *Behavioral Science* 1(4), 251–264.

Bertheleu, H., Dassié, V. and Garnier, J. (2014) Mobilisations, ancrages et effacements de la mémoire. Contextes urbains en région centre. In Barbe, N. and Chauliac, M. (eds) *L'Immigration aux Frontières du Patrimoine*. Éditions de la Maison des Sciences de l'Homme, Paris, 25/42.

Boissevain, J. (1992) *Revitalizing European Rituals*. Routledge, London.

Chélini, J. and Branthomme, H. (1982) *Les chemins de Dieu: histoire des pèlerinages chrétiens des origines à nos jours*. Hachette, Paris.

Claverie, É. and Fedele, A. (2014) Incertitudes et religions vernaculaires/uncertainty in vernacular religions. *Social Compass* 61(4), 487–496.

Durkheim, É. (1960) *Les formes élémentaires de la vie religieuse: le système totémique en Australie*. Presses Universitaires de France, Paris.

Eade, J. and Sallnow, M.J. (2013) *Contesting the Sacred: the Anthropology of Christian Pilgrimage*. Wipf and Stock Publishers, Eugene, Oregon, USA.

Elias, N. and Scotson, J.L. (1965) *The Established and the Outsiders: A Sociological Enquiry into Community Problems*. F. Cass, London.

Etienne, G. (2013) Un pèlerinage local entre communalisation religieuse et communalisation ethno-culturelle. *Les Cahiers de Cost* (2), 101–108.

Etienne, G. (2015) Devenir autochtone quand on est 'français d'origine étrangère'. *Revue Européenne des Migrations Internationales* 31(3 and 4), 187–208.

Fournier, L.S. (ed.) (2013) *Les jeux collectifs en Europe: transformations historiques*. L'Harmattan, Paris.

Goffman, E. (1963) *Stigma: Notes on the Management of Spoiled Identity*. Penguin Books, London.

La Semaine Religieuse (8 June 1895), 23.
La Semaine Religieuse (12 June 1897), 24.
La Semaine Religieuse (10 June 1911), 23.
La Semaine Religieuse (17 May 1913), 20.
La Semaine Religieuse (6 June 1914), 23.
La Semaine Religieuse (5 June 1920), 23.
La Semaine Religieuse (21 May 1921), 21.
La Semaine Religieuse (6 May 1922a), 18.
La Semaine Religieuse (27 May 1922b), 21.
La Semaine Religieuse (10 June 1922c), 23.
Lautman, F. (1985) Fête traditionnelle et identité locale. Terrain. *Revue d'ethnologie de l'Europe* (5), 29–36.
Le Petit Berrichon (15 June 1919), 23.
Le Petit Berrichon (21 May 1921), 21.
Le Semeur du Berry (22 May 1937).
Le Semeur du Berry (11 June 1938).
Nolan, M.L. and Nolan, S. (1989) *Christian Pilgrimage in Modern Western Europe*. University of North Carolina Press, Chapel Hill, North Carolina, USA.
Zonabend, F. (1977) Pourquoi nommer ? In Lévi-Strauss, C. (ed.) *L'identité*. Puf, pp. 257–279.

10 Mixing Sport and Religion in the Landes Area of France

Mathilde Lamothe*

Laboratory ITEM EA 3002, University of Pau and Pays de l'Adour, France

Introduction

In the area of Landes (France), certain features offer a surprising bridge between religion and sport, materialized through road signs indicating sites such as the 'Chapel of Our Lady of Rugby' at Larrivière-Saint-Savin, the 'Chapel of Our Lady of the Course Landaise'[1] in Bascons or the 'Chapel of Our Lady of the Cyclists' at Labastide-d'Armagnac. These chapels are real places of worship created in the middle of the twentieth century, where tributes are made to both sports and athletes, while attracting many visitors. But, since the local sports culture seems to undeniably influence the religious mesh of the territory, how can one build worship and religious pilgrimage through the phenomenon of this local sport identity? What role have members of the clergy (and lovers of sport) been able to play in the organization of pilgrimages to places of worship dedicated to sports and athletes? In particular it is interesting to explore the action or influence of these priest-founders through their patronage, but also the work of various associations of culture and worship such as the 'Friends of the Chapel of Our Lady of Rugby'.

The humanities and social sciences provide a historical depth and a particular heuristic analysis of society (Augustine and Sorbets, 1996); they allow one to question the origins of sport, its social and religious impact, not forgetting the way in which sport intersects with social and political issues. Sport can indeed be read as a 'social fact' if we consider that 'all traits of society, in general and in particular are found there [in sport]'[2] (Augustine and Sorbets, 1996, p. 12). In this chapter, I wish to propose an ethnological approach to religious practices and sporting events at these Landaise sports chapels. In particular, this work seeks to understand what has influenced or promoted the construction of this singular syncretism that authorizes jerseys of rugby players or cyclists to mingle with statues of the Virgin Mary, in these religious shrines dedicated to the memory of sports.

Territorial Footprint of Sporting Practices in Aquitaine

Brief reminder of the socio-historic process

In spite of a lack of causal or structural explanation (influenced by certain elements of tradition), rugby remains a sport strongly linked to the identity of southwestern France, even if its rapid implementation and adoption in this territory

---

*E-mail: mathilde_lamothe@hotmail.com

still remains a curious enigma in the history of French rugby. The phenomenon is often explained according to several factors: in the first place thanks to the British influence in the nineteenth century in Bordeaux, and in small British colonies such as Biarritz and Pau; then, second, thanks to networks of notable republicans and secularists (notably transmitted by l'École Normale de Dax, which introduced teachers to the teaching of art and the game of rugby), who supported the rugby clubs against the advance of football advocated and sponsored by Catholics. It is useful to explain that the oval ball constituted 'a symbol of republican France [...] the choice of secularists' according to Jean-Pierre Bodis: this last point explains the interest of the clergy, because of their opposition to the physical contact that characterizes rugby (Bodis in Cholvy and Tranvouez, 1999, p. 204), represented in a dialectic between north against south, between laymen with the oval ball against the parish priest of the sponsored round ball (Augustin and Garrigou, 1985). This religious–political conflict, however, disappeared before the beginning of the Second World War. Notwithstanding the passing of this dualism, rugby is seen as a 'sport-totem' in the southwest of France, and has become a distinctive sign of territorial affiliation that has generated a collective identity. Here, the work of Anne Saouter must be noted, which highlights the gender distribution of roles of men and women in this rugby micro-society (Saouter, 2000), while Jean-Pierre Augustin illuminates the socio-historical processes that have enabled the dissemination and the spatial distribution of these sports (Augustin, 1989).

In effect the footprint of sport in geographical space may apply, beyond rugby, to different sporting forms in the southwest of France. Basketball flourishes where football and rugby have not yet been established – in Chalosse (south of the River Adour), where the practice is strongly established in the rural areas where there is no rivalry between the secular and religious networks. This explains why, in Aquitaine, basketball clubs are more numerous than those of football and rugby (Augustin, 1989). To this could be added other more pragmatic explanations; for example, Chalosse is made up of many small villages and basketball requires fewer players than a football or rugby team. Thus, only cities such as Amou or Hagetmau have both a football and a basketball club, while most of the small Chalosse villages have a gymnasium and a basketball club.

In addition to these sports, other 'traditional' practices such as the Course Landaise exist – timeless customs, proudly practised since time immemorial in the southwest of France, as proclaimed on the internet site of the Fédération Française de la Course Landaise. Some historians of bullfighting note the existence of archives referring to 'les jeux taurins' as early as the Middle Ages, recording the custom of 'bull running' in streets or other approved places, in Bayonne or Saint-Sever.[3] Another argument proposes its establishment in the nineteenth century, with links to Spain (as well as links to other bullfighting cultures such as the Camargue). This latter theory connects local bullfighting to Castillan influences that are still evidenced in local vocabulary (words such as ganadería (breeding cattle), encierro (animal enclosure), paseo (a walk or a horse-ride), cuadrilla (gang or team of bullfighters), etc.), which seems to be derived from Castillian. Alexandre Fernandez follows this hypothesis by comparing the shows that are organized around the beast, that is, the Landes cow and the Spanish bull. Just as the British influence could be used to explain the introduction of rugby in cities such as Bordeaux, Pau or Biarritz, it is possible that certain Spanish influences of the Second Empire favoured the establishment of bullfights in Bayonne and Dax. The foundations of the 'taurine tradition' are anchored in the Landais taurine games, but also perpetuated by entrepreneurs behind the performances, just like their hispanophile counterparts, who at the end of the twentieth century revived a 'tradition' that was going into decline from the end of the war until the 1970s (Fernandez, 2007).

The distinction between street spectacle and formalized (and marketed) events in an arena has been highlighted by Frédéric Saumade (1995), for whom the process of reducing regional diversities – the geographic range of the Course Landaise, for example, extended from the areas of Lot-et-Garonne to Gers and Pyrénées-Atlantiques – derives from a bourgeois definition of local identity, influenced by a desire for spectacular traditions. Today, the Course Landaise is a cultural symbol of the Gascogne: it is on this rhetoric that the aficionados rely to counter the arguments of the anti-bullfighting groups (who are also against any sport related to the use of bulls),[4] whose opinions were particularly felt in

2011 at the time that bullfighting was registered in the inventory of intangible cultural heritage of France. Nonetheless, bullfighting remains a characteristic symbol of local culture and sporting practices connected with this particular territory, even if the livestock comes from Spain rather than the Landes (as it has since the nineteenth century).

Finally, sport, while being indicative of rivalries, asserts itself as a vector of identity. Each sport constitutes a privileged pole of community identification (Augustin, 1989) – even if this identity is not innate but is the fruit of a socio-historic construct. This link between sport and tradition has often been noted in the ethnological literature, but what is the link between sport and religion?

Sport and religion: A new 'opium for the people'?

Reflecting on the 'total social impact' of sport – and more particularly mass sports of the modern era – it can be seen to influence all elements of society in two interlinked dimensions: the practice of the sport, and the spectacle of the sport. This concept resonates favourably with Marxist theory in the field of physical education in the 1970s, which prompted the consideration of sport as the 'opium of the people', in other words, a powerful drug leading to an addiction or dependence. This theory – on sport as a spectacle and element of alienation – criticizes the society of (sports) consumption and its global capitalism that meets the needs of the system (we refer here, among others, to the work of sociologist Jean-Marie Brohm, 2006). Far from this concept of so-called 'sport tyranny', the anthropologist Marc Augé proposes a different symbolic perspective linking the spectacle of a football match to the idea of religious ritual. Taking the counterpoint of these Marxist-inspired theories, he observes in these passionate attitudes the designation of totemic values, religious fervour and motonymic identification of Group (Augé, 1982). If the definition of ritual is based on a break from daily, repetitive practices and norms, a specific spatio-temporal or even symbolic dimension, we would be inclined to support the analogy of the sporting spectacle that also brings together the elements of a religious ceremony (the faithful, a hierarchical

structure, a place to worship the 'cult', etc.). However, Christian Bromberger warns against this simplistic reasoning and offers the weight of the scientist in the analysis of this social game (and its intellectual construction), since, in football, there is 'no belief in an active and present "being" or supernatural forces – instead it is the ethnologist who intellectually applies the process of ritualisation' (Bromberger, 1992).[5] That is why this researcher proposes that the character of sports supporters presents an exaggerated representation of society, from theatrical scenes to social relationships and the fundamental values of our society, such as performance, chance, competition, solidarity, etc.

The analogy between rugby and religion has been underlined by Sébastien Darbon in his ethnography of the Tyrosse Rugby Club in Landes (Darbon, 1995). The playing field is compared to the elements of a church (choir, adjacent chapels, etc.) whose access is reserved only for the officiating clergy of worship; while the cloakroom remains a mysterious place where the layman is prohibited, which holds the appropriate clothing for the exercise of worship – undoubtedly reflecting a sacristy.[6] Local level clubs seem more open to the public in welcoming people after games, into facilities that contain the equivalent of holy relics on display for all (cups, flags, medals, photos, etc.).

Notwithstanding this, Darbon presents a warning on his ethnological supposition: his work tries not to lean in the direction of those who see the *ritual*, of the *sacred* and the *religious* everywhere [his emphasis]' (Darbon, 1995, p. 64). Rather, he attempts to consider ways in which these elements play a role in distinguishing between the formal properties of sport and the cultural context within which they are enacted (in other words, the context of Tyrosse rugby) and within which they fit. This heuristic perspective moves away from the risk of disenfranchising the societies being studied, while focusing in on the context of the study, which is the religious character or ritualized behaviour of society.

Certain introductory questions emerge when considering sport from the perspective of religion: are there values in sport similar to those advocated in religion? Or is this a form of idolatry or totemism, in a context of dechristianizing society, which transfers symbolic metaphysical values to new social objects? Particularly, in the case of football as in that of rugby, a note contradicts or, at least, tempers this relationship between sport and religion: even if many religious metaphors are used – in particular by sports journalists, who draw on the vocabulary of the Church – we cannot consider these teams or these sports, as genuine religions in the absence of a supernatural dimension, or explicit reference to a form of transcendence. However, other forms of religiosity are expressed in the framework of Catholic worship in the Landes: athletes living or deceased are put in the place of honour in chapels dedicated to the Virgin Mary, the figure of salvation and of maternal protection.

Reflection on Local Culture: The Chapels Dedicated to Sports

The Chapel of Our Lady of the Cyclists

The first chapel of sport, which appeared in the village of Labastide-d'Armagnac (Landes), was born from the inspiration of a priest who was a great amateur cyclist, who dared to combine the spiritual dimension and sports in the same place. The internet site of the Diocese of d'Aire-et-Dax tells us the history of the creation of this chapel, at the initiative of Father Joseph Massie: on 22 August 1958, the children of the local holiday camp were walking in the area. The heavy and persistent rain led them to seek refuge in a small rural chapel. The chapel was covered in ivy, and invaded by vegetation. The priest who accompanied the children took the opportunity to celebrate Mass and recounted afterwards that he had a distraction during the Mass, an idea came to him: to turn this little church into 'Notre-Dame-des-Cyclistes', as in Italy! This priest had already made the bicycle trip to the Italian Madonna del Ghisallo chapel, dedicated to the 'Universal Patroness of Cyclists' by Pope Pius XII in 1948. On 18 May 1959 (Pentecost Monday), Pope John XXIII fulfilled the idea of Father Massie by making the chapel of Larrivière-Saint-Savin, the National Shrine of Cyclists – under the protection of the Virgin – approved by the Fédération Française du Cyclisme and the Cyclotourisme organization: this is how 'Our Lady of the Cyclists' appears in the department of Landes.

Cycling does not figure as a regional sport in this area and does not have a dynamic local identity behind it; on the contrary, it exists on a wider scale that positions this site as the 'national sanctuary of cycling'. Approximately 850 jerseys of famous French and international racers (Jeannie Longo, Raymond Poulidor, Eddie Merckx, etc.), press articles and medals adorn the walls of the chapel, to which is added an exhibition of ancient bicycles. Located at the entrance of the chapel, the collection forms a mini-museum to the history of cycling from 1870 to today, juxtaposing a decor composed of sport and religious 'relics' in the nave of the chapel. This phenomenon established a certain acceptance to put religion and sport together – local this time – to be emulated in creating other chapels on this sporting–religious model, in the form of Notre-Dame-du-Rugby and Notre-Dame-de-la-Course-Landaise.

The Chapel of Our Lady of Rugby

The prohibition of rugby by the Catholic administration ended in the middle of the twentieth century, which allowed the emergence of figures such as Abbot Devert, a teacher-vicar who has 'married his faith with the passion of the Oval'. This priest is particularly famous – at the local level – for offering Masses in honour of the French Rugby XV and praying for their victory.

Reports on the origins of la Chapelle Notre-Dame-du-Rugby, in Larrivière-Saint-Savin (Landes) are like metaphors of apocryphal legend, and comprise two events: first of all, the reading of a section of the newspaper *France-Soir* by Abbot Devert, describing a stained glass window in an English church in Worcestershire dedicated to seven players from Manchester United Football Club who died in an aircraft accident; then a tragic car accident that killed three young rugby players in 1964 whom Abbot Devert had known in Dax when he was seminarian. He decided to build this chapel in tribute to these young people and to the families of deceased rugby players, and it was inaugurated in 1976. In 1966–1968, the first jerseys were deposited in the chapel and a museum, created in 2010, today contains approximately 450 players' jerseys, offered by collectors or lovers of rugby. Unlike the jerseys displayed in the museum, the donations from clubs or individuals, which remain in the chapel, embody a more symbolic significance in the local area – representing the famous 'family of rugby' – for example, via a shirt worn by the prematurely deceased son of one of the members of

Fig. 10.1. A nave decorated with shirts in the Chapel of Our Lady of the Cyclists (Labastide-d'Armagnac, France).

the association, 'les Amis de la Chapelle Notre-Dame-du-Rugby'.

Like the Chapel of Our Lady of the Cyclists, the decor represents this sporting–religious allegory: stained glass windows evoking rugby adorn the walls: the Virgin of the 'Lineout' and the Virgin of the 'Scrum',[7] a statue of the Virgin of Rugby stands at the entrance of the chapel, etc. There is also a prayer to Our Lady of Rugby written by Abbot Devert in 1967, in which the semantic fields of sport and religion intersect:

> Virgin Mary who taught your Child Jesus to play on your knee, look maternally on our game for larger children... Be with us, in the terrible melee of existence, in order that we emerge as winners of the great game of life, giving example as on the field, of courage, enthusiasm, team spirit... in the image of You. Amen.[8]

In addition, a set of 'mythical objects' (balls, jerseys, studded boots, etc.) are imbued with sacred qualities.

If we take the comparison a little further, other links or similarities seem to unite the Chapter of Our Lady of Rugby and the Chapel of Our Lady of the Cyclists, apart from the fact that both draw their inspiration from sporting–religious chapels seen abroad. The origin of these chapels is akin to a foundation or creation myth (a tragic car accident for one, heavy rainfall requiring shelter in an abandoned chapel for the other). The periodic evocation of these events brings together a community around a number of spiritual sporting values such as the commemoration of loss, sharing, the meaning of effort, respect for others, solidarity, etc. These values also develop and strengthen feelings of local community, often referred to as the 'family of rugby' or followers of 'la Petite Reine' (the 'little queen'), in effort and in the face of adversity.

Other Landaise sports chapels

The Chapel of Our Lady of the Cyclists has inspired imitators in other sports, particularly in the department of Landes, as seen from the examples mentioned earlier: the Course Landaise and basketball. I recall briefly here the history of the creation of these two memorial chapels, focusing in particular on the motivations for their foundation.

Fig. 10.2. 'La Vierge à la touche', Chapel of Our Lady of Rugby (Larrivière-Saint-Savin, France).

The Chapel of Notre-Dame-de-la-Course-Landaise in Bascons was originally dedicated to Saint Mary Magdalene, patron saint of the parish. When it was renovated in 1970 it took the name Notre-Dame-de-la-Course-Landaise (just after the dedication of Chapelle Notre-Dame-du-Rugby). As explained by one of the initiators of the project, Abbot Lafitau (Foulquier, 2014), this change is explained as a desire to:

> give the Course Landaise a worthy local sanctuary (of spiritual interest), similar to other sports; establishing a concept of unity and fraternity, a climate of understanding between all the members of this family of the Course

Landaise. The idea being, to create an important place of commemoration, with stone monuments inscribed with the names of all those who have been great servants of this Landais sport; a museum, bringing together glorious testimonials of the past; to organize each year, a religious ceremony to make solemn tribute to our dead.[9]

Similar to the sport of rugby, the Course Landaise can result in injury, sometimes fatal, despite an evolution towards making the game safer. The place to remember the past, and the dead, plays an important memorial at the present time. However, the chapel is only one of the elements of the site linked to the bullfighting, which also includes a museum (which seeks to be a showcase for this game of Gascony) managed by the municipality, a monument to the dead of the Course Landaise, as well as a monument erected to the memory of Bernard Huguet, a Landaise torero killed in 1987 in the arenas of Montfort-in-Chalosse. We also include two interesting facts: first, like many other cities of Landes and the southwest, the city of Bascons has arenas that were built in 1936; and second, the current mayor of Bascons, Raoul Laporterie, is also vice-president of the French Federation of the Course Landaise. This is significant, since, unlike the chapels of cycling and rugby, this chapel seems much more of a municipal expression – or at least, a project supported by the territorial authority – even if the desire of sport-loving priests representing Landes and the southwest were involved in the organization and running of the project.

La Chapelle Notre-Dame-du-Basket (basketball) located at Castel-Sarrazin has been in development for more than 10 years: the basketball players would also like to have a chapel where they could assemble and develop the equivalent of a museum and to leave memorials of the history of basketball in Chalosse.[10] The project of transforming the chapel of Bourcot into a chapel dedicated to basketball, however, remains aspirational.

Considering the spatial, temporal and social factors discussed above, sport clearly appears to perform as a territorial marker and symbol. These cultural particularities are invested in by local actors, be they lay or clergy, who have championed the emergence of sporting–religious places of worship. It is not just the celebratory achievements of individual sports that are important here, but the manner in which local identity is expressed through these sports. Understanding this desire to construct territorial identity must be understood in reference to its protagonists and their historical and social context.

The Actors in the Construction of Territorial Identity

The role of the clergy

I have mentioned already the patronage of the Church in this area and the role of mass popular education movements, such as the Jeunesse Agricole Catholique, with young people during the end of the nineteenth and the beginning of the twentieth century. Since the secularization of public primary schools (1882), parish clergy have focused their central patronage on pastoral actions with youths (Cholvy and Tranvouez, 1999), particularly if parish priests are passionate about sport, such as with Abbot Massie in the case of cycling or Abbot Devert for rugby.

In the social doctrine of the Church, multiple theories exist on the development and training of individuals according to papal discourse, which deserve to be reflected on elsewhere. Some patronage at the end of the nineteenth and the beginning of the twentieth century appears as a form of social Catholicism and involves a doctrine of organic societal reform: this two-pronged objective implies a concern for a combined religious and moral training, leading to human development without forgetting leisure (Zordan in Cholvy and Tranvouez, 1999). Thus, sport and entertainment can be integral parts of personal human enrichment. In addition, the integral human development, theorized by Pope Paul VI in 1967, appears precisely in the context of the creation of the Landaise sports chapels. However, it seems unlikely that it was applied so immediately in the actions of these priests (even if they were actively seeking to develop their ideas, both spiritual and intellectual). The doctrine in the encyclical *Populorum Progressio*[11] seeks to apply a humanist perspective to the process of globalization, claiming to consider the social aspects, a moral desire and a movement towards God while 'aspiring to the spiritual perfection of the human family' (Bertina, 2013), even if its limits were to be tested at the end of the twentieth century.

The associative fabric

Though priests were able to play significant roles in initiating these sports chapels, they were supported by a strong team: both les Amis de Notre-Dame-du-Rugby and les Amis de Notre-Dame-des-Cyclistes bring together committed lay people who weave a network of presence and material aid. As mentioned earlier, the place of Christian lay people in the Church has been strongly affirmed by the Second Vatican Council (1965)[12]: among the tasks of the apostolate is social Christian action, which focuses on maintaining Christian friendship, which lends mutual support in all necessities. The field of apostolic action is broad and can translate, for example, as assistance provided to those disabled by playing rugby. An example of this assistance is the rugby exhibition match organized by les Amis de Notre-Dame-du-Rugby in 1999, with the French team playing against the team of the Basque Coast, with the aim of collecting funds and financing the work of renovating the chapel and the creation of its museum. However, part of the earnings (5 million francs, or one-fifth of the profits) was paid to support people suffering disability as a result of rugby.[13]

Basketball has also imitated this associative model: in 2004, the association of les Amis de Notre-Dame-du-Basket was created (associated under the law of 1901), the objective of which is to 'dedicate this chapel to basketball under the name Notre-Dame du Basket in order to contribute to the radiation and the development of this sport, through sporting, cultural, tourist and social events' according to the official journal (statutes deposited on 24 January 2004). The presentation of these objectives highlighted a significant and gaping hole: there is an absence of a spiritual dimension among the events set out, which appears normal since there is no priest behind this initiative.

In the history of creating these sports chapels, the figure of the priest-initiator is often highlighted, but is inevitably accompanied by a strong team in the background, who support the project and participate in its realization and construction. These committed lay people are the pillars, working with the priests who are in charge of these chapels, supporting the organization of various activities and religious manifestations, such as pilgrimages and bringing to life these cult centres of worship.

Pilgrimages – Religious or Profane?

In la Chapelle Notre-Dame-du-Rugby, an annual pilgrimage has been created to commemorate deceased rugby players: the young, who died in car accidents (57 in the commune of Peyrehorade between 1957 and 2013), and former players who died of illness or natural death. A report that commemorates the rugby players who died in the year is carefully updated by the president of les Amis de Notre-Dame-du-Rugby. During the 'day of memories and pilgrimages' on Penticost day, commemorations are organized in the chapel. We were told:

> there are prayers for those who believe and a tribute-remembrance for those who do not believe in it, because there are some who come who are not believers but they come for the memory of their comrades.[14]

Thus, the link between the religious and the rugby communities is consolidated during this commemoration.

Similar to these testimonies and prayers in remembrance of deceased athletes, an annual religious ceremony also takes place at la Chapelle Notre-Dame-des-Cyclistes, on Whit Monday (on the anniversary of the consecration of the chapel by the ecclesial authorities). Prior to the Mass, a hike and two cycling circuits mark the alliance between sport and religion. However, the appellation 'pilgrimage' is rarely, if ever, used to qualify this event. The term is reserved for other types of event as we will see in the following.

With respect to the Course Landaise, a pilgrimage of coursayres ('distracters' and jumpers) and lovers of the Course Landaise has been held annually on the Ascension Thursday, following the same ritual: during the 'Morning of Remembrance' a posthumous tribute is made during the Mass to a coursayre (it should be noted that another religious tribute to the dead of the Course Landaise is celebrated on All Saints

Fig. 10.3. Stained glass window in Chapelle Notre Dame de la Course Landaise.

Day). A wreath is then placed at the monument to the dead of the Course Landaise, before a Course takes place in the afternoon in the arena of Bascons. I emphasize the term 'ritual', whose character is both lay or civilian and religious (the latter regarding only a part of the day – the morning Mass). In the present case, the sport plays the role of cultural and symbolic cement, even if part of the event takes place in a religious framework. On this point, I agree with the assumptions of Christian Bromberger on football, which he sees as a powerful catalyst for social identity and regionality, characterized by the double dimension of mimicry and catharsis (Bromberger, 1992).

Inscription on a Wider Scale

These chapels may become the reason to make a stop on a larger pilgrimage journey, for example pilgrim cyclists travelling to Lourdes (France) or to Santiago de Compostela (Spain) may add a stage in Landes in order to visit la Chapelle Notre-Dame-des-Cyclistes. Another form of 'pilgrimage', the Tour de France, has visited la Chapelle Notre-Dame-des-Cyclistes four times (1984, 1989 when it was the start of a 'stage', 1999, 2001), in tribute to the anniversary of the national sanctuary for cyclists who have died.

These chapels may also be linked to other important religious shrines in combining sport and sport for people with disability: for example, former rugby players are involved in the international pilgrimage of athletes to Lourdes, an initiative launched in 2003. Notable in this initiative is Michel Crauste, a former rugby player and captain of the French XV, who suffered a spinal injury and who currently presides over Lourdes Rugby Club. Links with these other French sanctuaries can also translate in the form of patronage. The Chapel of Our Lady of the Oval (Chapelle Notre-Dame-de-l'Ovalie) in Rocamadour is an initiative of the parish priest: this brings the link between religion and sport to a new level, since this priest is also a rugby player in the local team. That is why the chapel, devoted to injured or deceased rugby players (during or after matches), was inaugurated in 2001 in this great site of pilgrimage, in the presence of the presiding officials of the la Chapelle Larrivière-Saint-Savin and the president of les Amis de la Chapelle Notre-Dame-du-Rugby.

A semantic (or theological) point needs to be clarified with regard to these places of worship. In spite of the fact that the sports chapels bear the name of 'Notre-Dame', this Marian cult is tempered by the current parish priest of the Chapel of Our Lady of Rugby. According to him, the chapels are not considered as real cults of the Virgin as can occur, for example, in the pilgrimage of Our Lady of Buglose (Landes). In this latter case, the Marian cult is linked to the (re)discovery of a statue of the Virgin Mary by a shepherd, in the middle of a field in the seventeenth century: the Chapel of Buglose, located in close proximity, was then rebuilt and became a place of pilgrimage to pray to the Virgin. He justifies this 'do-it-yourself' ceremony nicely, considering that these 'testimonies between friends ... are genuine, with feelings coming from the heart'.[15] An exemplar of this faith dimension is that the events on the day of 'Testimony and Pilgrimage' at la Chapelle Notre-Dame-du-Rugby evoke natural prayers and testimonies from the attendees.

Conclusion

This new field of research, be it historical, sociological or anthropological, suggests an integration of 'sport' into various forms of study.

Various forms of research put forward that these identity markers or even ideological constructs found in the field of sports, oscillating between a pre-existing given, a colourful display of folklore and a reconstruction or intellectual invention, are part of the process of sportivization or heritagization. The traditional sports and games are a valid and relevant entrée into the study of society, its behaviour and its cultural values; sports appear as a watermark identifier of a territory, the characteristics of a specific society in a local geographical space.

On the whole, these individual chapels are in agreement with the social doctrine of the Catholic Church and offer a place in the spiritual formation of the individual but also facilitating leisure. However, the gap sometimes seems thin between cultural tourism and pilgrimage, in other words, between simple curiosity and devout intention: la Chapelle Notre-Dame-du-Rugby welcomes 10,000 visitors annually and 15,000 two-wheeled or two-legged visitor-pilgrims visit la Chapelle Notre-Dame-des-Cyclistes, to discover this church-museum. These places of reflection appeal to the sensitivity and affectivity of individuals. Certainly, they bring people outside of themselves and their daily subjective life, but do they experience the sacred?

This network of small shrines, however, reveals a certain mystical soul, blending both spirituality and sport within this territory. In this chapter, I have tried to present the vitality and the continuous representation of identity as demonstrated in these illustrations of Landaise sports chapels. These sites underline the convergence between sport and religion and cannot be separated from the historical and cultural framework in which they have evolved. In effect these sports chapels are anchored in modern society and its discourses, as demonstrated by the gesture of the president of lesAmis de la Chapelle Notre-Dame-des-Cyclistes, who had to remove the shirt of Lance Armstrong in 2012.

Many other research tracks could evolve from this chapter: for example, one could develop research around the Marian cult in Landes, or focus on how death is commemorated in each chapel where the walls are covered in objects that oscillate between functions of museum commemoration and votive offering.

Notes

[1] The 'Course Landaise' is a local, traditional form of bullfighting held in arenas, without bloodshed – unlike the Spanish equivalent, the 'Corrida': in the 'Course' men perform acrobatic jumps over the cow or dodge the animal at the last minute, in a show of artistic acrobatics.

[2] Original text: 'l'ensemble des traits structurants des sociétés s'y retrouvent dans leur généralité et leurs particularités'.

[3] The first references to the topic are the subject of historical nuances, since direct access to the sources seems difficult: to explain the history of the Course Landaise, Claude Martel cites Michel Laforcade, who quotes a text from 1282 discovered by Claude Pelletier at Bayonne, signalling the custom of 'letting go bulls, oxen and cows in the streets to make them run' (Martel, 1995).

[4] A linguistic challenge in translating the paper emerges in that corridas and tauromachies both refer to bullfighting; however, the latter is used in the context of the Course Landaise, which does not involve the slaying of a bull/cow.

[5] Original text: 'pas de croyance en une présence agissante d'être ou de forces surnaturelles. [...] C'est l'ethnologue qui est l'opérateur intellectuel du processus de ritualisation' (Bromberger, 1992, p. 239).

[6] Original text: 'lieu mystérieux interdit au profane, [...] où l'on endosse les vêtements appropriés à l'exercice du culte – faisant incontestablement penser à une sacristie' (Darbon, 1995, p. 64).

[7] Original names: La Vierge à la touche et La Vierge à la mêlée.

[8] 'Vierge Marie qui avez enseigné votre Enfant Jésus à jouer sur vos genoux, veillez maternellement sur nos jeux de grands enfants. [...] Soyez avec nous, dans la terrible mêlée de l'existence, afin que nous sortions vainqueurs du grand jeu de la vie, donnant l'exemple, comme sur le terrain, du courage, de l'entrain, de l'esprit d'équipe, en un mot d'un idéal à l'image du Vôtre. Amen.'

[9] Original text: 'donner à la course landaise un sanctuaire pour que les écarteurs landais soient aussi dignes d'intérêt (un intérêt spirituel) que les autres sportifs; établir un principe d'union et de fraternité, un climat de compréhension entre tous les membres de cette famille tauromachique qu'est la course landaise; créer un haut lieu du souvenir, avec gravés dans la pierre les noms de tous ceux qui ont été les grands serviteurs du sport landais; un musée où seraient rassemblés les témoignages glorieux du passé; organiser chaque année une cérémonie religieuse pour rendre un hommage solennel à nos disparus'.

[10] From an article in the newspaper *Sud-Ouest* from 12 December 2013.

[11] Elle 'naît d'une volonté de compléter cette quête de prospérité par une vision nouvelle du développement qui promouvrait "tout homme et tout l'homme" (Paul VI, 1967, n 14), revendiquant ainsi une part délaissée par le développement économique' (Bertina, 2013).
See also la *Lettre encyclique de sa Sainteté le Pape Paul VI sur le développement des peuples*, available at: www.vatican.va/holy_father/paul_vi/encyclicals/documents/hf_p-vi_enc_26031967_populorum_fr.html (accessed 4 September 2014).

[12] See the Decree on the apostolate of the laity: *Apostolicam actuositatem* : 'Le Concile exhorte instamment les laïcs, chacun suivant ses talents et sa formation doctrinale, à prendre une part plus active selon l'esprit de l'Église, dans l'approfondissement et la défense des principes chrétiens comme dans leur application adaptée aux problèmes de notre temps'. Available at: www.vatican.va/archive/hist_councils/ii_vatican_council/documents/vat-ii_decree_19651118_apostolicam-actuositatem_fr.html (accessed 1 September 2014).

[13] Interview with G. Dubois, of the association of les Amis de la Chapelle Notre-Dame-du-Rugby, 12 December 2013, in Peyrehorade.

[14] Interview with G. Dubois, of the association of les Amis de la Chapelle Notre-Dame-du-Rugby, 12 December 2013, in Peyrehorade.

[15] Interview with Abbot Lavigne, 5 August 2014, at Grenade-sur-l'Adour.

References

Augé, M. (1982) Football. De l'histoire sociale à l'anthropologie religieuse. *Le Débat* 19, 59–67.

Augustin, J.-P. (1989) Les espaces des sports collectifs: l'exemple du département des Landes. *Mappemonde* 2, 29–31.

Augustin, J.-P. and Garrigou, A. (1985) *Le rugby démêlé. Essai sur les associations sportives, le pouvoir et les notables.* Le Mascaret, Bordeaux.

Bertina, L. (2013) La doctrine catholique du 'développement humain intégral' et son influence sur la communauté internationale du développement. *International Development Policy, Revue internationale de politique de développement* 4. Available at: http://poldev.revues.org/1320 (accessed 4 September 2014). DOI: 10.4000/poldev.1320.

Bromberger, C. (1992) Pour une ethnologie du spectacle sportif. Les matchs de football à Marseille, Turin et Naples. In: Althabe, G., Fabre, D. and Lenclud, G. (eds) *Vers une ethnologie du présent*. Maison des Sciences de l'Homme, Paris, pp. 211–243.

Cholvy, G. and Tranvouez, Y. (1999) *Sport, culture et religion. Les patronages catholiques (1898–1998)*. Centre de Recherche Bretonne et Celtique, Brest, France.

Darbon, S. (1995) *Rugby, mode de vie. Ethnographie d'un club Saint-Vincent-de-Tyrosse*. Jean-Michel Place, Paris.

Diocèse d'Aire et Dax. Notre Dame des Cyclistes. Available at: http://landes.catholique.fr/Notre-Dame-des-Cyclistes (accessed 2 February 2015).

Fernandez, A. (2007) Du ballon ovale et des taureaux comme marqueurs identitaires de l'Aquitaine?. In: Cocula, A.-M., Figeac, M., Guillaume, S. and Loupès, P. (eds) *Entre tradition et modernité, l'identité aquitaine. Mélanges offerts à Josette Pontet*. Centre Aquitain d'Histoire Moderne et Contemporaine, Bordeaux, France, pp. 337–343.

Foulquier, C. (2014) *Analyse et valorisation du patrimoine naturel et culturel du Pays Grenadois*. Sous la direction de P. Heiniger-Casteret, mémoire de master professionnel, Université de Pau et des Pays de l'Adour, France.

Martel, C. (1995) The vocabulary of 'bovine people' related to the Course Landaise: first lexicographical approach. *Cahiers Ethnologiques* 17(2), University Press of Bordeaux, Bordeaux, France.

Saouter, A. (2000) *'Être rugby': jeux du masculin et du féminin*. Maison des Sciences de l'Homme, Paris.

Saumade, F. (1995) Les rites tauromachiques entre culture savante et culture populaire. *Cahiers Ethnologiques*, 17(2), Presses Universitaires de Bordeaux, Bordeaux, France, pp. 41–56.

11 An Ethnology of the Foreign Traveller to the Shrine of St Nicholas of Bari, Italy

André Julliard*

IDEMEC – Institut d'ethnologie méditerranéenne, européenne et comparative, UMR 7307 – CNRS/Aix-Marseille Université, Maison méditerranéenne des sciences de l'Homme, Aix-en-Provence, France

Introduction

Each year, on 7 and 8 May, thousands of people 'show up' at the port of Bari on the Adriatic coast bordering the region of Puglia (southern Italy).[1] They come by ferry from Croatia, Serbia, Montenegro, Albania and further, from Greece, Romania and Bulgaria. Others arrive by plane from Russia or Georgia. Parishes, especially in the Neapolitan region, charter an impressive number of buses. Finally, even small groups of parishioners from Abruzzo arrive in the regional capital by foot after only a few days' walk along the traditional transhumance paths.

The vast majority of these travellers go directly to the basilica of St Nicholas celebrating the translation of the relics[2] (Bouet, 2011; Julliard, 2015a) from the Mediterranean port of Demre (formerly Myra in the Antalya region of Turkey) where he was bishop from 280 to 325 AD approximately (Cioffari, 1987). Devotion is expressed through a variety of practices that recall both Catholic and Orthodox (both Greek and Russian) traditions, albeit expressed in the vernacular practices of the pilgrims' home regions.

Standing in the Basilica

These practices produce small gatherings of people who engage in various activities (prayers, discussions, preparation of banners, etc.). The number and size of these groups grow as the morning service approaches. In the gathering churn, concentrations of murmurings swell only to fade back into the surrounding murmur. Unlike the queues that form and reform around devotional objects to impart a sense of movement, the gathering excitement and devotional effervescence overtake the muted pilgrims. The atmosphere intensifies. When the altar bell finally signals the start of Mass, the crowd merges and movement becomes problematic. The crowd now forms a horizontal mass of uniform thickness, carpeting the nave down the stairs into the crypt to the height of the statuary and sarcophagi. *Carabinieri* and soldiers in dress uniform cordon off a passageway from the portico to the chancel holding the crowd back and preserving a corridor for the procession and relics.

Between the opening of the doors at 5:00 am and the start of the service, one can discern comings and goings within the basilica that provide a sort of devotional mapping. I counted four

*E-mail: pamjulliard@wanadoo.fr

stations: one in the chancel, on the gospel side (left) where pilgrims offer a prayer and leave an offering of cut or potted flowers before the (inaccessible) statue; a second in the nave, where the pilgrims say a prayer, lay on hands and kiss two glass-encased icons of St Nicholas; a third stop just to the right crypt entrance where the pilgrims lay on hands and pass a written prayer through a wrought iron grill protecting 'the prodigious column';[3] and finally, the tomb itself at the back of the crypt, where pilgrims spend a long time in prayer (sitting, kneeling or standing) and light candles at the grill of the (inaccessible) tomb. The pilgrims combine these four stations in a sort of micro pilgrimage in which a pilgrim might move from the chancel station to the back of the crypt and later that same day stop at the icons before returning to the tomb. There is also a framework for an informal devotion that, without ritual or chronological constraint allows the pilgrim to follow his or her conscience and 'prayer intentions'.

Meanwhile, along the lateral aisles, confessionals are busy up to the morning service. After Mass and accompanied by several brass bands, a large procession carries the imposing statue to the port, where it is placed on the deck of a fishing boat that will anchor in the harbour. Throughout the day, pilgrims and families rent boats to bring envelopes containing an offering and a prayer or intercession. At sunset the statue of the saint is returned to the quayside, where it is welcomed with much joy and taken by procession to the Old Town Square, where it will spend the night under a tent with an honour guard of carabinieri and representatives of the Army, the Navy and the Air Force. Following commemoration of the miracle and 'the distribution' of the manna[4] in the basilica, families, groups of friends, teenagers and even children come together to see the statue. Regardless of age, all will have made at least one stop at the metal bars of the cage behind which three and sometimes more employees greet the public, sell an official portrait of the saint or otherwise act as relays between the statue and those offering flowers. Sometimes, yielding to the insistence of a pilgrim, one of these attendants will agree to rub a devotional photograph on the hem of the bishop's alb, thus ensuring the pious quality of an image of Saint Nicholas. A lively party atmosphere invades the square until late after midnight.

The summer season is still far away and few tourists will follow trails leading into the back country or along the coast where they will find Byzantine churches and rural architecture. Yet in the early hours of the morning, some enter the basilica: 'We came early', a retired German couple offered in French, 'because we plan to spend the day cycling along the sea'. The wife added, in German, that the owners of the house where they were staying had warned that the basilica would be crowded with pilgrims and they might not see the statue. Besides, she continued, they were leaving the following day. One might guess that their interest in Saint Nicholas was not the main reason for their presence.

Also and with apparent indifference, three other couples (Julliard, 2015b) make their way through the narrow rows of chairs. What differentiates these individuals from everyday ferry passengers is not their clothing or their backpacks. Only an ethnographer would discern the contrasting behaviours: they are in the midst of a 'basilica tour' when they are caught up in a scuffle of pilgrims arriving for Mass. The visiting couples even seem a little static in the midst of the growing crowd, who proceed to reserve seats, arrange seats for the elders, mill about waiting for a confessional, look for a spot where they can kneel before the statue or drink from a thermos, snack on pastries from a paper bag, greet friends or encourage latecomers to hurry up, etc. Through all of this the backpackers assiduously study the paintings and statuary as if by mimesis. They admire the columns, capitals and vaults: in short, we might say they continue to gaze at the ceiling while all the ambient energy is focused on the gathering crowd.

Despite their brevity, these early field observations allow for some comparisons between tourists and pilgrims. First, the time factor plays an important role for each of these groups, even if it means something technically different for each. For the tourist, taking one's time (Cassou-Noguès, 2013) is part of a break from the ordinary, including the individual's professional and family life. Conversely, for the pilgrim, time is regimented by the liturgical programme and he or she has no time to lose if he or she is to 'succeed' in his or her quest.

Both tourists and pilgrims experience emotion as they look upon the historical monument and take in the church decor, but it is not the same emotion. The tourist contemplates the statue of St Nicholas for itself as an assemblage of wood and colourful fabric (dating from the eighteenth century) – a remarkable artistic and folk expression of religious belief. In passing, some tourists will pause, discreetly cross themselves, even stand for a moment in silence (a sign they are meditating?), but they are not there to pray, only to admire the heritage! For the pilgrim however, the look is different because the pilgrim does not distinguish between the statue and demand for intercession (demand for protection, reassurance, comfort, etc.). It is not an object to be described (analysed or commented on), but an object of mystery, the Word incarnate; the pilgrim looks to Nicholas in prayer. We might say that the statue does not appear as an object of art but as an object that invokes a deeper system of religious belief (Pomian, 1990).

Finally, both pilgrims and tourists (Boutier, 2005) share the condition of being outsiders. Whatever the motivation for their presence, both remain strangers to the space, whether as a sacred place or simply as an attractive space such as a picturesque village, a historic city of art culture or a typical landscape. For example, unlike the natives, the non-Apulian pilgrim can be recognized as coming from afar, because he rarely brings armfuls of flowers for Saint Nicholas. He may be familiar with the space and time of the pilgrimage, but he remains a stranger to local customs. Moreover, like the tourist standing before the icon, he feels no need to perform a devotional action. The pilgrim's culture is sufficient to commune with the mystery of Saint Nicholas, and justification enough for the pilgrimage and recognition of the devotee's status as a pilgrim.

We should note, however, that both are highly variable ethnographic objects, always inclined to steal away and disappear only to reappear in another form. As we observed elsewhere (Julliard, 2015b) a tourist can adopt pilgrim-like behaviour during the course of a visit, such as devotional behaviour before 'the prodigious column' or during the rite for the distribution of manna and, between the ceremonial liturgy (Mass and procession) and Vespers, window-shop the stalls along the waterfront, explore galleries and temporary exhibits or even treat family, children and friends to fair rides organized on the harbour.

Within the time frame under consideration, it would be futile to try to account for the complexity of festive and devotional rituals in Bari that, moreover, extend from late April to late May and rotate among the surrounding villages and Abruzzo. I must confine myself, then, to a few reflections on an eminently anthropological question: in what ways do tourist practices differentiate and define devotional practice?

Within the Basilica Walls

Once at the basilica, tourist and pilgrim itineraries will vary. For the tourist, the visit is just another element in the discovery of the destination. Visitors will see 'what there is to see': that is, the artistic and historical treasures contained in the basilica. For the pilgrim, however, crossing the threshold into the basilica represents achievement, the culmination of a process that began with commitment to follow a path of personal devotion to St Nicholas. From this perspective, the prodigious column, the tomb and the holy icons have a drawing power at least equal to that of the more ornate statue, which for the pilgrimage is exhibited in plain view.

Whether from Greece, Romania or a nearby Puglia village, whether a returning pilgrim or a pilgrim making the pilgrimage for the first time, a pilgrim never really discovers the site because from the beginning the pilgrim would have visualized the site on previous visits or through various oral or photographic channels (family, neighbours, parish), web research (Julliard, 2015c) or by enquiry directly to the Dominican trustees of the shrine. Consider as a quick example, the itinerary followed by six faithful of the Ukrainian Greek Catholic Church, making their first St Nicholas pilgrimage in 2010. These faithful entered the church, ignored the statue erected in the choir and headed confidently towards one of the two holy icons barely visible in the dim light of a mid-May dawn. Each having kissed the icon, they stood in a half circle around the icon to quietly recite prayers from a missal. Upon approach, one of these pilgrims handed me her open missal and I noticed that they were reciting prayers addressed to the Virgin and that on the next page were prayers addressed to 'Christ crucified'. I found these pilgrims much later, kneeling before Saint Nicholas' tomb at the back of the crypt. Rising, my interlocutor explained, 'We go statue now'.

These modest observations will mark the central role played by the basilica spatial volume, whether for the tourist or for the pilgrim. Also, and for purposes of comparison, I propose that we consider Davallon's semiotic definition of what may be considered a Catholic pilgrimage: '[a pilgrimage] is the subjective assimilation of a universe of values (more emphatically, a participation) for which space is the preferred medium' (Davallon, 1988). The parallel with cultural tourism invites an examination of three key notions: 'a spatial medium', 'a value system' and 'participation'.

The basilica of St Nicholas is undeniably a *medius locus* without being a *sacer locus* for the European cult of St Nicholas. Permanently accessible to all, the basilica places believers (regardless of personal practice) and visitors (whether or not believers) in a central and flexible position between material reality expressed in the socio-cultural diversity of behaviours that co-exist particularly on Saint Nicholas' feast day, and several 'value systems'. These systems are as much spiritual (Roman, Byzantine Catholic, Greek or Russian Orthodox) as they are cultural (art, Italian and Mediterranean history, classical, baroque and even esoteric philosophy).[5] The sanctuary is the channel of communication, a medium that provides a great variety and amount of information. Appropriation of this information does not require the same effort of the tourist as it does the pilgrim. For the tourist, the contribution is provided as an initiation to 'another culture' that heightens the individual's general knowledge in a recreational manner. The pilgrim's relation to the object of his or her visit is more dynamic however, and the basilica itself is transformed into the centre of highly devotional activities where the pilgrim is called to commune with the saint. We can say that in this unity of time and place, the tourist consumes 'gratifying' knowledge (Brown, 1999) contrary to the pilgrim, who, as we have said, is simply accomplishing his task. As unstable as it may seem, the traditional distinction between tourist-consumer and pilgrim-producer highlights two aspects of the rapport between the pilgrim's approach and the built religious space (MacCannell, 1976). At the time of the celebration, the basilica is vested with points of physical signage (flower presentations of the statue,

crypt lighting and easel for the icons in the nave) facilitating a personal discovery of the saint. Such signage, however, has no intermediary function, as just mentioned: it does not prescribe 'strict' instructions as to the devotion (i.e. no posted itineraries or one-way signs). It is not the building that serves as a link, but the pilgrim who, directly and without 'intercession' enters into a trusting relationship with St Nicholas. To be perfectly accurate, mediation is 'achieved in silence' through apprehension of the word or an epistolary reading (an intercession, a petition or some other means). Since access to the statue and tomb are not permitted, a 'letter' is slipped into the screened cage enclosing 'the prodigious column'. If in the past, Nicholas spoke with his devotees, today the saint is most likely to respond 'offline', which is to say by sign (miracle, providence, fate) interposed.

By the time the morning service begins, two visitor attitudes comingle under the basilica arches practically unaware of each other. The tourist 'naturally' adopts the attitude of an observer of architectural elements and religious adornments, a posture that captures the monument, first as a unique object of historical value, and then as an object somewhere between church and museum. The observant gaze and hushed voice serve as models of appropriate behaviour, transforming by an air of reverence otherwise ordinary religious objects, so that when the tourist discovers, it is not without some sense of novelty. A Walloon (Belgian) retiree from the textile industry confesses in a whisper: 'I put my hand behind the grill [of the column]. I don't know if it's forbidden here for foreigners, but I was curious whether I would feel something in my fingers ... [I asked for an example] ... such as pins and needles or heat or something like that.' The 'tour' inside the basilica is studded with such loops in which visitors will approach an object only to move away from it, their imagination and sensitivity captivated by it, just like my interlocutor was motivated by the materials of the column. Gradually, the visit turns into a story that meets at least two cognitive functions: first, it shapes an elsewhere or, if you will, 'a probable imaginary' (Vax, 1987) that, although personal, describes 'another', in this case, the culture of the Byzantine basilica. Second, it provides materials appropriate to the visitor's cultural 'universe' (memory) and spatial sense of that universe (recollection of place).

From the beginning, the organizer and pilgrimage planner becomes the first subject of the Saint Nicholas pilgrimage act (by imagining and promoting the pilgrimage act). One should not however, mistake the founding act for an act of devotion. Multiple factors are considered, such as the choice of itinerary and the means of transport, factors that are primarily concerned with getting to Bari in the best conditions possible for the available budget. The logistics of organizing and preparing a round trip leave little time for reflection upon or commemoration of the encounter with the holy. On ferries and parish buses, families and small groups of friends rarely benefit from the services of priests or laymen who lead prayers or stimulate religious fervour (songs, readings, recitations of the rosary) on the trains to the Grotto of Massabielle (Lourdes) and coaches for the visionaries of Medjugorje (Bosnia and Herzegovina).

No sooner across the square, each pilgrim-producer performs his or her personal devotion without delay before moving on to other tasks entrusted to him or her 'back home', much like the Ukrainian group encountered (see above) before one of the framed Nicholas icons. Following prayers, one of them will unfold a paper that lists six or seven full names: 'People to stay in my country', she said, running her finger down the list. Now the 'pilgrim delegates' resume the recitation of prayers for each of the sponsors, for whom no doubt, they ignore the true prayer intentions.

Consequently, it is only within the basilica that intercession is made (connection and expression) with the universe of St Nicholas. At this moment, actor and producer roles become inseparable. The 'subject' now occupies, not the centre of the sanctuary (as from a desire to see), but the heart of devotional practice and a 'desire to do'. As I have already discussed, at that moment the devotional activities are transformed into short sequences of busy activity followed by all pilgrims: 'We must tend to San Nicola. It will be impossible to talk during the rush, we will be too busy. We can talk later,' I am told in French, by the priest from Abruzzo. Upon arrival, a pilgrim will focus on the saint with an urgency that betrays his fear that at any moment his pilgrim fervour and justification

for the pilgrimage will be snatched away in the collective excitement of the liturgical ceremony or diluted in the plurality of the intercession-waving crowd that continues to grow in the nave. Finally, the superposition of pilgrim movements among the five 'stations' of the saint (the column, the crypt, the statue and the two icons), defines the only true locus of personal devotion to St Nicholas.

Leisure and Pleasure in the Basilica

Anthropological studies commonly recognize similarities between pilgrim and tourist behaviours: construed as rite of passage (Graburn, 1977). Indeed, it is easy, too easy, to rationalize the three phases of tourism behaviour theorized in 1909 by Arnold Van Gennep (1981):

1. Preliminary (separation from the group): this is the period that includes the announcement, preparation and travel time. Among preparatory activities one may cite parish and family gatherings and occasions for counselling pilgrims and participants; presentation of the hospitality organization; or even issues related to the maintenance and surveillance of the house during the pilgrims' absence.
2. Liminality (or marginalization) is the period during which the pilgrim encounters and intercedes with the saint or makes contact with elements of another culture.
3. Post-liminality (return to the group but with a new social status): for example, a pilgrim will complete intercession on behalf of prayer sponsors much as a tourist will describe 'destination sights and sounds' among friends.

The parallel raises a number of issues regarding tourism as a contemporary substitute for pilgrimage frequently understood in its medieval form, as great crowds of people pressing along the roads to the great shrines (Dupront, 1987). The feast of Saint Nicholas is little concerned with such analyses because, although a 'mass' movement, it is driven by individual practices, but for the feast day itself, tour operators abstain from organized tours of the basilica. Yet, by assimilating the sanctuary visit to a (brief) period of liminality, one raises the scientific question of 'efficiency', especially if both the visit and participation in the mystery of Saint Nicholas are equally qualified as ritual.

For the pilgrim, the extent of the social interlude may be limited to those moments of crowded frenzy when in communion with the saint. However, there is no liminality of practice because St Nicholas is part of the pilgrim's everyday world, without which there is no conceivable pilgrimage. The celebration of the translation of the relics to Bari fits as a likely event at least in the life of Catholic and Orthodox families installed on the perimeter of the Adriatic and Europe's Mediterranean shores.

Similarly for the tourist, the visit to the basilica is far from being experienced as a marginal event within a holiday schedule. Entrance into the sanctuary is merely one activity among other anticipated leisure activities. The visitor is not only free to choose the timing for the visit but free in every respect in view of his original commitment to visit the basilica. The tourist can choose to visit the basilica or not. He may do so in full (make a complete visit) or in part (see what he wants to see) and even episodically (visiting highlights), and he is free to end a visit at any time. Standing in the central aisle, jostled by the comings and goings of the faithful, a Belgian tourist remarked, 'We have seen enough... There is almost nothing to see, and one hardly sees the tomb... The church is pretty but there is nothing in it' (Cioffari, 2010, pp. 27–48). I respond by indicating the entrance to the treasury (Cioffari, 2010, pp. 59–65), 'we went there but [the showcases] are always the same [...] we will go to the Fair'. This short testimony encourages comments that easily fit an ethnographic description of tourism behaviour, although here it raises two thoughts on the attitude of the pilgrim: one on the notion of strangeness, the other on desire.

Before the May 2010 procession, I spoke more or less at length with half a dozen tourist couples of English, German, Swiss, Belgian and Cypriot origin. Some were struck by the realism of animal sculptures on the Romanesque capitals, while the twelfth-century ciborium, the late sixteenth-century frescoes in the presbytery and the seventeenth-century paintings on Nicholaian themes did not raise strong feelings – 'too cold', 'too busy' or even 'we couldn't make out the characters on the roof paintings'. It seemed that these tourists sought to be surprised by one aspect or another of the object detail: from the columns and the telluric foundations to the unusual feeling of emptiness in a church.

In 2005, in Seyssel (France, Ain department), a small port on the right bank of the Rhône River and the point at which the Rhône becomes navigable almost continuously to the Mediterranean, I had already noted that 'taste for strangeness'. The parish church has a black Virgin Mary (Our Lady of the Bridge) dating from the thirteenth century and an eighteenth-century statue of St Nicholas in polychrome wood with a tub and three children (Julliard, 2013). On my first visit, a parishioner who was cleaning around the altar offered me a postcard of the black Madonna, which is particularly difficult to photograph because it was placed high on a bracket attached to the choir loft as an anti-theft measure. I asked her whether she had any postcards of Saint Nicholas for sale. 'We don't have any [...] there is no demand. The statue rarely interests people passing through. They come to see the Virgin and they leave without even visiting our [nineteenth-century] church. Nobody has ever even asked for St Nicholas.' The mystery of the black virgins (remnants of the cult of Isis and Moorish representations of virgins, etc.) invoke the extraordinary, while the wonders of Nicholas, today transformed as promotional legends of the Rhône, represent little more than the ordinary work of a saint.

Returning to the basilica of Bari... Arguably, and without engaging in a quest, the tourist is waiting to be surprised by what he will see: something that will feed the story of his visit. Neither the pilgrims nor the procession practices are sufficiently 'extraordinary' to capture his attention: Nicholas is not San Domenico Abate, the body covered with snakes in procession during the first days of May in the streets of Cocullo (Abruzzo).

Conversely, research into a 'sense of the strange' totally escapes the concerns of the Catholic or Orthodox pilgrim because he has no need to 'become a stranger to himself' (Vax, 1993, p. 13) to increase the intensity of his visit to the saint. On the contrary, the pilgrim must remain completely himself,

> we must say what we came to tell St Nicholas, and then for me, my sons and daughters-in-law, my grandchildren [...] we must remain civil [because] there are some who are not polite

[with the saint], I do not know why? And that's it. We will return [at dusk] to take a little manna [if] we are not too tired.

The pilgrim is seeking his family history through a contact that, while endowed with super human resources to aid in 'intimate' areas of protection, healing(?), financial success, etc., nonetheless remains at a 'human scale'. The patron saint is the protector, healer, intercessor or all three simultaneously, ever present in the social relationship without which the encounter is merely pious (praise, glorification, etc.). My two interlocutors perfectly express this reality: 'Saint Nicholas did a lot of things and a lot of good', said the relative who translated into Italian the sentence to my interlocutor. 'It's true, he did many things we do not even know the words to express it [...] you will see what he has done if you stay this afternoon, it's nice' (Cioffari, 1996, pp. 13–14, 21–26). When the time comes to act, the pilgrim does not consult St Nicholas in the light of his miracles: both are situated directly in the field of practical 'concerns' generated by work and family life.

Ultimately, the conduct of the pilgrim is dictated solely by the 'desire to do good', to not disappoint the expectations of the saint. My interlocutor suggests a responsible attitude on the part of supplicant is crucial for the effectiveness of mediation. The pilgrim should not beat around the bush ('be polite') with respect to his intercession and, therefore, should not shrink from recognizing his personal situation. In other words, the devotion to St Nicholas does not fit into a ritual pattern that would freeze the symbolic gestures and obligations and thereby risk failure of the process of intercession for the slightest error or fault of conduct. The pilgrim comes to Bari endowed with the mutual respect that is proper to his social standing, and with examples of conduct (family, village, parish, etc.) that allow the faithful considerable freedom of action in finding his or her own way to Nicholas. Such attitudes do not escape the eyes of others, who may find cause to modify or adjust their behaviour at any time, even completely revise their approach. For example, and before I lost sight of him in the procession, a priest from Abruzzo explained that 'in 2009 the group had not wanted to stay together and that after their first prayer, the group had disbanded with each person returning to the village on their own that evening by train'. This year in anticipation of the need for flexibility he had asked the group how they wanted to organize themselves for the pilgrimage. The priest had in this way, become aware that individual requirements for free time needed to be accommodated and that they would somehow disrupt the 'congregation's way' of making the Bari pilgrimage. The congregants had agreed they would share the group hike (with some religious songs) and stay together for the prayer 'on arrival'. In the end the group found their own balance between leisure and religion! In 2010 the congregants dispersed after the procession behind the parish banner, proceeding individually or in small groups to perform their devotional duties. That evening and no doubt by prearrangement, they regrouped behind the apse of the basilica, and, following the distribution of manna, returned together to the railway station.

During the first morning of the feast of the translation of the relics of St Nicholas, the pilgrimage assembles returning pilgrims and first-time pilgrims to enact fully or partially the devotional practices of older and more recent memory combined with the latest innovations in devotional practices. The group movement functions as a conservatory and meets three functions: it is a catalogue (a recollection) of the 'way things have been done' yesterday and today; an integration of new uses (promotion); and, in a way, a pedagogy for 'encountering the mystery' of the saint inside the basilica. From a sociological perspective, this pilgrim conservatory inhabits the historic monument that the tourist visits, even if not crowding, turn into a conservatory of cultural and religious heritage of medieval Christianity in southern Italy.

Heritage conservation is really only apparent through the eyes of those who are outside of the conservation and site maintenance process. The disappearance of the basilica and cessation of the pilgrimage would be deplorable but not fatal for those who have visited or who plan to visit: the loss would be irreparable only as a world heritage site. It would be a very different story for devotees. As part of their devotional practice, not only do they 'form the basis for a collective memory' (a pilgrim conservatory), above all they sustain it through religious times and local histories.

The pilgrimage practice maintains local narratives 'away from' the cultural heritage and a skilled culture of the 'immaterial'. As for believers, whether regular, occasional or potential, Orthodox or Catholic, the disappearance of the Bari pilgrimage would open a breach in the sense borne by St Nicholas that beyond religion, the larger environment is attached to the person.

What Does One Say upon Exiting the Basilica?

On the morning of Saint Nicholas' celebration, tourists and pilgrims in the basilica do not really see one another because their eyes are completely focused on 'the useful' (Bergson, 1972), on their respective (conservatory) activities: the object as a cultural heritage reality for some and the saint as a pilgrimage reality for others. Yet they rub shoulders, brush past one another, move away, swerve and again move closer to blend undetectably in the eyes of the outside observer. Only the flash of a camera at the foot of a column or a posture of kneeling in prayer by the altar may tell them apart.

Through slow, steady observation, frequently halted by the crowd, similarities in behaviours are revealed. Among those: 'the expression of pleasure'. I shall not comment about tourists such as the Belgian couple whose visit to certain sites proved boring – not, however, to the point of spoiling an otherwise entertaining, pleasurable stay. Indeed, that couple will 'fill' the void left by the visit to the basilica with a gratifying experience at the Festival of Saint Nicholas! For their part, the pilgrims punctuate their practice of devotion with enjoyable moments that combine relaxation and pleasure. This was clearly implied by the shopkeeper I spoke to in Bari. Once their request is made 'with care', the faithful feel that they have satisfied their need to talk to the patron saint: 'we said what we had to say', she stated. She paused during the meeting without, in the words of a French priest, 'filling the holy water fonts', to indulge briefly in some of her pastimes before Mass such as wandering in the nave, engaging in casual conversations with people 'next to her' or making a thorough study of the flower arrangements surrounding the saint's statue.

Ultimately, three groups are active in the basilica space: a largely minority group of tourists, a group of Catholic and Orthodox faithful coming to worship, and a group of pilgrims who have completed or are about to complete their meditation session. Everyone is aware of the presence of 'those who are not like them' yet they do not view this as an 'otherness' that might cast doubt upon or interfere with their own current activity. Few or no words are exchanged between the pilgrims and tourists, who mostly remain unconcerned with matters relating to the individual. What's more, the pilgrimage is not sufficiently organized as a collective ritual to be disturbed by external intrusions.

One could say that St Nicholas, the religious heritage and the diversity of cultural practices create a kind of indivisible transcendence that makes it possible for everyone to accept diverse and multiple presences, by raising the Saint Nicholas feast 'above' any determination of place, belief or culture. In this sense, a tourist might be considered an associate pilgrim and vice versa; such an association, which is only real through its potential attainment, somehow instils an 'atmosphere' that energizes the religious aspect of the Saint Nicholas feast.

I shall end my presentation without conclusion because these observations are in a developing phase, but I should like to recall that specialized literatures offer a view of pilgrimage and sightseeing as rites of passage. I have focused only on time spent in the basilica, which I then interpreted as a preliminary stage that places tourists and pilgrims outside ordinary life, and in Bari, outside each membership group. I suggest this as a working hypothesis because it raises questions as to whether the element common to any phase of marginality – that is, the transmission of an original message – is also present in the Bari context. When cutting oral testimonies short (to be brief) we can easily see that everyone leaves the basilica having received no teaching or revelation that would not otherwise be accessible to man's common knowledge (philosophical reason). Prayer requests do not call for an immediate response from St Nicholas and tourists are satisfied with some photographs of general cultural references. Accordingly, each one 'returns to the world' with their own interpretation of the visit or pilgrimage; that is, with questions for future visits to monuments, new encounters with the bishop of Myra and other patron saints.

Notes

[1] This research has been supported by Cirelanmed – ANR-12 TMED-0002-01.

[2] In May 1087, sailors removed the skeletal remains of the saint in order to safeguard them from the Ottoman Turks. Around the middle of the first decade of the twenty-first century, a formal request to return the remains of Saint Nicholas was presented by the Turkish government, who consider that this heritage was stolen from Turkey.

[3] I use this qualifier because, to my knowledge, the monolith does not perform any sort of miracle. According to several accounts, the stele comes from the basilica of Myra and floated behind the boat that brought the relics to Bari. In close proximity to the tomb, the column is seen as a historical testament to both the miracle-working power of Nicholas and his attachment to his native land.

[4] An oily fluid that oozes from Nicholas' skeleton and is used by the clergy as an ointment to mark the sign of the cross on the foreheads of the faithful who request the blessing.

[5] Several days after the 2006 feast of Saint Nicholas, when I was taking a picture of the nave furnishings, a Swiss couple from Neuchâtel asked me about my work. During the conversation, the man asked whether I was interested in 'organic telluric waves' (sic) upon which were built, according to my interlocutors, medieval cathedrals in general and Bari in particular, especially since, 'the basilica was built at water's edge'!

References

Bergson, H. (1972) Madrid lecture on the human soul, 2 May 1916. In: Robinet, A. (ed.) *Mélanges*. Puf, Paris.

Bouet, P. (2011) Orderic vitalet the translation of the body of St. Nicholas. In: Cioffari, G.G. and Laghezza, A. (eds) *Alle origini delle'Europa. It culto di S. Nicola tra Oriente e Occidente*. Nicolaus Studi Stori, Bari, pp. 109–142.

Boutier, J. (2005) Le "Grand Tour" des élites britanniques dans l'Europe des Lumières. La réinvention permanente des traditions. In: Martinet, M.-M., Conte, F., Molinie, A. and Valentin, J.-M. (eds) *Le chemin, la route, la voie. Figures de l'imaginaire occidental à l'époque moderne*. Presses Universitaires de la Sorbonne, Paris, pp. 225–242.

Brown, D. (1999) Des faux authentiques. Tourisme *versus* pèlerinage. *Terrain*, 33, Paris, pp. 41–56.

Cassou-Noguès, P. (2013) *La mélodie du tic tac et autres bonnes raisons de perdre son temps*. Flammarion, Paris.

Cioffari, G. (1987) *S. Nicola nella critica storica*. Centro Studi Nicolaiani, Bari, Italy.

Cioffari, G. (1996) *Saint Nicolas l'histoire et le culte*. Centro Studi Nicolaiani, Bari, Italy.

Cioffari, G. (2010) *La basilique Saint Nicolas. Petit guide historique et artistique*. Editions des Pères Dominicains de la Basilique, Bari, Italy.

Davallon, J. (1988) Les chemins de la mémoire. Réflexions pour une approche sémiotique des circuits culturels. In: Cerclet, D. and Gachet, L.-J. (eds) *Patrimoine ethnologique et tourisme. A propos des circuits culturels*. Acts of the ARA Meeting, Lyon, France, pp. 25–35.

Dupront, A. (1987) *Du Sacré. Croisades et pèlerinages. Images et langage*. Gallimard, Paris.

Graburn, N. (1977) Tourism: the sacred journey. In: Smith, V. (ed.) *Hosts and Guests: The Anthropology of Tourism*. Blackwell, Oxford, UK, pp. 17–32.

Julliard, A. (2013) *Ora pro nobis*. Réflexions ethnohistoriques sur les voyages et pratiques religieuses en Bresse et Bugey (Ain, fin XIXe–début XXe siècles). In: Cano, D. (ed.) *La route. Le Bugey. Le monde*. Publication of the Conseil Général de l'Ain/Departmental Museum Conservatory, Bourg-en-Bresse, France, pp. 124–141.

Julliard, A. (2015a) Saint Nicolas: du tombeau à la place publique. Modernité des fonctions de saint patron dans les politiques régionales et les relations internationales entre l'Europe et la Turquie (2009–2013). In: Gazeau, V., Guyon, C. and Vincent, C. (eds) *En Orient et en Occident, le culte de saint Nicolas en Europe (Xe–XXIe siècles)*. Cerf, Paris, pp. 461–488.

Julliard, A. (2015b) Flussi devozionali, atti politici e visite turistiche nei pellegrinaggi in onore di un santo patrono regionale: l'esempio di San Nicola di Bari. In: Albera, D. and Blanchard, M. (eds) *Pellegrinaggi del nuovo millennio*. Mesogea, Messina, Italy, pp. 221–246.

Julliard, A. (2015c) La mission d'internationaliser St Nicolas. Regards ethnologiques sur le site 'stnicholas-center.org' de culture religieuse anglicane. In: Duteil-Ogata, F., Jonveaux, I., Kuczynski, L. and Nizard, S. (eds) *Le religieux sur Internet.* L'Harmattan, Paris, pp. 127–139.

MacCannell, D. (1976) *The Tourist, a New Theory of the Leisure Class.* Schocken Books, New York.

Pomian, K. (1990) Musée et Patrimoine. In: Jeudy, H.-P. (ed.) *Patrimoines en folies.* Maison des Sciences de l'Homme, Paris, pp. 177–198.

Van Gennep, A. (1981) *Rites de passage.* Picard, Paris.

Vax, L. (1987) *La séduction de l'étrange.* Puf, Paris, (1961), pp. 153–168.

12 Healing Tourists with Religion: Saint Rita's Cult in Poland

Inga B. Kuźma*

Institute of Ethnology and Anthropology of Culture, University of Łódź, Łódź, Poland

A Historical Outline of Veneration of St Rita in Poland

The veneration of St Rita in Poland is not massive (yet). It is spreading quite slowly, but steadily. The cult began to grow around the year 2000, even though some Church sources date it back to the seventeenth century. Central to this veneration is the church of Saint Catherine of Alexandria, located in Kracow. The church belongs to the Augustinian friars, and is adjacent to a convent of the Augustinians, the order that St Rita herself entered a few centuries ago.

Augustinians were brought to Kracow from Bohemia in the years 1342/3 (Droździk and Kwiatkowska-Kopka, 2008, p. 12). At that time they were considered the most learned people in Europe. Their location in Kracow was spurred by the desire of the king of Poland, Casimir the Great, to found a university there. The king intended to entrust the development of the university to the Augustinian friars. The building complex of the monastery and the church of St Catherine of Alexandria, patroness of universities, was modelled on the architectural design of the then existing college in Bologna, Italy.

The cult of this saint grows owing to individual people who recommend her to others. It is also thanks to the initiatives of individuals that chapels, paintings and statues of St Rita are funded in small towns in Poland. Therefore, devotion to this saint may be considered a spontaneous grassroots phenomenon that stems from individual veneration. During my conversations with the Kracow friars in the years 2009–2011, they showed their surprise at people's interest in St Rita and at a number of the 'folk' practices of the faithful. This made them rethink the forms of organized devotion so as to shape it appropriately, that is, according to theological precepts. For this reason, more or less since the year 2000, special celebrations have been organized on 22 May, the feast of St Rita (Abramczuk, 2011, p. 56).

Polish monks and nuns of the Augustinian order issue their own publications with prayers to the saint, the story of her life and devotion towards her (Modlitewnik, 2004 (wydanie 3); Pierwsza Pobożna Unia, 2009; Curzydło, 2011a). In addition, there are also books about St Rita by lay authors. Such publications are works for the general public, some of them verging on reportage and documentary journalism. Over the past few years they have appeared in large numbers. A new publication is published almost every year (cf. Konderak, 2009; Sieńczak, 2009; Murzańska, 2011; Bilska, 2013; Machalica, 2013; Majdan, 2014). However, there are almost no critical works (Dawidowski, 2008). Before Polish authors

*E-mail: inga.kuzma@uni.lodz.pl

started writing about St Rita, the Catholic Church-related publishing houses had published translations of books by both clerical and lay authors (e.g. Lemoine, 1994 (second edition, 2009); Eberhard and Back, 2000; Di Gregorio, 2006; Govetti, 2010).

In their sermons, the Augustinian friars inform the congregation how to venerate the saint and how to approach her life. There are often stories told about her as a victim of domestic violence, which are strongly denied by the Church. What is interesting, however, is that such grassroots stories have been invented (modelled on the ancient apocryphal legends) about her unfortunate life with her brutal husband, even though this interpretation is rejected by the Church. Similar scepticism and a desire to gain control over the grassroots activities of the congregation are shown with regard to roses blessed in the name of the saint. Blessed flowers are very popular among the faithful. Some use the roses in accordance with the principles of folk medicine, that is, treat the flowers as a cure (by brewing the roses like tea, eating them, applying them to the aching spots, etc.). People also bring flowers before the statue of the saint as votive offerings. This behaviour is, however, induced by the friars, who use roses in their teaching about St Rita, as the rose is a symbol of long-standing religious tradition.

The internet is another space where Saint Rita is present. Websites in Polish include private webpages and blogs dedicated to this saint.[1]

Initially, the veneration of St Rita in Poland was limited to the Augustinians and mainly to Kracow. In the above-mentioned church in Kracow, the main altar dating back to the seventeenth century contains a statue of the saint, but it is not the object of cult. Another altar, one devoted exclusively to St Rita, was built in the eighteenth century. It contains an image of the saint from the same period (Abramczuk, 2011). The painting shows St Rita receiving stigmata from the crown of thorns in front of the Holy Cross. Until the Second World War, this image was kept in the south nave of the church. Then it was moved to the chapel of the Augustinian nuns and remains the subject of their veneration (Curzydło, 2011b, p. 31).

In 1900 St Rita was canonized. Since then the veneration of this saint has been growing in Poland, yet it remained within the circles associated with the Augustinian friars and nuns. In 1902 the first Polish edition of Novena to St Rita

was released by the nuns (second edition, 1916). Over time other prayer books and pictures meant to cultivate private devotion were published, and not only by Augustinians (St Rita often appears in prayer books with patrons of difficult cases such as St Jude and other saints; e.g. Kałdon, 2002).

In 1944 a 2-m wooden statue of the saint (designed by the Kracow-based architect Adolf Szyszko-Bohusz) was put in the southern nave. This event was preceded by the establishment of the first parish by the church (in 1942). The parish was to serve the Christian inhabitants of the Kazimierz and Stradom districts, whereas the other former residents of this area, that is, the Jews, were removed before 1942 and sentenced to extinction by the German Nazis. On 20 September 1941 the Augustinians, who initially, although very briefly, ran the parish, were also taken out. The monks were deported by the Nazis to Auschwitz-Birkenau.

In 1950 the Augustinian order was dissolved. However, the cult of the saint was kept as far as possible by priests who ran the parish and by the Augustinian nuns who had survived. They told stories of St Rita during religious education classes (catechesis) and distributed publications about her.

During the Second World War, petitions directed to St Rita mostly concerned the regaining of freedom from the occupation by the Nazis. St Rita was therefore incorporated into the mainstream of the Polish religiosity, which strongly accentuates the theme of regaining sovereignty by the nation.

Although a small group of people were involved in this cult, the monastery archives hold evidence that Masses with various intentions have been celebrated by the altar of St Rita since the beginning of the twentieth century. The accounting ledgers and correspondence gathered over a few centuries contain proof that the faithful made offerings for a Novena to St Rita, or that they gave funds for flowers to her altar, for oil, etc. (Abramczuk, 2011, pp. 52–54).

The most common requests for the intercession of the saint were private matters such as curing a disease, helping out, family matters, a happy death, finding a job, etc. Today's requests are no different, as the same prayers have been recurrent over the past decade, as has been corroborated by the results of my investigation into the recent intentions of the faithful. Petitions and intentions are sent via postal mail or email and are submitted to a special mailbox in the church at the altar of St Rita. They are all collected by the Augustinian friars and nuns.

Urban Sacred Topography: The Urban Veneration

The specific nature of veneration is to a certain extent also affected by its placement in space. The church is located in Kracow's old town. Aside from the past of the Jewish district of Kazimierz and coexistence of their communities with the neighbouring Christians, quite specific institutions have been established in the vicinity of the church more or less from the nineteenth century onwards. Currently these include the University Hospital, Brothers Hospitallers of Saint John of God, who are involved with healthcare, and the Albertine Brothers, who help the homeless people and the poor by giving out food to them, for example. There is also a therapeutic centre for children and an orphanage.

Each of these institutions was founded at a different time in history. They were also established by various Church-related, municipal or national institutions and non-governmental organizations (NGOs).

Kazimierz, a district influenced by the church of the Augustinian order and the parish of St Catherine of Alexandria, has always been quite poor. This area of the city is highly interesting for tourists, though, due to the Jewish past and revival of this culture since the 1990s. As I noted, the previous inhabitants of Kazimierz were killed during the Second World War, and the area has undergone a demographic change since the mid-1940s. The Jewish Kazimierz was surrounded by Christian enclaves, however, one of them being the church of St Catherine and its veneration of St Rita.

Before the cult of St Rita developed, there was another image that had been brought to Kracow along with the monks from Bohemia and their traditions rooted in their order in Bologna, namely the image (and veneration thereof) of Our Lady of Consolation.[2] A separate chapel is devoted to her, the image being renowned for its graces, and therefore of much value. Currently, Marian devotion in the Augustinian church is perhaps less visible in comparison with the cult of St Rita. However, the image of Our Lady of Consolation also attracts the faithful and without any doubt it is more rooted and better established in this place. A special lay confraternity devoted to Our Lady of Consolation dates back to the Middle Ages and is still active in the parish. The cult of St Rita is grassroots and spontaneous, but the same people who come to venerate her also come and visit the chapel of Our Lady of Consolation (and the other way round).

In addition, Our Lady of Consolation and Saint Rita, due to the extent of their patronages (Mary: consolation, Rita: help in hopeless cases), combine together to make a whole.

As already mentioned, in the area of the Kazimierz district where the church with the statue of St Rita (and the chapel of Our Lady of Consolation) is located, there are also institutions that provide aid to people affected by different forms of exclusion and marginalization: children from pathological communities, the sick, the homeless, the poor.

This institutional and social environment covering just a few streets has hardly been planned. Due to the nature of the said aiding establishments, densely located in the vicinity of the place of veneration of St Rita, at first glance they seem to blend in to make a whole in spatial and social terms. This is all the more true as the Kracow setting is nearly identical to what can be found in Barcelona and Paris, the other two inner-city places of veneration of St Rita. On the Boulevard de Clichy and in Raval there are also statues of St Rita, who is a popular saint there as well. In these locations, there are facilities and activities targeted at excluded groups and those in need of various kinds of aid.

Below you will find a brief description of selected places of veneration of St Rita in Paris and Barcelona. First, however, I would like to stress that despite all similarities between the districts and the problems of their inhabitants, it is difficult to indicate the actual diversity of veneration of St Rita resulting from the specific combination of social, demographic and economic factors.

In Barcelona, the statue of St Rita stands in the parish church of St Augustine at Saint Augustine Square. This place is located in Ciutat Vella,[3] the oldest district of Barcelona. Ciutat Vella contains four subdistricts, including Raval, where said church can be found. The right altar thereof is devoted to St Rita. Raval used to be farmland located outside the city walls. Its agricultural character remained unchanged until the turn of the fifteenth and sixteenth centuries when many monasteries started to appear there. The biggest change came with the Industrial Revolution. Raval was the cradle of this revolution: fields and gardens gave way to walls of workshops and factories. A new division of urban space appeared, and the local population began to turn into the working class. More immigrants were coming, also from outside Europe, which is why in 1925 the writer Angel Marsà called the southern part of Raval the 'Chinese quarter'[4] (a name that is also in use today). Poverty, economic crises, which initially affected those of modest means, that is, mainly the residents of Raval, as well as the specific socio-ethnic characteristics of this area (a large percentage of immigrants) have made this part of the city truly multicultural. This was a distinguishing feature of Raval and so also of Ciutat Vella. This was also the factor that has brought about the most profound changes in this part of Barcelona. Nowadays, the largest groups of immigrants in Raval come from Pakistan, the Philippines, Morocco and Ecuador. Obviously, they are not the only ones to make up the ethnic and religious mosaic of Raval, but they are presently the largest groups (Tarpia Gómez, 2006). Another characteristic of poor city areas is the prostitution of women. Brothels were officially banned by the municipal authorities in 1956,[5] however this hardly changed anything. It remains a 'traditional profession' of women in Raval, nowadays pursued by migrants, mostly minors. The researchers in this field point out that until recently local middle-aged women had been prevalent in this group (Torner and Comulada, 2007).

The Augustinian order has been present in Raval since the eighteenth century. At the beginning there was only a monastery there, and a parish was established in the nineteenth century. The monks disseminated the cult using its most characteristic feature – the blessing of roses on 22 May. The statue of the saint is located in the side altar, which is decorated with a great number of roses. In front of the altar, there is a place to kneel down, write your intention and put it into a box designated for this purpose. The same spatial organization is used in the church in Kracow.

According to the descriptions of 22 May celebrations in Raval, the entire square and nearby streets are filled by people with roses. Women come there in the first place. They are not only the local inhabitants. Many of them come from other parts of the city and from the outside of Barcelona. Every half an hour a priest comes out of the church to bless the roses and sprinkle them with holy water. The crowd is so great that the blessing is held in several rounds.

According to local tales, the prostitutes of Raval treated St Rita as their main protector and advocate. This belief is still vivid today, as perhaps best illustrated in an article 'El fenómeno de Santa Rita'[6] by Isabel Olesti, which appeared in *El País* (on 26 May 2000). Olesti describes an argument between the faithful, which broke out when one of the women told a reporter that 'St Rita was a prostitute'. Another woman became annoyed and upset, so she responded ironically: 'Maybe you will also tell us she lived in Raval?'

Such a grassroots affiliation of the saint is captivating as it reveals the local religious folklore. It is closely associated with the local customs and specific community of Raval, that is, mainly poor people, often socially relegated for various reasons, such as their status as immigrants, migrants or non-Catholics, or their pursuit of taboo activities (prostitution). The excluded make up about 80% of Raval's population. Due to the intensity of social problems in Raval, nuns from the congregation of Mother Teresa's Missionaries of Charity set up their regional house there in 2003. There are also many other centres that provide help to the addicted and homeless (night shelters and soup kitchens), youth support centres, etc.

Raval is specific in social terms and makes one wonder how the local community may influence the perception of the saint. The patronage of St Rita, a mediatrix assisting in hopeless cases, which are humanly impossible, takes on a very special meaning in Raval.

In Paris, the place of cult of St Rita is also located in a very specific environment that is somehow similar to Raval in Barcelona and that in a sense corresponds with the area around the church in Kracow where this saint is venerated.

The Paris statue of St Rita stands in a small chapel at 65 Boulevard de Clichy, on the borderline of districts 9 and 18. This place is historically classified as Montmartre. The chapel is situated across from the Moulin Rouge, a few steps away from the Place Pigalle.

The place of St Rita's veneration is situated in a district associated with a specific environment (Prado, 1993), where you can meet the homeless, criminals, pimps, prostitutes, 'exotic dancers' and tourists, who sometimes seek unconventional forms of tourism (sex tourism).

The Paris chapel was erected in 1956 and is part of the Holy Trinity parish church. The figure of Saint Rita is quite small; it is made from raw wood and it is approximately 1 m tall. The largest of the three is the wooden statue in Kracow, which, as was mentioned above, is 2 m tall.

In Paris, a solemn procession and blessing of roses are held on 22 May, whereas the faithful submit written petitions in front of the statue of the saint all year long (Pedron-Colombani, 2007; Prado, 1993). What distinguishes the Paris place of veneration is the evangelizing action carried out by the parish group Emanuel. Its members go out to the streets of the city every week (except school holidays). Every Wednesday evening they take part in the adoration of the Blessed Sacrament at the Boulevard de Clichy, and then they set out in pairs for a walk around Pigalle and Montmartre. The chapel is located on the ground floor of a building at the Boulevard de Clichy. By the door there is also a display cabinet with an image of St Rita (and, according to one of the priests, the image of Saint Thérèse of Lisieux). Numerous prayers are posted next to it. In 2010 Father Wilfrid d'Angleville,[7] who is in charge of evangelization, said that the evangelization activists form a cross with candles on the pavement in front of the chapel. The cross attracts a number of people. The Chapel of St Rita often turns out to be a real refuge for those who are in dire straits.[8]

The chapel and its vicinity are a space where different social worlds meet, as evidenced by for example, tourists and residents of the district. Diversity also consists of religious differences. Father d'Angleville mentioned that evangelizers go to the Muslims who live in large numbers in this area of the city, and try to find people who are open to prayer or conversation about faith.

The above characteristics of the place of veneration of St Rita in Paris show that it may also be a venue of interreligious meeting. This is similar to Raval, where St Rita attracts followers also among non-Christians who live there and come from different ethnic and religious groups.

The increase in popularity and veneration of St Rita among these people may stem from her universal patronage. The scope of intercession of St Rita does not refer to the virtues or values related to the narrow religious context of Catholicism. This makes it open to various interpretations, content and intentions.

Certainly, local social factors that provide a specific context also give a special meaning to hopeless causes, which are entrusted to St Rita in Raval and Boulevard de Clichy. Kazimierz district in Kracow is no different.

The areas of Kazimierz, Raval and Pigalle are immensely popular among tourists visiting Kracow, Barcelona and Paris, respectively. Most of them, however, do not make any special pilgrimage to the local places of St Rita's veneration. It was only in the Polish centre of her veneration that I observed the most common forms of organized pilgrimage. With a second class relic located in the altar of St Rita, it is a central place for devotion to this saint in Poland. Tourists who are familiar with St Rita and come individually or in groups, often from abroad, turn into pilgrims in each of the above-mentioned places. When they see a representation of this saint, they take a moment to pray in front of her statue. I have witnessed such transformations, which is especially striking as regards their behaviour and way of being. I spent most time making such observations in Kracow.

In such situations, it was becoming clear that the intention with which a person came to a given place influenced his or her behaviour and stature. People's reactions in a space interpreted by them as sacred differ from their behaviour in a historic place understood as a tourist attraction.

What I described as social and environmental convergence regarding the veneration of St Rita in Paris and Barcelona, is to some extent also present in Kracow. However, in the former locations I did not notice any striking popularity of St Rita among people who visit aid centres such as the homeless, children or poor. The statue in Kracow is far more frequently visited by the sick and their families, and by employees of the previously mentioned hospital, which is located just two blocks away from the church. Health problems seem to be prevalent in the Polish place of veneration.

Characteristics of the Veneration - the Saint as a 'Healer', 'Therapist' and 'Coach'

My area of study included the petitions sent to the Augustinians in the period from 2000 until the beginning of 2012. As the requests varied from a few dozen to over 100 almost every month (their number increasing subtly over time), I have examined only some of them, selecting a few months per year (and looked into petitions submitted more or less every other year). The months were chosen at random, but I particularly strived to have a look at requests submitted in May (when a parish fair of St Rita is held) and from the months that followed the parish fair.

Petitions concerning health do not mention any specific disease and do not differ from requests made by the faithful in such matters in other shrines. Thanks to the internet, large-scale comparative studies of this kind may now be conducted online. I have conducted this type of investigation as well. I have read posts that appeared on the official forums and websites of the shrines dedicated to Our Lady. In Poland she enjoys the most common and strongest devotion. No saint can match the popularity of Mary. In addition, I looked at forums and private blogs of people who declare themselves believers.

No major differences could be found between petitions made to St Rita and other saints. In general, the faithful ask for health, successful personal and family life; sometimes they mention matters at national and supranational levels (making peace in the world, ending wars, stopping crises). This is hardly changed by the patronage of St Rita, that is, hopeless, difficult, humanly impossible cases, which include a wide range of issues. It is up to the faithful to determine which matters are hopeless and as such can be presented to the saint, which depends, in turn, on cultural and social conditions occurring at a given time and place.

It is important to note that the wording of petitions is highly structured. They represent a distinct type of language and writing (Kowalski, 1994), and contain specific phrases that are characteristic of religious petitions. They sometimes resemble a biographical story. Such texts are governed by the purpose and function they are supposed to serve. This is evidenced by common linguistic traits that can be observed in them. For that reason, when compared with other prayers and examples of veneration, it is hardly possible to prove the uniqueness of the petitions to and veneration of St Rita based on the very structure of this type of expression.

However, the attitude to health, sickness and accidental events presented by the faithful to St Rita is quite interesting. In the context of her patronage, the faithful generally treat these things as hopeless and most difficult. The loss of physical and mental health is seen as a misfortune, evil, an unpredictable and unavoidable thing. You can only minimize the losses suffered as a result of such events. Therefore, the faithful ask St Rita for an accurate diagnosis of their disease, for the care of good doctors, possibly for the diagnosis to turn out to be wrong and for the disease to prove less serious. The most common ones are requests for health recovery and for being healed, for ending the suffering of the petitioners and their loved ones (also for death, which frees from pain and suffering). The petitions are underlain with fatalism of views on illness, the body, aches and pains, and medical care.

Another issue that seems independent of human beings and is seen as hopeless is failures in relationships. The faithful list in this category unrequited love, breakdown of a relationship, emotional distance between parents and children or between partners, loneliness, divorce, childlessness, lack of love, lack of friends, emptiness of life and lack of purpose in life.

People cannot fully control health and disease. The latter may be considered independent of people's wishes, desires, preventive actions and healthy habits. Diseases are most frequently associated with 'objective reasons' (act of God, genes, the environment – depending on individual interpretation). As for matters related to mental welfare, in the submitted requests there are no signs the faithful see any possibility of influencing their life situation or that they ever had any such influence. The texts show that people do not associate failures in relationships with their own behaviour and choices. The difficult issues they experience appear to them as insuperable as the loss of health. Both happy events (such as love, birth of a child) and misfortunes (such as divorce, job loss) are therefore twists of fate, because good and evil happen to man regardless of what he is like and what he does. The attitude of the faithful is that they must bear the burden of suffering (as they assume it is probably what they deserve) or give thanks for good events (as they assume they must have deserved them). Many of the faithful who venerate St Rita treat human relationships and mental states as something beyond their own control.

Nowadays, remarkable medicalization and psychologization of the language of petitions can be observed. In many of the texts the faithful reveal their dilemmas. However, I would call them mental rather than spiritual. They write about their emotions and feelings, so they describe issues related to their mental lives. The requests demonstrate that St Rita gains the status of 'healer', 'therapist' and modern 'life coach' in the eyes of her followers: she is to address and direct the fate of the penitent. The faithful very often refer to her life experiences, particularly regarding bad interpersonal relationships (cf. Giacalone, 1996).

The purpose of the requests is to get help, or improve their life situation and well-being. Followers believe that St Rita, experienced in matters of fate, harassed by nuns and suffering in her own family as she was, can understand the position of a person who also feels rejected.

This emotional structure of aiding that the faithful create is strengthened by the miraculous image of Our Lady of Consolation. The patronage of the latter, to console and provide comfort, and the patronage of St Rita, to rescue in desperate cases, reinforce each other and combine to make a meaningful whole.

The expectation of protection in difficult situations means a desire to recover to the desired mental state, to obtain a balanced life and to find a solution. Descriptions of the faithful draw from the language of psychology or counselling rather than religious discourse. In the latter case, terms relating, for example, to salvation, Christ's sacrifice, sinfulness, purification of sins, following Jesus, forgiveness, etc. would be used. Such phrases are still present in the Polish requests to St Rita, but the 'language of psychology' is equally visible. This certainly reflects not only the quality of contemporary Polish religiosity, but it also shows how various fashionable cultural trends, such as the popularization of psychological knowledge, shape religious functions, perception of holiness and the manner of prayer.

Conclusion

Although similar social problems (poverty, exclusion) occur in the districts of Kracow, Paris and Barcelona, where the veneration of St Rita is cultivated and spread, the cult found in Kracow nullifies an assumption that St Rita has her 'specific' followers, that is, the faithful coming mainly from the underclass and various 'margins of society'. The followers in Poland do not belong to this social layer. This is a characteristic feature of quite a large number of the faithful from Paris and Barcelona, but even there they are not the only followers of the saint in question.

Kracow's place of veneration is the youngest in comparison with Paris and Barcelona. Although the Augustinians came to Kracow earlier than to Barcelona, the popularity of St Rita – which has spread over the city district and local area – has become apparent over the past dozen years. As for the cult around the Boulevard de Clichy in Paris, it is moderated by parish priests rather than the monks.

The examination of the Polish petitions of the faithful has shown that most requests concern physical and mental health. This is not necessarily linked with the patronage of St Rita, that is, aid in impossible and desperate cases, because requests for curing diseases, etc., are directed to all other saints, too. However, diseases and other disasters are regarded by the faithful as problems that are impossible to solve by humans, hence they prevail among the requests addressed to this saint. Consequently, this tells us more about the contemporary attitude to unhappiness, weakness, suffering, pain and the body than the perception of St Rita and the nature of piety exhibited towards her.

Notes

[1] http://swietarita.blogspot.com; www.swietarita.pl/; https://pl-pl.facebook.com/SwietaRita (accessed January 2015). Villages and small towns, in whose local parishes the veneration of St Rita is cultivated and spread, also have their own websites: http://swietaritawewlosani.pl/galeria-wydarzen/; http://parafia.bielawa.pl; www.swjerzy-rydultowy.wiara.pl/; http://blociszewo.archpoznan.pl; www.mbnsacz.diecezja.tarnow.pl/; www. nsj.srem.pl; http://parafiamaszkienice.pl; http://antoni-kielce.pl/; www.czarna110.republika.pl/; http://bozecia-lozawiercie.republika.pl/; www.brynow-wujek.wiara.pl/; www.sw-barbara.katowice.opoka.org.pl/; www. jankanty.jaworzno.pl/pl/; www.parafia-brzezie.pl/; www.parafiaradoszowy.pl/; www.krzyz-zawada.katowice. opoka.org.pl/; www.parafiagalew.pl/; www.parafia-nspj.pl/; http://borowymlyn.parafia.info.pl/; www.milbo. wiara.org.pl/; www.bieliny.parafia.info.pl/; www.golkowice.tarnow.opoka.org.pl/; http://pksul.parafia.info.pl/; www.wol.bydgoszcz.pl/; http://swroch-lipkow.pl/; http://parafiar.drl.pl/; www.parafiapcim.republika.pl/;

www.franciszkanie-konin.pl/; www.parafiakrzyza.pl/; www.nmp-kp.pl/; http://parafiaswjerzego.pl/aktualnosci/
26/swieta-rita-w-naszej-parafii. Most of these temples, chapels and even parish churches named after St Rita
already have relics of hers. Information about them and their web addresses have been collected by Augustinian nuns (www.augustianki.pl/index.php/augustianscy-swieci/swieta-rita/osrodki-kultu/, accessed January
2015).

[2] www.augustianie.pl/historia-augustianow-w-polsce-3/ (accessed August 2014).

[3] http://w110.bcn.cat/portal/site/CiutatVella (accessed March 2012).

[4] http://w110.bcn.cat/portal/site/CiutatVella (accessed February 2012).

[5] http://w110.bcn.cat/portal/site/CiutatVella (accessed February 2012).

[6] www.elpais.com/articulo/cataluna/fenomeno/santa/Rita/ISABEL/OLESTI/elpepuespcat/20000526elp-
cat_2/Tes (accessed September 2012).

[7] www.anuncioblog.com/2010/03/18/wilfrid-d-angleville-quelle-joie-d-annoncer-le-christ/ (accessed June 2012).
An interview by Jean-Baptiste Maillard of 18 March 2010.

[8] The followers of St Rita are depicted in an ethnographic film *Sainte Rita de Montmartre* by Patrick Prado
and Jacques Giumet, France (1995).

References

Abramczuk, K.O.S.A. (2011) Z klasztornego archiwum. In: Curzydło, M. (ed.) *Pielgrzymi świętej Rity.
O początkach i rozwoju kultu świętej Rity w Polsce.* Wydawnictwo Polskiej Prowincji Zakonu św.
Augustyna, Krakow, Poland, pp. 43–58.

Bilska, M. (2013) *Kochaj i walcz. Święta Rita – patronka spraw trudnych i beznadziejnych.* Wydawnictwo
WAM, Krakow, Poland.

Curzydło, M. (ed.) (2001a) *Pielgrzymi świętej Rity. O początkach i rozwoju kultu świętej Rity w Polsce.*
Wydawnictwo Polskiej Prowincji Zakonu św. Augustyna, Krakow, Poland.

Curzydło, M. (2011b) Pod opieką świętej Rity. In: Curzydło, M. (ed.) *Pielgrzymi świętej Rity. O początkach
i rozwoju kultu świętej Rity w Polsce.* Wydawnictwo Polskiej Prowincji Zakonu św. Augustyna, Krakow,
Poland, pp. 27–42.

Dawidowski, W.O.S.A. (2008) *Święta Rita.* Wydawnictwo WAM, Krakow, Poland.

Di Gregorio, M.O.S.A. (2006) *Święta Rita z Cascii: patronka spraw beznadziejnych.* Wydawnictwo Diecez-
jalne i Drukarnia, Sandomierz, Poland.

Droździk, P. and Kwiatkowska-kopka, B. (2008) *Augustianie z miasta Kazimierza.* Drukarnia Goldruk
Wojciech Gołachowski, Nowy Sącz, Poland.

Eberhard, E. and Back, S. (2000) *Święta Rita: matka, wdowa, zakonnica.* Zgromadzenie Sióstr Świętego
Augustyna, Instytut Teologiczny Księży Misjonarzy, Krakow, Poland.

Giacalone, F. (1996) *Il corpo e la rocca. Storie e simboli nel culto di Santa Rita.* Meltemi, Rome.

Govetti, P. (2010) *Rita z Cascii. Święta od spraw niemożliwych.* tr. it in. K. Stipa, Edycja Świętego Pawła,
Częstochowa, Poland.

Kałdon, S.M.O.P. (2002) *Nabożeństwa do świętych szczególnego wstawiennictwa w sprawach najtrud-
niejszych i beznadziejnych.* Wydawnictwo M, Krakow, Poland.

Konderak, E. (2009) *Św. Rita i nasze sprawy beznadziejne.* Stowarzyszenie List, Krakow, Poland.

Kowalski, P. (1994) *Prośba do Pana Boga. Rzecz o gestach wotywnych.* Towarzystwo Przyjaciół Polo-
nistyki Wrocławskiej, Wrocław, Poland.

Lemoine, J. (1994) *Rita: święta od spraw trudnych i beznadziejnych.* Wydawnictwo Instytutu Teologicznego Księży Misjonarzy, Krakow, Poland.

Machalica, A. (2013) *Święta Rita: anioł nadziei.* Wydawnictwo eSPe, Krakow, Poland.

Majdan, M. (2014) *Święta Rita z Cascii: życiorys, nowenna, modlitwy.* Promic – Wydawnictwo Księży Marianów
MIC, Warsaw.

Modlitewnik. (2004) *Modlitewnik. Święta Rita – patronka spraw trudnych i beznadziejnych.* Polska Prowinc-
ja Zakonu św. Augustyna, Krakow, Poland.

Murzańska, A. (2011) *Święta Rita: cudowna historia patronki od spraw beznadziejnych.* Dom Wydawniczy
"Rafael", Krakow, Poland.

Pedron-Colombani, S. (2007) Procession Sainte-Rita à Paris, mai 2005. *Ethnologie Française* 37(1),
57–59.

Pierwsza Pobożna Unia (2009) *Pierwsza Pobożna Unia Świętej Rity.* OO. Augustianie, Krakow, Poland.

Prado, P. (1993) Sainte Rita de la place Blanche, la sainte au, bout du rouleau. In: Belmont, N. and Lautman, F. (eds) *Ethnologie des faits religieux en Europe*. EHESS, Paris, pp. 203–206.

Sieńczak, D. (2009) *Św. Rita*. Wydawnictwo Instytutu Teologicznego Księży Misjonarzy, Krakow, Poland.

Tarpia Gómez, M.C. (2006) *Superposición de realidades. Colectivos minoritarios en el espacio público de Ciutat Vella – Barcelona*. Universitat Politècnica de Catalunya, Departament d'Urbanisme i Ordenació del Territori, Barcelona, Spain.

Torner, I. and Comulada, I. (2007) *El fenómeno religioso. Presencia de la religión y la religiosidad en las sociedades avanzadas*. Centro de Estudios Andaluces, Seville, Spain.

13 A Transnational Cult: St Rita of Cascia

Fiorella Giacalone*

Department of Political Science, University of Perugia, Perugia, Italy

Introduction[1]

The cult of Saint Rita of Cascia, who lived in Umbria at the end of the Middle Ages, has become widespread in the past 50 years, as the saint is considered to be thaumaturgic by her many devotees, to the extent that she is known as 'the saint of the impossible' and 'the advocate of desperate cases'. The wide distribution of the cult of Rita (in Italy, France, Spain, Switzerland, Ireland, Lebanon, the Congo and Brazil) is due to the power attributed to her to intervene when devotees are faced with illness, operations and family problems. The votive offerings at the sanctuary in Cascia attest to the provenance of the faithful, who come from many continents, while the diffusion of her reputation as a healer can also be seen in the stories of healing that her devotees send to the monastery magazine, *From Bees to Roses*. A dream vision of Rita, dressed in monastic robes, often accompanies the stories of those who consider themselves to have been healed and protected by the power of the saint.[2]

One interesting aspect of the cult is its extension – this has resulted in the building of churches dedicated to Rita in several cities, such as Turin in Italy, Nice and Paris in France, Monachil (Granada) in Spain and Fribourg in Switzerland. There are also several churches dedicated to her in Lebanon. Indeed, in 2015 the city of Cascia was twinned with Dbayeh, an event that takes place every year in the name of peace. The devotion to Rita in Lebanon was reiterated recently through the gift of a 6-m-high statue of Rita (weighing 30 tonnes) that was donated by a Lebanese artist to the city. The inauguration of the statue occurred in Cascia on 18 October 2016, in the presence of the Patriarch of Antioch, Bèchara Boutros Raï, after he had spent a few days in Rome.

The cult of Rita is approaching the level of the Marian cult, in part thanks to her human and maternal story, as exemplified by the use of roses in devotional practices.

The Places Associated with the Saint and Her Healing Power

The pilgrimage to Cascia has always been important to those who consider themselves protected by the saint, and want to travel to the towns where she lived. Significantly, to speak of Cascia means, at the same time, to speak of Rita, the sign and symbol of the city. The 'space of pilgrimage' coincides with the places associated with the saint, the sanctuary and the city. It can be said that Rita created Cascia, making it a city worth knowing and visiting, and that her figure

*E-mail: fiorella.giacalone@unipg.it

has had a particularly complex economic impact. Not only in terms of the network of hotels, gift shops and restaurants that profit from the phenomenon of pilgrimage, but also the presence of an important hospital and dedicated accommodation structures for infants.

There are therefore many perspectives from which to view the city: first the standpoint of the local community, which has built its own identity and distinctiveness around the saint (streets, crests, tourist images); the position of economic agents, which aim to make use of the environmental resources of the area; and the viewpoint of the travellers, who arrive attracted by the economic–religious circuit that revolves around the saint. Cascia has found its identity as the destination for national and international pilgrimages, and has also had to reinvent itself over the years, in order to adapt to the dynamics of religious tourism, and learn to interpret the territory in a modern way.

In the process of the self-representation of the city, the saint remains the main resource, becoming the *topos* that has brought together the various historical and cultural aspects of the place, such as the historic centre and environmental resources. In a process that involves a connection between tradition and innovation, Rita represents an image that can be used in the different forms of capitalization of the town. As she is a pacifist, naturalist, medieval saint, Cascia can valorize the historical and cultural context of the natural beauty of the Valnerina area, and play the role of city of peace, competing with Assisi, which is much better known, and more important in artistic terms. If tourism is a *process of the creation of locations*, then Cascia has made parts of the city sacred, and also invented new ways to promote the territory.

Cascia has also developed an ecological dimension by creating the path of pilgrimage (the Path of St Rita) that runs from Cascia to Roccaporena on a pathway of about 6 km. This path, which runs through a landscape of rare beauty, is based on the longer and more complex pathway in Assisi (the Path of Francis), and manages to combine ecological pilgrimage with the valorization of the natural area and the cult of the saint. In this light, the *ecological myth* (of 'uncontaminated' nature) is associated with that of the simple and everyday Middle Ages, in a form of *sanctification of the territory*, thanks to the presence of the pilgrims who, in passing through

such a rugged environment, feel they are participating in the 'magic' dimension associated with Rita.

As the town is inevitably linked to its saint, Cascia has made the icon of Rita its own image, the hallmark of its historic and environmental reality, and robust rural traditions. The reproducibility of this image is therefore tied to the hagiography of the saint, to its versatility and the capacity of the local community to transform her image, always in connection with religious tourism, and the legends of the visionary women of the Valnerina (Piccolpasso and Cecchini, 1963) and the nymph Porrina (Morini, 1933)[3] that have been passed on for generations.

Hagiographies and Media Coverage

Little information exists about the life of Rita Lotti. What is known is that before entering the monastery, she was the wife of Paolo di Ferdinando Mancini, a man of arms and Ghibelline during the political–religious struggles of fifteenth-century Cascia (between the white and black factions), in the rebellion against the papacy. Her husband was killed after his religious conversion, which Rita had arranged. Following the death of her husband, her two teenage children died of disease. Based on the available evidence, her birth can be traced back to 1381, in Roccaporena. After her husband's death, Rita tried to end the conflict between the factions that had resulted in Paolo's murder, and prevented her children from avenging their father's death, but the lack of a resolution to the conflict remained at the root of the refusal to accept her into the convent.

The element that unites the first part of her life (as wife, mother and widow) with the second (as a nun), is the 'nocturnal flight'. Tradition has it that when Rita asked the monastery to accept her, she was faced with refusal by the nuns, and Rita miraculously entered by night, accompanied by three saints: St Augustine, St Nicholas of Tolentino and St John the Baptist. Her saintly protectors transported her from the 'Rock' of Roccaporena, a spur of rock where it is said the prints of her body remain, into the monastery in Cascia. The narrative involving the presence of the saints made Rita's flight acceptable in the eyes of the monastery, as, when performed by other contemporary women, they were held to be witches. It should be noted that the first trial for witchcraft in Umbria occurred in 1438 (Matteuccia di Francesco), while the 'transportation' of Rita dates back to 1407. Once in the convent, Rita performed a number of miracles, involving the transformation of a bush into vines, and roses that flowered in the winter, elements involving plants that were part of the contemporary cult. Rita was a nun at the Monastery of St Mary Magdalene in Cascia for 40 years, and was injured by a thorn, which broke away from a painting depicting the crucifixion of Jesus. This thorn caused a wound that remained for 15 years, as evidenced by the iconography of her funeral casket in 1457.

Rita managed to heal the wound on her forehead, and came to be considered a healer, to the extent that the women in the area turned to her for their health issues; for centuries the 'fur' (a goat skin used for cover in winter) was used to help women in childbirth.

The oral element is critical to understanding the wealth of legendary elements to be found in the biography of the saint, and the need to rewrite a story that appears to resemble a nineteenth-century *feuilleton*, which contains elements such as the death of her husband and children, the Mater Dolorosa (Lady of Sorrows) and the healing nun.

The account of the life of the saint has been adapted over time. It was first narrated through written biographies, and more recently through modern audio-visual media: the 1960s and 1980s saw the production of two photo story narratives (1966 and 1985), followed by videotapes and audio cassettes in the 1990s, and DVDs and USB flash drives today. Several films have been produced on the life of St Rita, for cinema and television, the most recent in 2004.

The evocative power of the imagery, the narrative of an exemplary story, and the interweaving of fiction and reality, of cinema and documentation, strengthen both the cult and, at the same time, its media coverage. Votive practices found new impetus thanks to the media, which can be purchased as a complete package, ready to be enjoyed whenever the customer-devotee wants to watch and access it. On the DVDs, the filmed pilgrims attest to their experiences at the holy place, where grace can be granted, and confirm the power of the saint and her thaumaturgic abilities. The recounting of the story by living and present witnesses confers reality to the narrative.

As an example of a different relationship with religion, experienced as more intimate individual research, the monastery website (www.santaritadacascia.org) also represents the more modern type of devotee, who is sensitive to the influence of the faith, and ready to share their beliefs online as well as on pilgrimage.

Celebrations: Between Institutional Events and Religious Kitsch

The festival season takes place in May, and every year Cascia is 'twinned' with other cities where the cult of Rita is also strong. The involvement of other cities in the celebration of the festival serves to encourage the presence of devotees from such places, and reiterates the *popular* dimension of the initiatives and the *international* character of the saint.

A series of events takes place on 22 May: the human story of Rita is honoured through 'living pictures', which outline the essential moments in her biography: as a little girl, young woman, wife, mother, widow and nun. Women and girls from Cascia, in fifteenth-century costumes, offer a face and a context to the life of the saint. The historic procession arrives in mid-morning, when the tourist flow is at its peak. The use of a procession in costume is not only reminiscent of other sacred representations (live Nativity scenes, Good Friday processions) that take place in a number of towns in the region, but can also be associated with the medieval re-enactments of other Umbrian festivals. The Middle Ages are presented as a large container, capable of reconstructing local identities in a single framework of reference, in which art and culture, political history and religious events, scenic beauty and ecotourism are brought together.

The centres of pilgrimage are no exception to the logic of the package tour, in which lunches and prayers, and commerce and devotion, appear to be combined without contradiction. Moreover, festivities involving patron saints have always been associated with local fairs, because they represent a moment that involves both economic activities and symbolic practices. The fair remains a presence in Cascia, with stalls occupying a square in the town, a continuation of a tradition that can be traced back to the earlier rural culture.

Since 1988, as established by the Municipality of Cascia, the Saint Rita International

Recognition Award has been presented. The award is given to five women who bring the message of Rita to the world. The women are rewarded for their engagement in society, or because they have distinguished themselves in family and social life, or are involved in the struggle against the Mafia and organized crime – they are women of peace, or have forgiven the killers of their husbands and sons, like Rita.

The morning of 22 May ends with the impressive *blessing of the roses*: thousands of pilgrims, lining the avenue leading to the sanctuary, raise the roses that are blessed at the end of the religious ceremony that takes place in the sanctuary. For the rose, defining symbol of the saint (and the Marian month), this is the apex of its beauty and power: the blessing will confer a therapeutic value that will be put to use in dangerous situations, or be collected in prayer books, accompanying the devout in their daily lives. Originally, the monastery sold the roses; now plastic roses are bought at the stalls. The roses are then deposited at stops along the pilgrimage.

Cascia, like all towns associated with therapeutic sanctuaries, is no stranger to the spread of shops and stalls selling souvenirs of Rita. Statues of the saint proliferate: plaster statues in Augustinian clothing, or plastic representations of the saint in ecstasy. It is also possible to see the saint in her funeral casket, surrounded by small bulbs that light up. Such objects, of questionable taste, are intended for private votive activity, and are placed in homes, in the kitchen or bedroom, creating a kind of 'domestic shrine' for the protection of the house.

Many items are aimed at children: bibs with the inscription 'protect me', baby clothes and sachets of pulverized rose petals (similar in appearance to the small cloth bags containing miraculous medals that were known as 'brevi'), as well as pens, pencils and even household products such as tea towels, wooden spoons, cups and ashtrays (Fig. 13.1).

As part of a process of deculturation and the fetishization of objects, Christian kitsch represents an area with specific connotations. First, this is emblematic of a progressive decline in works of sacred art, as the works produced are not always of a high formal value. This in turn also influences the commercial production of votive objects. Furthermore, religious kitsch is not limited to a defect (or excess) of form, which is characteristic of kitsch in general, but also has

a theological aspect: indeed, this leads to a loss of substance that is not only aesthetic, but also of a theological nature (Moles, 1977).

People who buy such objects in Cascia do so both out of devotion, as a keepsake of the journey they have made to honour the saint, and as a tourist souvenir, the value of which seems to transcend the banality of its form, as it reminds the devoted, in its daily use, of the path of penance they have completed.

The Devotional Forms of Pilgrimage

The path that pilgrims follow at Cascia traces practices of popular religiosity relating to a request for an intercession, or to give thanks for a favour that was granted, according to a process through which the worshipper goes directly to the centre of the cult, in the presence of the *body of the saint*, where its *potentia* is expressed (Brown, 1981). The relationship with Rita is made more meaningful by retracing her steps and visiting the places of her life, where her body lived and suffered; this journey involves full psycho-physical involvement for those who undertake it, in terms of travel, time, emotions, expense and effort, and this discomfort is central to the expression of the devotional procedure. The longer the journey, and the more arduous the road, the more the encounter with the saint becomes a pleasure, almost a long-awaited meeting.

The devotion to Rita was born and remains a popular tradition, in terms of both votive forms and the style of worship. The journey to Cascia and Roccaporena, somewhere between an excursion and the search for an answer to the pilgrim's own suffering, involves several milestones of diverse importance and tone. The sanctuary, a modern structure, is an obligatory stop, in order to stand in front of the chapel that hosts the urn of the saint (dating back to 1930), which is protected from the devotees with a rugged grille. The pilgrims parade in front of the body, which is visible but inaccessible, throwing coins over the grate towards the catafalque, in order to obtain the protection that comes from the body of the saint.

The itinerary of the pilgrimage continues inside the monastery, which traces the steps of St Rita's monastic life. The pilgrims listen to the guides that recount the life of the saint, and look at the cell where the saint lived for many years,

Fig. 13.1. Examples of religious kitsch, available from many stalls and shops.

admiring the crucifix associated with the thorn, and the bush that became a vine.

The sacred itinerary of the pilgrimage to Roccaporena, where the saint lived her previous life as a wife and mother, takes on other aspects. The tiny village is invaded by crowds of pilgrims who arrive by bus, with organized tours or come by private car, to follow a biographical itinerary made up of a succession of stops in close proximity to one another. An obligatory visit, in both Roccaporena and Cascia, is to the office for pil-

grims, to leave an offering in exchange for 'packages' prepared by the monastery. It is common to meet pilgrims from the south of Italy or foreign countries who stop by at the office, bringing with them the 'offerings' of friends and acquaintances who were not able to come all the way to the sanctuary. Lists of devotees and their names have emerged, some donating €10, some €20, some €50: in exchange the monastery offers a 'package' that, according to the amount offered, may contain a small statue of Rita, a rosary, rose dust and prayer cards with blessed medals (Fig 13.2). Through their monetary donations, even the distant devout can have an active presence, and through those who have come all the way to the sanctuary, they can count on the possibility of Masses and objects that are considered *therapeutic transmitters of power* (Salmann, 1996).

The most difficult path, and therefore the most significant from an institutional perspective, is the climb to the *Rock*, the huge boulder on which it is believed that the imprint of the knee and elbow of the saint can be recognized, and from where the saints accompanied her to the monastery in Cascia. This place, heavily sacralized

in this century, stands high on a rocky outcrop, the highest point of the village. A staircase has been built to enable access, which is punctuated by the Stations of the Cross. The ascent to the Rock thus becomes a pilgrimage of prayer, which many undertake barefoot, stopping at the various Stations of the Cross. The wide handrail that leads to the top is composed of blocks of marble, on which are inscribed the names of donors and the date of their donation, as an imperishable memory of all the pilgrims who climb.

In my most recent study (2014) I also noticed the presence of knotted handkerchiefs on

Fig. 13.2. Examples of prayer cards with blessed medals.

the branches of the trees. These are another connection with Rita, a knot that binds the request for the intercession of the saint with the votive resolution: until a few years ago, handkerchiefs were also present in the Garden of Miracles, another place of pilgrimage.

Having laboriously arrived at the top, the pilgrim arrives at the chapel that is built around the Rock, which is now surrounded by Plexiglas railings and unapproachable. The research carried out in the 1990s revealed that the faithful threw anything that might enable a relationship with the saint onto the Rock: handkerchiefs, clothing accessories (hats, glasses) that had been in contact with their bodies, photographs, requests for graces written on slips of paper, votive expressions, and banknotes and coins of various denominations, according to the practice common at many shrines (Giacalone, 1996a).

While objects are no longer left on the boulder, hundreds of roses bought at souvenir stalls are still thrown. Each of these attests to the presence of a single devotee, much like the numerous photographs left on both the boulder and the walls and windows of the small chapel (Fig. 13.3).

These objects represent a testimonial to the pilgrim's presence, a way to mark the site of their personal and spiritual journey. This space,

which might appear to have been 'invaded' by the quantity of roses and photos, is a place marked by the presence of those who have arrived that far, and left photos representing their own bodies, signs of a journey that unites the human body with the holy body, and words with gestures, according to a therapeutic mechanism associated with *litholatry practice*. Rubbing a stone that bears the imprint of a saint, and placing fingers or body parts in perforated blocks, for the treatment of specific diseases, are phenomena present in many shrines. This is true in particular in the Valnerina, where litholatry therapies, especially for the treatment of bone diseases, have a long and profound tradition (Preci, Sellano, Rasiglia) (Fig. 13.4).

The belief in the impression left by the body of the saint on the stone is part of a viewpoint in which the relationship between cause and effect breaks down, and miracles are possible, such as a rock 'marked' by divine intervention. For this reason the place is charged with power, a power that has already been expressed and, therefore, can be expressed again, in accordance with a procedure that automatically reinforces the place, creating a symbolic network which confers identity and memory to a space that has left the ordinary behind, in order to enter into a sacred

Fig. 13.3. Testimonial photographs and personal items left on the walls.

Fig. 13.4. Rubbing the statue of Rita, to 'bring home' some of her power.

dimension. Mountains and grottoes, spaces above and below ground, are projected in dimensions other than the 'here and now' of man, and are therefore difficult to 'anthroposize'; this makes possible mythopoietic constructions, which allow the transformation of 'natural reality into sacred reality' (Di Nola, 1972, p. 1617).

The pilgrims perform another ceremony in the *Garden of the Miracles*, a small rose garden planted in memory of the miracle of the rose that flowered in winter. This path, which runs uphill towards a small grotto, also features the Stations of the Cross. At the top of the hill, behind the rose garden, there is a small grotto that is home to two bronze statues, depicting Rita and her cousin, who is offering her a flowering rose. In this small area, which has limited connotations with historical elements, or relics of the saint, the pilgrims have the opportunity to express a devotional gesture.

While undertaking my earlier research (1990–1994), the statue of Rita was almost completely covered with handkerchiefs, which were tied around the arms and the body. Inside the handkerchiefs were cards with votive requests, as well as banknotes, photos, rosaries and flowers. In performing this gesture, the devout touched and kissed the statue. In addition to this practice of 'bandaging', they wrote (and

still write today) requests for graces on any sheet of paper available to them, to insert into cracks in the (particularly porous) wall of the small grotto, holes that are then carefully 'sealed' with candlewax, as it is important that the pages are not lost.

Today the ritual practices involving the statue have changed somewhat. The noteworthy presence of handkerchiefs on the two statues has disappeared, perhaps due to the intervention of religious institutions that did not appreciate the proliferation of objects and money. As on the Rock, the pilgrims lay roses purchased in souvenir shops on the statue: each rose represents a person and their request for grace. Yet the handkerchiefs remain, to a limited extent, now placed inside the containers of the candles, accompanied by a note bearing the request, along with the name of an individual or their entire family.

The number of photographs inserted into the crevices of the rock surrounding the statues has increased. They are accompanied by numerous papers, which by now have covered every available space. The handkerchiefs are wiped on the face and body of the statue that represents the saint, to be later used on the body of the person who is to be protected or healed. The ceremonies involving those present are held in silence, through a procedure, repeated many times, which gives the place a particular sanctity. Some of those present say they have come regularly for several years, in order to find Rita, and attempt to bring home some of that power; these are the women who arrive laden with the clothes of the relatives they want to protect, through the ritual of rubbing the statue, after the necessary offerings have been made to the sanctuary.

Dupront writes, with reference to the cult of Rita:

> Through acts, gestures and words, which also represent requests for intervention, the practices of popular religion auto-exorcise the drama, anguish and entangling obsessions of those who implore assistance. [...] The present cult of the saint from Cascia, with her forehead bloodied by a thorn from Christ's crown, is one of the most expressive testimonies of the passionate and anxious impulses that torment our time, and is an example, which is within our grasp, of a beneficially therapeutic fixation. (Dupront, 1987, pp. 440–441)

The hundreds of papers, photos and roses are a demonstration of the thaumaturgical power that the pilgrims attribute to the saint, and their desire for a direct relationship. Every pilgrimage finds a sense through a journey, which finds its conclusion in the encounter with the miracle-working saint. To be able to bear the marks of that power, and be able to return home with a sign, an object, as a reminder of that 'presence', is the value of the journey, of the encounter that was expected, sought and found, and then renewed through the handkerchief touched by the face of Rita.

As Turner notes, pilgrimage is a *liminoid phenomenon*, a liminal experience of religious life, an 'externalized mysticism': to perform the Stations of the Cross makes the pilgrimage a path of 'stations', consisting of successive steps relating to the life of the saint. Those who undertake the voyage decide to 'expose themselves' to the *tangible sacrality* of the sanctuary, to live the physical experience in all its complexity. Moving, walking, climbing, hearing and touching are experiences of the body (not only of the mind), something that engages the senses in their perceptual intensity, which makes the pilgrim listen to their body and its requirements: all this has a value for those who believe that their salvation/health is conditioned by their faith (Turner and Turner 1978, pp. 53–57).

The gaze of the pilgrims, caught in their photographs, can meet that of Rita, which, as it is thaumaturgic, is a gaze that guards, 'watches over' and protects.

This is the context in which to interpret the spread of the 'prayer cards' sold by the institutions at the sanctuary, to be placed in cars or on buses, in wallets and handbags. On every holy card, the image of Rita, in front of the crucifix and surrounded by roses, seems to reach the gaze of suffering mothers, sick children, women in labour, travellers and all those who invoke her in their suffering. She seems to establish a personal relationship with each of them, through a visual and tactile dimension, within the small ceremonies that the faithful perform.

The little picture is to be touched and gazed upon, and the prayer that accompanies it recited; it should not be discarded, or damaged. As a devotee from Perugia writes in the Cascia magazine:

> One day, going down to the garage, I found an image of St. Rita on the ground that had been there for some time. It was a sign. She looked at me, and asked me to pray to her. It was a difficult period for me, and I found that renewing my devotion to Rita, which I had put aside until that moment, really helped me to get through that ordeal. (*Dalle api alle rose (From Bees to Roses)*, no 5, 1992)

The holy picture, once lost, and now found, becomes the means to re-establish an interrupted relationship, a sign of supernatural assistance that is to be understood and solicited. This relationship between man and divinity is to be nourished by glances, words, gestures and prayers, in order to arrive at a condition of expectation and hope. The saint, in turn, requires constant devotion.

According to Dupront, the sacred image is ambivalent: on the one hand it is silent, timeless and passively decorative, while on the other it stirs and calls upon the imagination, and nourishes the soul. In its dual nature it is therefore not only a support, but also a means of communication, a witness of sanctity and represents a resource of religious imagery (Dupront, 1987, pp. 440–441).

Belting underlines that the devotee, rather than a miracle, wants the image to help him to initiate a dialogue in his imagination. There is an expectation that the image (or vision) will speak, as happened to Rita, who had spoken to and interacted with other saints (the three saints who transported her to the monastery).

'This act could have been directed to the observer as *coming* from the image, or being developed *within* it, addressed to the observer, if its characters spoke to each other *about the observer*' (Belting, 2001, p. 503). In this context, the image does not appear distant from the devotee, but rather sets in motion a dialogue; the image changes to adapt to the eye of the beholder, to leave space for a subjective moment. The dialogue takes the form of an anecdotal narration through images, with the images becoming external guarantors of an interior disposition (Belting, 2001, p. 504).

According to Spera it is possible to speak, in these specific contexts, of *iconodule*, similar to that found in popular forms of Orthodox worship, and forms of *icon therapy*, in which the holy picture itself is used directly on the patient's body, as a form of medication (Spera, 2008).

Together with the word, uttered in prayer, or sealed on a sheet of paper in the rock, the image creates a relationship of mutual glances, which expresses reciprocal attention, and a commitment, as is the case with all miracle-worker saints, which involves attentive devotion and relational depth. The gaze of the saint testifies to the importance of the relationship, which calls for solicitude. One stares, and one is stared upon (also by other pilgrims), and in this gaze the perception of one's own uniqueness is recognized, in the need to feel protected. The martyrdom of the living finds a match in the suffering endured by the saint, in a kind of 'micro-hagiography' parallel to that of Rita. The familiarity with which the devotees turn to her ('my second mother', 'my sister who leads me by the hand to God') expresses an intense private relationship, almost of kinship, made up of glances and trust (Giacalone, 1996b).

Pilgrims or Tourists?

For many years the debate has tended to identify pilgrims with tourists, albeit with some degree of nuance, above all recognizing the dimension of the consumption of the sacred in relation to the place of worship, as is the case with visits to cities of art. Collins-Kreiner (2010) underlines the difference from the perspective of religious

motivation, which sees the pilgrim move for spiritual reasons, as opposed to the standpoint of the hospitality and restaurant sector, which is orientated towards the tourist as consumer; in her opinion religious motivation should be distinguished from economic and touristic motivation. Cohen (1992) differentiates those heading to a religious centre from those who travel for art tourism, although the sanctuaries are often also museums, with the result that the tourist may visit religious places for historical and artistic reasons. Eade and Sallnow consider it essential to define the specific nature of each pilgrimage, and the various historical perspectives that are contextual to the sites (1991). However, Gastrell and Reid (2002), Coleman (2002), Coleman and Eade (2004), Albera and Eade (2015) and Albera and Blanchard (2015) assert that economic processes take place in the same socio-cultural space, and that the differences depend on perceptions and expectations at the local level; therefore, the theoretical perspective cannot be generalized without taking the ethnographic aspect into account.

I share this view, as economic aspects have by no means always been a secondary element in Catholic pilgrimages, as evidenced by the restaurants and hospitality that develop around shrines, not to mention fairs and markets. In reality, the pilgrim has never been just a spiritual traveller, but rather has always been a traveller who also needs to nourish the body and engage in social relations. Nolan and Nolan (1989) divide pilgrims into three groups: traditional pilgrims, members of organized religious tours and tourists interested in cities of art, who also visit churches and shrines.

The role attributed to the saint changes the perspective of the visit, which involves different perceptions, expectations and experiences. There is not only a difference in terms of the places of arrival, but also a distance, in terms of the perspective from which the pilgrim relates to a miracle-worker saint. In the dimension of popular religiosity, travellers to Cascia are pilgrims that await answers to their problems, and at the same time consumers of the sacred and souvenirs, much as at Lourdes (Reader, 2014).

The difference persists when the ethnographic analysis differentiates the modes of collective rites, the specificity of the type of pilgrimage and place of arrival, and the story of the individuals and their expectations. Cascia is not a town that can boast of important works of art, and its geographical location, far from the main transit routes, requires that the trip, be it individual or collective, be organized in advance. Therefore, those who visit Cascia go because they want to find St Rita, rather than undertake a tour of places of art, an option that is available in other towns in Umbria.

In reflecting on the phenomenon of pilgrimages, Eberhart, with particular reference to cases in Germany, stresses the importance of moving the focus from the place of arrival (the history and identity of the sanctuary) to the place of departure, and the travel experience of groups of pilgrims (Eberhart, 2005). This is a change of perspective, from the 'essentialist' approach of the culture of pilgrimage, to a vision that centres on the territorial and social reasons for travelling (Eberhart, 2005, pp. 95–96).

The provenance of most of the pilgrims is from the southern regions of Campania, Puglia, Sicily and Calabria, as well as Lebanon and Spain: this is evident from the data collected in the ethnographic analysis, the twinning arrangements for the festival and narratives of miraculous events. The age of the female pilgrims is also of interest. The women are often middle aged and elderly, evidence of the persistence of the cult among groups of the devout throughout their lives, as a form of 'affection' that lasts over time.

This proliferation of centres demonstrates the widespread diffusion of the cult, according to recurring modalities in southern votive practices, such as parades, processions, ceremonial clothing, special bread and votive offerings in honour of St Rita (Bitotto, Bitetto, Conversano).

In recent years there has been a decrease in the number of pilgrims from Puglia. They are more likely to visit the places associated with Saint Pio in San Giovanni Rotondo, another miracle-worker saint who has recently been canonized.

This also affects the organization of the cycle of events that celebrate St Rita, and the attention paid to keeping the relationship with these centres of worship alive. The cycle of festivals in Cascia maintains its popular dimension, despite having been transformed over time, and has still not become a form of religious tourism, at least not in the sense of a place associated with the consumption of the sacred.

It is possible to compare the rituals in Umbria with those in other chapels dedicated to Rita, in order to highlight the differences. The cult in the chapel of Pigalle, in Paris, while retaining some characteristics, has moved towards the presence of immigrants and prostitutes (Prado, 1993) and the blessing of animals, as attested by Brisbarre (2003). Marlène Albert-Llorca, on the subject of the notes written to Rita in the chapel of Pigalle, stresses that the writing does not just involve the 'supplicant', but also involves the 'intercessor'. Writing promises and expectations is therefore a way to oblige the saint to satisfy the demands (Albert-Llorca, 1993, p. 199).

The church is frequented by people from various walks of life, who invoke her grace, including charismatic Catholics (la *Communauté de l'Emmanuel*). They attempt to lead the faithful along more institutional paths, as the cult of the saint is expressed in popular, not orthodox forms. As Father Picard writes on devotees of the saint: 'parfois, des médiums m'envoient des gens. D'autres viennent demander de prières de délivrance. Il y a un danger d'idolâtrie, nous sommes aux frontières de la foi' (At times, mediums send me people. Others come to ask for prayers of deliverance. There is a danger of idolatry, and we are at the frontier of faith). (La Croix, 20 May 2016).

On 22 May 2016, the holy door for the Jubilee of Mercy was opened, at the behest of the Archbishop of Paris: this move by the diocese was dictated by religious motives, and directed against the decision of the owners of the building to demolish the chapel to build a private car park. There had already been protests by the faithful, who occupied the church, and were ejected by the police. The church is therefore at the centre of a legal conflict, which also sees political positions taking sides, as Catholic protesters see the closure of the church as an extreme form of the secularization of the country, which proposes the closure of Christian spaces and places of worship, while at the same time there is much greater sensitivity to mosques and the presence of Islam.[4]

In Lebanon, Christians see hope for change in their country in the parable of the life of Rita (Cheaib, 2011). It is therefore evident that the cult has been transformed and adapted, according to both the place of departure and of arrival, which highlights the different votive ways in which pilgrims of various nationalities and backgrounds can transform the meaning and practices of their devotion.

If the meaning of the pilgrimage is in the dynamics of the journey, in ritual and emotional practices, and individual expectations and stories, then the cult of Rita meets a plurality of needs, including the search for a place in which to find expression for discomfort, and the need for the sacred in a heavily secularized world. The places of departure and arrival, the travel strategies and the diversity of practices create a *web of meanings*, in the Geertzian sense, which indicates the variables of the 'sanctuary system' in its local and transnational organization, and modes of expression that cannot be reduced to a single meaning. This represents its strength and its continuous mediation with ecclesiastical institutions.

Notes

[1] This chapter was translated by Liam Boyle.

[2] The popular hagiography tells of how the saint has protected the city of Cascia from tragic events, such as the plague, and, more recently, the earthquake of 30 October 2016, which did not result in any fatalities, despite the severity of the event. In the past the powders of her funeral casket, oil from the lamp and the veil placed over her body were used as therapeutic means to cure the sick and demon-possessed. The small bread rolls made by the monastery that bear the imprint of the saint were also sent to distant countries, and were said to calm storms on land and sea (Tardi, 1927, 177–178). In my previous research on the saint I analysed stories relating to her healing powers in the years 1987–1994 (Giacalone, 1996c).

[3] Piccolpasso observes that the Valnerina area was a land of mediums and clairvoyant women, and home to the Sibyls of Norcia. Morini presents the legend of a local nymph, the sibyl Porrina, who lived in a cave in Roccaporena. A seer and protector of births, she would announce the coming of a 'daisy', or a 'precious stone'. The standard of Cascia features the depiction (based on a bas-relief) of a woman who holds in her hands a lily and a snake (the symbol of medicine), which is believed to represent Porrina (Giacalone, 1996c, pp. 188–190).

[4] See https://it.zenith.org/articles/parigi-cattolici-sulle-barricate-per-difendere-una-chiesa-dalla-demolizione.

References

Albera, D. and Blanchard, M. (eds) (2015) *Pellegrini del nuovo millennio. Aspetti economici e politici delle mobilità religiose*. Mesogea, Messina, Italy.

Albera, D. and Eade, J. (eds) (2015) *International Perspective on Pilgrimage Research: Itineraries, Gaps and Obstacles*. Routledge, London, New York.

Albert-Llorca, M. (1993) Le courrier du ciel. In: Fabre, D. (ed.) *Ecritures ordinaires*. P.O.L., Paris, pp. 183–221.

Belting, H. (2001) *Il culto delle immagini. Storia dell'icona dall'età imperiale al tardo Medioevo*. Carocci, Rome (original edition Bild und Kult, Beck, Munich, 1990).

Brisbarre, A.M. (2003) La messe des animaux. Sainte Rita, patronne des causes désespérés. *Communications* 74, 139–158.

Brown, P. (1981) *The Cult of the Saints*. University of Chicago Press, Chicago, Illinois, USA.

Cheaib, R. (2011) Una santa che profuma di cedri. *Dalle api alle rose* 1.

Cohen, E. (1992) Pilgrimage and tourism: convergence and divergence. In: Morinis, A. (ed.) *Sacred Journeys: The Anthropology of Pilgrimage*. Greenwood Press, Westport and London, pp. 47–61.

Coleman, S. (2002) Do you believe pilgrimage? *Anthropological Theory* 2(3), 355–368.

Coleman, S. and Eade, J. (2004) *Reframing Pilgrimage: Cultures in Motion*. Routledge, London.

Collins-Kreier, N. (2010) The geography of pilgrimage and tourism: transformations and implications for applied geography. *Applied Geography* 30, 153–164.

Di Nola, A. (1972) Pietre. Florence, *Enciclopedia delle Religioni* 2, 1616–1626.

Dupront, A. (1987) *Du sacré. Croisades et pèlerinage. Images et langages*. Gallimard, Paris.

Eade, J. and Sallnow, M.J. (eds) (1991) *Contesting the Sacred: The Anthropology of Christian Pilgrimage*. Routledge, London.

Eberhart, H. (2005) Pellegrinaggio e ricerca: tendenze e approcci attuali. *Lares* LXXI(1), 73–100.

Gastrell, J.D. and Reid, N. (2002) The cultural politics of local economic development, the case of Toledo jeep. *Tijdschrift voor Economische en Sociale Geografie* 93, 397–411.

Giacalone, F. (1996a) *Il corpo e la roccia. Miti e simboli nel culto di Santa Rita da Cascia.* Meltemi, Rome.

Giacalone, F. (1996b) Le regard bénéfique. Les images de Sainte Rita de Cascia. *Xoana* 4, 85–92.

Giacalone, F. (1996c) Le guarigioni attribuite a Santa Rita da Cascia. Un confronto fra antropologia religiosa e antropologia medica. A.M. *Rivista della Società italiana di antropologia medica* 1–2, 179–214.

Moles, A. (1977) *Psychologie du Kitsch. L'art du bonheur.* Maison Mame, Paris.

Morini, A. (1933) La leggenda di Roccaporena. *Latina Gens* XI(4), 1–11.

Nolan, M.L. and Nolan, S. (1989) *Christian Pilgrimage in Modern Western Europe.* The University of North Carolina Press, Chapel Hill, North Carolina, USA.

Piccolpasso, C. and Cecchini, G. (eds) (1963 [1565]) *Le piante e i ritratti delle città e terre dell'Umbria sottoposte al Governo di Perugia, ristampa anastatica, Roma.* Arti Grafiche Panetto e Petrelli, Spoleto, Italy.

Prado, P. (1993) Sainte Rita de la place Blanche, la sainte du 'bout du rouleau'. In: Belmont, N. and Lautman, F. (eds) *Ethnologie des faits religieux en Europe.* EHESS, Paris, pp. 203–206.

Reader, I. (2014) *Pilgrimage in the Marketplace.* Routledge, London, New York.

Sallmann, J.M. (1996) *Santi barocchi, Lecce, Argo* (original edition Naples et ses saints à l'âge baroque (1550–1750)). Presses Universitaires de France, Paris.

Spera, V. (2008) Iconoterapia: pictures that heal. In: Viesca, C.T. and Tricot, J.-P. (eds) *Analecta Historico Medica.* vol. II. Memorias 41 Congreso Internacional de Historia de la Medicina, Facultad de Medicina de la UNAM, Mexico City, pp. 113–122.

Tardi, L. (1927 [1864]) *Vita della Beata Rita da Cascia.*, Tipografia di Domenico Sensi, Assisi, Italy.

Turner, V. and Turner, E. (1978) *Image and Pilgrimage in Christian Culture.* Columbia University Press, New York.

14 Saint Rita of Cascia: An Evolving Devotion in Dublin's Inner City

Tony Kiely*

*School of Hospitality Management and Tourism, College of Arts and Tourism,
Dublin Institute of Technology, Dublin, Ireland*

Introduction

Within the broad hierarchical Church, it has
long been acknowledged that popular devotion
by way of pilgrimage participation, processions
and novenas, the Rosary, the Angelus, Stations
of the Cross and the veneration of relics has
played a crucial role in fostering ceaseless
prayer. Indeed, since the advent of Christianity,
devotional practice has been enacted along an
evolving continuum ranging from prescribed
adoration of saints and martyrs who lived to an
impossibly high standard (Hoever, 2005; Martin,
2006; Bangley, 2009; Kasten, 2014), to alignments with ordinary saints whose lives resemble
that of the devotee (Ghezzi, 2007; Ganzevoort,
2008; Mayblin, 2014). For generations of Irish
Catholics, prescribed devotional routines were so
intertwined with their daily lives, that devotional
avoidance became almost impossible, as a consequence of attendance requirements being applied within families and schools to what were
by and large, captive audiences (Ellsberg, 2006;
Winstead, 2011). However, within today's more
capricious and ephemerally driven societies, it
would seem that traditional devotional intensity
has been somewhat replaced by more populist
alignments (Cotter, 2005; Coles and Harrison,
2012). Examples of such behavioural evolution

is evidenced in the 'popularity' of St Michael the
Archangel (articulating the contemporary fear
of terrorism), St Patrick (justifying a momentary
alcohol fuelled desire to be 'Irish'), St Francis of
Assisi (following the media-generated popularity of the current pope) and St Valentine
(acquiescing with a commercial conduit for ar-
ticulations of love). Furthermore, opportunistic
forms of devotion arise in situations wherein
those experiencing challenging situations become acutely 'aware' of saints who are associated with the assuagement of their 'worries',
and that a 'chosen one' even has the power to
deliver on ephemeral requests, without the
'plaintiff' having any devotion to the targeted
saint (Cotter, 2005; Coles and Harrison, 2012).
Worried students for example will often be encouraged by their parents or grandparents to
pray to St Joseph of Cupertino on the eve of their
examinations to help them answer questions
that they have not sufficiently prepared for,
while others will casually promise St Anthony
a 'reward' to find lost items for them. Similarly,
habitual recourse to St Blaise is evident in Ireland
on 3 February each year, when significant numbers 'invest' in his protection from throat infec-
tions for the following 12 months. Equally, the
rise in popularity on the internet of a third-
century Turkish saint (St Expeditious), patron of

*E-mail: tony.m.kiely@dit.ie

long drawn out legal cases and 'other' emergencies, has attracted a significant virtual following among those with impatient needs for speedy resolutions of their difficulties.

On the other hand, saints deemed 'ordinary', due to their trials and sufferings being representative of those of the sufferer, often become starkly relevant for traumatized and stigmatized souls. In such instances, devotional co-alignment with the 'ordinary', rather than the 'extraordinary', happily occurs, and a more appropriate devotional relationship is seen to be at play (Ellsberg, 2006; Ghezzi, 2007; Ganzevoort, 2008; Jansen and Kuhl, 2008; Mayblin, 2014). Mayblin (2014, p. 272) also suggests that, while devotion is often characterized as an association with the sublimely holy, devotees themselves are peculiar in that they alternatively champion the human form, or indeed, how 'likeable' divine figures ground their devotional motivation. Furthermore, she argues that 'within Catholicism, sanctity is not the exclusive property of an intangible God, or formless Holy Spirit, but rather, a constituent part of an entire material panoply that includes relics, priestly vestments, ritual paraphernalia, the architecture of an ecclesiastical system, and by no means least, the gendered bodies of clergy and saints'. This would suggest the possibility that intimate devotion is grounded in the 'ordinary' as opposed to the 'extraordinary', wherein the saint's weakness ultimately becomes their strength. For example, in contextualizing the significance of devotional co-dependency among Catholics in northeast Brazil, Mayblin (2014, p. 272) argues that when saints are perceived by devotees as having 'suffered like them', they 'become like them', which drives the devotion towards an intimacy, wherein devotees 'enjoy regular conversations' with their co-suffering saints. Such intimacy is instanced in their portrayal of a local 'folk saint' Frei Damiao (1898–1997), as 'snoring loudly' and 'cracking jokes', which for his devotees, heightens the probability of his understanding the daily sufferings of ordinary people.

Equally, more contemporary representations of 'ordinariness', particularly in St Therese of Lisieux, St Pio, St Angela Merici, St Jane de Chantal, St Joan of Arc, St Mary McKillop and Pier Giorgio Frassati, have created deeply rewarding devotional conduits for those impacted on by issues associated with persecution, social injustice, gender discrimination and rejection (Ellsberg, 2006; Ghezzi, 2007; Coles and Harrison,

2012). In addressing the significance of gender discrimination, Ellsberg (2006, p. 15) argues that in acknowledging the provenance of women saints as merely 'providing the perfect framework for religious devotion', the Church has been guilty of overtly characterizing them in terms of their 'feminine virtues of purity', rather than in terms of their 'wit in surmounting the obstacles put in their path'. For example, in exploring devotion to the Virgin Mary among Muslim women, Jansen and Kuhl (2008, p. 295) found that in their pursuit of 'shared womanhood', they viewed Mary not as virginal and pure, but more as 'an ordinary mother, who suffered herself'. Accordingly, in perceiving Mary as a mediator between themselves and a distant and judging God, they were particularly attracted to her strong feminism, which made her 'nearer and more approachable, especially during intimate moments such as childbirth'. Equally, in her 'understanding of their need to feel responsible for the direct physical, moral, and social wellbeing of their family', she would undoubtedly help them to 'overrule parental power, escape from a violent partner, assist sick family members, or face loneliness within a hostile society' (Jansen and Kuhl, 2008, p. 295).

Hagiography and Devotional Inducement

While differing in their motivational depth, each devotional conduit creates a personalized identification with a saint of choice (Cotter, 2005; Carroll Cruz, 2006; Ghezzi, 2007; Coles and Harrison, 2012; Kasten, 2014). Accordingly, while for some, 'blind devotion' may be considered old fashioned or naive, in that unquestioning loyalty is disproportionately one directional, and exclusively associated with the holiness of saints, alternative devotional formats may instead be activated by a sense of hopelessness or desperation (Tari and Vanni, 2008; Trueb, 2009). For example, the creation of modern fictitious saints has opened tailor-made devotional channels, wherein situational commonality facilitates devotional intent (Jansen and Kuhl, 2008; Tari and Vanni, 2008). So, while a number of saints are born, or revived for utilitarian reasons (typically associated with revenue generation or tourism development), San Precario of Milan has since February 2004, been 'appropriated' as the patron saint of those with zero hour contracts of employment, by a group of Milanese activists. The creation of this fictitious 'saint' acknowledges the fact that those in difficult or traumatic circumstances (not being able to gain full-time employment in Italy, France and Spain) are no different from other traumatized devotees, in that they need someone to pray to (Tari and Vanni, 2008). Thus, the fictionalized 'saint' is utilized to create a critical public awareness of changes in work conditions (moving people from permanent to casual positions), which cleverly aligns with the sufferer's need to pray, in these particular countries. Again, the hagiography is significant, in that it grew from the Italian expression 'non so a che santo votarmi' ('I don't know which saint to pray to'), a phrase that captures the utter loss of hope among the dispossessed, and that in turn, unites and narrates a community into existence.

A number of additional factors may also contribute to shaping the efficacy of a devotion; for example, an embedded emotional attachment, a simplicity of format, an engaging hagiography or a social interaction with others who are regularly engaged in the same devotional practice. Equally, serendipitous reasons, such as the fact that someone you know also likes a particular saint, and has introduced you to their story, can trigger longitudinal devotion, which in a sense creates a form of 'brand identification' with the saint of choice. In Dublin for example, a strong intergenerational devotion to St Anthony of Padua still exists, where on his feast day (13 June), parents bring their children to a Franciscan church in central Dublin at 4:00 pm for the saint's blessing. This practice is bound up in an embedded hagiography which posits that at exactly 4:00 pm on 13 June 1231, the children of Padua ran into the streets shouting 'Il Santo é Morto' ('the saint is dead'), proclaiming in the process a 'santo subito' ('an immediate saint'). What is interesting here is that the adults, who themselves were brought as children for a blessing, now bring their own children, and in doing so, nourish the ancient hagiography. Furthermore, many women who were educated in Ireland's Holy Faith Convents, of whom, St Brigid is the patron, believe the hagiography that on her asking for a plot of land on which to build a monastery, the mythical spreading of her cloak covered more than enough land for the monastery. Similarly, St Patrick, Ireland's premier national saint, despite evidence to the contrary, is blindly acknowledged to have driven the snakes from Ireland.

It would seem therefore that the way in which the hagiographical representation of a particular saint has been communicated and absorbed can determine its relevance for devotees. Such pertinent alignment is often associated with acute medical or psychological traumas, which in turn instigates a comforting bond with saints who have experienced similar sufferings (Kunz et al., 2009; Trueb, 2009; Mayblin, 2014). Indeed, Martin (2006) contends that Roman Catholic tradition has made particular saints the protectors of various aspects of human frailty, resulting in their powers being invoked for specific needs. For example, St Blaise is associated with throat ailments because he allegedly saved a child from suffocation caused by a fish bone being stuck in their throat. For others, devotion is associated with the alignment of their trauma with the saint's martyrdom, exemplified in the invocation of those suffering from burns to St Lawrence of Rome, who, legend has it, was martyred by being roasted on a gridiron (Hoever, 2005). A similar co-identity, relating to stigmatization (being classified, or classifying oneself as a social outcast), is common among devotees to particular saints. Accordingly, Trueb (2009) cites devotional relationships to St Bartholomew and St Rose of Lima (for those suffering with troubling skin diseases), to St Charles of Borromeo (for skin ulceration), to St Agatha and St Peregrine (for skin cancer), and to St Vincent de Paul (for leprosy). In championing a case for the appointment of St Agnes of Rome (a virgin martyr of the Roman Catholic Church) as the patron of women suffering from the trauma of hair loss, Kunz et al. (2009) suggest that her powerful hagiography could well facilitate a therapeutic co-identification bond for women suffering from the traumatic experience of hair loss. This hagiography suggests that on 21 January 304 AD, following her refusal to marry the son of a local Roman prefect, Agnes was dragged naked through the streets before being publicly beheaded at a stake, where legend has it that her hair copiously grew to cover her body, thus protecting her from the prurient gaze of onlookers. Similarly, Ganzevoort (2008, p. 19) communes with the attractiveness of communality in suffering when suggesting that stigmata (physical manifestations of divine grace) can become 'powerful metaphors for exploring the interaction between scarring, trauma, and identity' in the lives of ordinary people, by facilitating 'a narrative construction of one's woes with re-spect to those of a respected other'.

Hagiography and St Rita

A strong hagiographical connectivity epitomizes devotion to St Rita, wherein a chronological series of vivid stories reflect her sanctity, obedience, suffering, grief, endurance, ostracization, neglect, reconciliation and belated recognition. Indeed, aspects of this hagiography have been employed by her devotees to ameliorate similar experiences within their own troubled lives. Known as 'the saint of the impossible or seemingly impossible cases', Rita of Cascia (Fig. 14.1) was born in 1381 in Roccaporena, a tiny village in an earthquake-torn region of Umbria in Italy. Throughout her life, she experienced rejection, loss, pain and serenity in numerous guises, initially, as a reluctant, yet compliant wife, in motherhood and widowhood, and in her later years, in the frustration and fulfilment of her desire to become an Augustinian nun (Rotelle, 2000). Paraphrasing the complexity of her life, Heather and Heather (2003, p. 189) suggest that while 'some saints enter into a cloistered life at an early age, and live in relative innocence of the world, others experience all the trials and tribulations of secular life before they are called to a life with God'. What is peculiar about devotion to St Rita is that contemporaneous evidence

Fig. 14.1. St Rita.

of her life is so scarce that it is impossible to construct the 'facts' associated with her story. This brings into focus an almost blind illogicality, wherein cognitive dissonance trumps logical proof. Accordingly, while her biography was never written, devotion to her flourished among the simple and uneducated people of Cascia after her death. It is not difficult to imagine therefore, how a number of legends sprang up around her name as the local people tried to express her greatness and sanctity in concrete terms (Corcoran, 1985).

Nonetheless, for regular devotees of St Rita, the story of her life has become a series of life enhancing attributes that comfortably bind them with her. For example, the miracle of the bees informs us that at her baptism, Rita's mother noticed a swarm of white bees hovering around, and entering the infant's mouth as she lay sleeping in her cradle. However, her alarm was allayed when she noticed that they did not sting the infant (Corcoran, 1985). This incident was retrospectively interpreted by her contemporaries as a portent of her subsequent sanctification. Interestingly, an accompanying legend has grown over the years, which details how a swarm of stingless bees occupy a fissure in the convent wall in Cascia, midway between St Rita's cell and the place of her sepulchre to this day, appearing only during Holy Week, and on St Rita's feast day, which adds to the allure of the original legend. A second narrative illustrates that while still a teenager, despite her long-expressed desire to become a nun, Rita was promised into an arranged marriage by her ageing parents to a difficult and violent man, for whom she bore two sons. Sadly, 18 years into her marriage, Rita became a widow and a single mother, when her husband was brutally murdered in an interfamily feud, which under the unwritten medieval law of 'La Vendetta', obligated her sons to avenge their father's death. Tortured by this prospect, Rita prayed that her sons would not succumb to carrying out this horrendous act, and her prayers were swiftly answered when both died from a fever on the same day, before they could engage in vengeance (Corcoran, 1985; Rotelle, 2000; MacNiven-Johnston, 2009). For her devotees, the significance of this story is that Rita, despite her grief, was unavoidably cast in the role of a reconciler between her own family, and those of her husband's murderers, an attribute

that in later years would become the source of many petitions from her devotees to reconcile quarrelsome differences in their own lives.

Following her husband's murder and the death of her two sons, Rita was finally free to fulfil her long-held desire to enter religious life. However, she tasted rejection when repeatedly refused entry into the Augustinian convent in nearby Cascia, which was possibly due to her being deemed 'a widow and a woman of the world' (Heather and Heather, 2003, p. 190), or perhaps because relations of her husband's murderers were nuns in the convent at the time (Corcoran, 1985; MacNiven-Johnston, 2009). Accordingly, a third narrative relates to how Rita entered the convent as a novice in most unusual circumstances. Legend informs us that when praying in her own kitchen on Ascension Thursday, she was visited by St Nicholas of Tolentino, St Augustine and St John the Baptist, (her three favourite saints), who miraculously transported her through the locked convent doors, much to the consternation of the congregation of nuns who had impeded her access. Furthermore, although finally accepted as a novice, Rita experienced greater trials – when she asked if she might be involved in the normal routines of the convent, she was instead required to water a dry stick on a daily basis, which she did with a patient resolution. Legend has it that the dry stick eventually grew into a great vine, which to this day, bears much fruit. These incidents were subsequently interpreted as showing Rita's gifts of patience and perseverance despite disappointment, which is encapsulated in many of her devotees accepting that she will undoubtedly grant their petitions, albeit that they might possibly have to persevere. What is interesting here is that despite the fact that the vine was carbon dated to a time after Rita's death, and that Augustinian guides tell this to visitors to the convent, many pilgrims believe the original story, which in illustrating a contemporary dissonance, fits better with their image of Rita's triumph over her attempted subjugation.

The concluding years of Rita's life produced the most iconic images in her fascinating hagiography. On Good Friday 1442, following intense prayer before an image of the crucified Christ (Fig. 14.2), Rita was the recipient of a partial stigmata, when a loosened thorn, in penetrating her forehead, created a putrified wound,

Fig. 14.2. St Rita praying.

which never healed, resulting in her being confined to her cell for the final 15 years of her life
(MacNiven-Johnston, 2009). Characterizing the
life of St Rita of Cascia in a contemporary context, wherein a combination of her life's experiences (violence, rejection, pain and devotion)
culminated in her being the recipient of a partial
stigmata, Ganzevoort (2008) contends that ordinary people can feel stigmatized through their
not being accepted within the confines of what
they perceive as normal society. Thus, the sufferer will often find solace in being in the company of many who have travelled that road. The
final hagiographical incident illustrates for many
the defining symbol of her life. Nearing death
during the bitter winter of 1457, Rita requested
a rose from her family garden in Roccaporena.
Believing, as the nuns did, that Rita had lost
possession of her senses, a visiting relative

nonetheless acquiesced with her request, only to
find to her astonishment, a rose bush in full
bloom in the snow-covered garden (Corcoran,
1985; MacNiven-Johnston, 2009). During the
annual triduum in honour of St Rita each year,
the distribution and blessing of rose petals is of
major importance to her devotees, who believe
that the rose and the thorn symbolize her life.
Finally, after her death (22 May 1457), Rita still
experienced continued rejection, when, despite
her acknowledged saintliness, albeit at a local
level, and the contemporaneous attribution of
many miracles to her, calls for her beatification
and canonization were ignored by the papacy
for approximately 450 years. Corcoran (1985,
p. 19) argues that the reticence of the Church to
acknowledge the sanctity of Rita over many
centuries was primarily due to the nature of the
devotion to her, and that because 'her clients

came from simple people rather than the educated class, the significance of Rita was expressed in concrete rather than abstract terms'. Nevertheless, on 24 May 1900, following years of patient exhortation by devotees, notably Blessed Maria Teresa Fasce (Papalini, 1997), Rita of Cascia, an extraordinarily ordinary woman, who is associated with heroic stoicism through her patient acceptance of tragedy and rejection, was the first woman to be canonized in the twentieth century.

The Devotional Site

Simply known to locals as John's Lane (Fig. 14.3), the Church of St Augustine and St John the Baptist is the location of a weekly devotion to St Rita of Cascia. This beautifully ornate church, which stands on the twelfth-century site of a hospital for lepers, was originally administered by the Knights Templar and a group of like-minded men, who lived according to the rule of St Augustine in about the year 1080 (Butler, 1983). The Augustinians, who originated in Umbria in the thirteenth century, arrived in Dublin in 1280, and occupied a number of well-known sites across the city including Crowe Street in Temple Bar, Trinity College and Christchurch Cathedral (which was a monastic foundation in pre-Reformation times). After much movement, the friars finally agreed to settle on their original site in Thomas Street, which was by then part of Dublin's Liberties, and a bustling shopping area of the city. Although funding for the new church was in short supply at the time, the foundation stone was laid by Cardinal Cullen (who was responsible for the explosion of post-Catholic Emancipation church building in the city), on Easter Sunday, 1862 (Butler, 1983). Edward Welby Pugin, and his equally talented brother-in-law George Ashlin were architects on the building, which was described by artist John Ruskin as 'a poem in stone'. The church was opened to the public in 1895. On entering through the doors, visitors are instantly struck by its artistic beauty and hypnotic light patterns, much of which comes from a suite of strategically positioned stained glass windows, attributed to stained glass manufacturers Meyers (Munich based), Harry Clarke and Michael Healy. The rich marble shrine dedicated to St Rita (Fig. 14.4) was erected in 1936 (Butler, 1983). Among the very fine mosaic tiling in the shrine,

one scene depicts the saint pleading for, and receiving a thorn from the Crown of Thorns, which embedded in her forehead and remained there until her death (See right panel in Fig. 14.4). Furthermore, while there are the obvious representations of the great Augustinian icons such as St Augustine, his long-suffering mother St Monica and St Nicholas of Tolentino (Fig. 14.5), there is an undoubted Italian feel to the church, epitomized in the shrine to the Mother of Good Counsel, which was constructed in 1898 by Edward Sharpe (Fig. 14.6). Here, one can view the most maternal depiction of Mary listening to her child, which is a copy of the famous fifteenth-century painting by Troija, housed in the replicate shrine in Genazzano (Butler, 1983). Another striking Italian representation is encapsulated in the four-panel Harry Clarke window, which documents the life of St Clare of Montefalco, a lesser known Italian Augustinian nun (Fig. 14.7). The window depicts her kneeling before Jesus, with two hearts beating in her breast, one of which bears the imprint of His cross. Legend has it that despite the wearying disregard for her suggestion that she felt the beat of two hearts throughout her life, such was found to be the case following a post-mortem after her death. Other Augustinian stained glass representations in the church include those of St Thomas of Villanova, a Spanish Augustinian, famous for his devotion to the poor, St Monica receiving the purifying cord for her wayward son and Michael Healy's masterpiece, which documents incidents in the life of St Augustine. But, despite the availability of such an impressive array of devotional opportunities, St Rita is the most celebrated figure among a community of regulars who gather in John's Lane every Saturday at 11:00 am for a novena Mass that has been celebrated in her honour for over 60 years.

The Devotional Ritual

Considering the protracted neglect of St Rita by the Church authorities over the centuries, and the fact that devotion to her was contained at a local level in her native Cascia, it is not particularly surprising that there was little to no awareness of her in Dublin during the late nineteenth century. For similar reasons, it is understandable that Rita was the last of the great Augustinian icons to be publicly represented in the city's

Fig. 14.3. The Church of St Augustine and St John the Baptist – St. John's Lane Church.

Fig. 14.4. Shrine of St Rita.

Fig. 14.5. St Augustine, St Monica and St Nicholas of Tolentino.

Fig. 14.6. Shrine to the Mother of Good Counsel (with insert detail of main icon).

Fig. 14.7. Harry Clarke window – St Clare of Montefalco.

Augustinian church. Nonetheless, devotion to St Rita commenced in John's Lane in 1962, and was led for many years by a Limerick-born priest Father Frank O'Shaugnessy, who, when stricken with a serious illness, promised St Rita that he would initiate a devotion to her if she cured him of his illness. This serendipitous alignment bore fruit when following his cure, the weekly devotion commenced, with a small congregation of no more than 50 in attendance (Butler, 1983). However, following the addition of a 9-day retreat in the period approaching her feast day (22 May), and later by an annual triduum in her honour, the number of devotees exponentially grew, and were nourished by the stories of her life, which were recounted on successive evenings of the triduum. Accordingly, for many of her devotees, it was the continuity and the consistency of the hagiography that became the cornerstone of their devotional alliances. Illustrating that point, at a triduum some years ago, the visiting preacher, on viewing the crowded pews prior to commencing his sermon was heard to comment 'I won't bother to tell you the story of St. Rita yet again, as I'm sure you must know it by heart by now'. However, a small group of women in the first row instantly responded by springing to their feet and shouting 'no, we want you to tell us her story; we want to hear it again', as if this were the most integral part of their devotional need. Typically, the first 2 days of the triduum were concerned with the reading of personalized petitions, while a feature of the final day was its reservation for thanksgiving, and the blessing of roses, which her clients would later distribute to those who were not well enough to attend. Indeed, such were the crowds at these early triduums that the Knights of the Shrine who guided devotees to their seats, were issued with packs of smelling salts, which were to be administered should any of the attendees faint during the proceedings.

These days, thanks to the generosity of Father Pat Gayer, a Cork-born friar who generously facilitated the continuation of this important Dublin tradition after the passing of Father Frank, the weekly devotion has remained relatively unchanged, much to the delight of Rita's devotees. Accordingly, there are a number of chronologically identifiable rituals enacted in the Mass. For example, there is a public reading of petitions, most of which have the name of the petitioner attached. Many of the petitions speak to the life of St Rita in being associated with cures from illnesses, seeking employment, the successful outcome of a court case, for a family to be reunited, for finding a life partner, for the conception of, or the safe delivery of a baby or simply to offer thanksgiving. Moreover, this tradition affords the opportunity for communal prayer for those named in the petition. Equally, the traditional blessing with the relic of St Rita (Fig. 14.8),

Fig. 14.8. Relic of St Rita.

which contains a precious bone fragment of the saint, is a core element of the novena Mass. Moreover, an opportunity is afforded to devotees after the Mass to take a private blessing, which, in many cases, involves personal contact by touching or kissing the sacred relic. During the Offertory, the congregation ritually sing the following hymn to their 'own Saint Rita', which recalls her neglect by the Church, and their belief that she will listen to them as a mother would.

> O glorious name, our own St Rita,
> O glorious name, sweet name of love.
> Throughout the years, thy name forgotten,
> Thy children now, thy grace implore.
> O glorious name, our own St Rita,
> O glorious name, sweet name of love.
> What priceless gifts, what endless treasures,
> Now flowing from, thy boundless store.
> In all our joys, in all our sorrows,
> No prayer of ours, shall thou ignore.
> O glorious name, our own St Rita.
> O glorious name, sweet name of love.

Similarly, the special prayer said during Mass serves as a reminder of her acceptance of the wound in her forehead.

> O Glorious St Rita,
> Who didst so wonderfully participate
> In the sorrowful passion of Our Lord Jesus Christ,
> Obtain for me the grace to suffer with gentle resignation,
> The trials of this life,
> And protect me in my necessities,
> Through Christ Our Lord, Amen.

Furthermore, despite taking an hour out of their busy Saturday schedule to participate in devotion to St Rita, there is also an important social element to the weekly gathering. Accordingly, devotees will often gather after Mass in a local coffee shop to discuss issues of the day, or simply to assuage each other's worries in a communal social activity, which they know that Rita 'would fully understand'. Equally, as John's Lane is situated in a busy shopping area of Dublin, a number of Rita's devotees either arrive with their shopping completed, or go shopping after the Mass, thus integrating a happy mix of satisfying the needs of both the soul and the body. This ritual enactment of pre- or post-novena shopping activity would appear to bear testimony to their belief that St Rita, in being like them by way of her ordinariness, would fully understand the practicalities of having to shop for the family for food, while fitting in some devotional time in John's Lane.

Participant Testimonies

Testimonies as to why devotees were attracted to St Rita were gathered over a 12-month period at the triduum and the weekly novena Mass. Regarding devotional inclination, evidence of a strong alignment with St Rita emerged, wherein respondents attributed significant motivational importance to their devotion, in terms of its longevity and its regularity. Asked how long they had been devoted to St Rita, periods ranged from 'three years' to 'fifty six years', with the majority of those interviewed having been committed for over 20 years. A related question enquired about the regularity of their attendance at the weekly novena Mass. Again, enthusiastic responses such as 'every Saturday', 'it's part of my week' and 'I would be lost without it', testified to both devotional determination and the importance of its regularity, continuity and consistency. In endeavouring to rationalize this ubiquitous devotional commitment, attendees were probed to elicit if the ritual of weekly devotion ever drifted into being merely habitual. However, all respondents strongly disagreed, with one stressing that his weekly attendance was purposeful rather than habitual, when insisting, 'I definitely don't see it like that. You see I have specific reasons for coming here every week, so it's not just a habit that I have grown into.'

Enquiring what initially triggered devotion to St Rita elicited a tapestry of responses. For most, devotion was intergenerational, in that they were introduced to the devotional practice by their own mothers or grandmothers. Yet, for others, devotion grew out of a chance, almost casual interaction. This expression of the drawing power of St Rita was illustrated in statements such as 'I wandered into John's Lane church one Saturday, and I liked what I heard; things like petitions and thanksgivings'. Addressing the serendipity of her contact, another commented that she had 'picked up a prayer card of St. Rita in a church in Armagh during a down time in my life, and after saying the novena prayer, all seemed well again'. Relating to an illness, another lady recalled that she was 'recovering from cancer, and I met a woman on a bus who told me about St. Rita, and when I went to John's Lane, I just knew that she would look after me'. When pursuing how devotees petitioned with St Rita at the weekly novena Mass, the easing of acute and temporal worries emerged as common devotional conduits, with one lady stating 'my niece was very ill in hospital, and I prayed for her to get better. St. Rita answered my prayers, so I have been devoted to her ever since,' while another humorously commented 'years ago I was worried about passing my examinations, when I met a woman who told me about St. Rita, and said that she was the Patron Saint of the Impossible, and that was music to my ears'.

Regarding Rita's hagiography, interviewees spoke openly of how well they knew her life story. Here a strong unanimity was ubiquitous, illustrated in responses such as 'of course we know her story', and 'some of us have been coming here for years, and know the story off by heart because Fr. Frank told it to us every week, and now Fr. Pat is doing the same'. However, while extensive knowledge of Rita's story appeared to be a given, alignment with particular hagiographical highlights was selective, with one woman commenting 'I know her life story, but I mostly identify with her devotion to the cross, and the thorn in her poor forehead'. Another communed with the story of Rita being a renowned peacemaker when stating 'I come here every week to pray to her for another week's peace in my family'. Another associated with the miracle of the rose, when answering 'I bring roses from my own garden to Cascia to have them blessed, and I distribute them to anyone who is sick when I get home'. Additionally, the legend of Rita's ability to overcome obstacles and rejection also appeared to confer a special status on her, with one woman being quite direct in commenting 'look, she was forced into a marriage by selfish parents who just wanted to be looked after in their old age, and she just got on with things'. A similar alignment was evident in another commenting that, 'I like the way she accepted life as it unfolded', while pausing to admit 'I try to emulate her in accepting what comes my way, but it's never easy'.

Devotion to St Rita also appeared to fuse with perceptions of her ability to understand and resolve more intimate feminine worries and concerns, with one lady commenting 'My mother had a difficult first pregnancy, and prayed that my birth would be easier and it was, thanks to St. Rita's help, and when I became a mother, she helped me too'. However, by far the most popular devotional driver related to the devotee's need to align with what they viewed as a likeness between St Rita's life and that of their own. Here, comments such as 'I had a difficult marriage, and things seemed to be getting worse', and 'my life has some similarities, broken marriage, alcoholic husband and son', appeared to align their need with the ability of St Rita to support them. Articulating a view that St Rita does not offer easy solutions, another lady commented that 'a lot of women won't deal with her, because they say that she can also give you a thorn, but I don't mind, because, that's what our lives are about; good days and bad days'. Interestingly, in depicting Rita in such ordinary terms, one woman visualized her as being 'just like a woman who would go shopping with you', while another concluded, 'she could write the life story for everyone here in one way or another because she is just like us'.

Conclusion

This chapter explored the evolution and anatomy of devotional practice among a predominantly female congregation who attend a weekly novena Mass to seek favours and support from a medieval Italian saint. Accordingly, Rita of Cascia is for all the world a saint with a complex hagiography, who, despite being forgotten for centuries, has grown to become an inspirational figure for troubled and marginalized women. Within John's Lane, the devotional routine appears to be a mix of the traditional hagiographical format, wherein the stories of Rita's life nourishes the devotion, and a more applied format wherein the saint moves from being adored to being just like the devotee. Thus, the relevance of Rita can be rationalized in the pragmatic application of devotion to her, wherein many of those who attend find themselves in similar life situations to those experienced by Rita. Indeed, the fact that Rita was beset by everyday problems, in that she was disproportionately put upon by the expectations of the material world, suffered much rejection and physical pain, had a wayward husband and troubled sons, and experienced bereavement, widowhood and neglect, appear to distil a cohesive identification with her among her devotees. Furthermore, unlike other saints, there is not a universality about devotion to Rita. Instead, for many of her devotees, she is just another woman like them, who understands their ongoing practical worries. As a result, her followers have developed an unshakeable devotion to one they perceive as an ordinary saint, a devotion that overrides any chronological or hagiographical errors in the depiction of her life. Furthermore, as this devotion is embedded in their psyche, through reliving Rita's iconic hagiography over many years attendance at the weekly novena Mass and annual triduum held in her honour, they have become the carriers of the devotional flame.

During the testimonials, devotion to St Rita emerged as being both strong and traditional among many of those interviewed, wherein a gritty devotion created a powerful alignment with their 'saint of the impossible'. And while a minority of interviewees stated that they had accidentally discovered St Rita, the findings suggest that devotional alignment was primarily intergenerational (as is the case with most saints for devotees of a particular age), exemplified in how most spoke of being introduced to St Rita by their own mothers or grandmothers. Interestingly, none of those interviewed alluded to being influenced by their fathers or grandfathers, which would suggest that the intergenerational devotion was predominantly gender based. However, the main impetus for devotional intent was encapsulated in the motivational power of communing with the ordinary (Ghezzi, 2007; Ganzevoort, 2008; Mayblin, 2014), wherein these women co-identified with Rita's life and suffering, resulting in their perception that she would be ideally positioned to listen to their petitions and worries. At an operational level, the cohesiveness and consistency of the devotional ritual as evidenced in the weekly Mass, is of particular importance for devotees. Accordingly, the anatomy of their devotion appears to create a community of devotees who are in the habit of sharing their suffering, while at the same time, offering their support to like sufferers. This *modus operandi* is evidenced in the social context of the devotion, wherein their shopping routine is tied in with their devotional routine, and capped off with an enjoyable and informative coffee break. In conclusion, it is found that devotion to St Rita in Dublin is inextricably linked with aspects of Rita's hagiography being absorbed on a weekly basis, which in becoming seamlessly embedded within devotional practice, creates the perfect devotional conduit to their favourite 'extraordinarily ordinary' saint.

References

Bangley, B. (2009) *Butler's Lives of the Saints: Concise*, modernised edition. Paraclete Press, Orleans, Massachusetts, USA.

Butler, T.C. (1983) *John's Lane: A History of the Augustinian Friars in Dublin 1280–1980*. Good Counsel Press, Dublin, Ireland.

Carroll Cruz, J. (2006) *Saintly Youth of Modern Times*. Our Sunday Visiting Publishing Division, Huntington, Indiana, USA.

Coles, R. and Harrison, T. (2012) *Lives of Improbable Saints*. Darton, Longman, & Todd Ltd, London.

Corcoran, G. (1985) *Saint Rita of Cascia, Saint of the Impossible*. Augustinian Press, Villanova, Pennsylvania, USA.

Cotter, B. (2005) *Scandalous Saints and Spirited Sinners*. Veritas Publications, Dublin, Ireland.

Ellsberg, R. (2006) *Blessed among All Women: Women Saints, Prophets and Witnesses for Our Time*. Darton, Longman & Todd Ltd, London.

Ganzevoort, R.R. (2008) Scars and stigmata: trauma, identity and theology. *Practical Theology* 1(1), 19–31.

Ghezzi, B. (2007) *Saints at Heart: How Fault Filled, Problem-Prone, Imperfect People Like Us Can be Holy*. Loyola Press, Chicago, USA.

Heather, J. and Heather, C. (2003) *The Pilgrim's Italy: A Travel Guide to the Saints*. Inner Travel Books, Nevada City, California, USA.

Hoever, H. (2005) *Illustrated Lives of the Saints*. Catholic Book Publishing Corporation, Totowa, New Jersey, USA.

Jansen, W. and Kuhl, M. (2008) Shared symbols: Muslims, marian pilgrimages, and gender. *European Journal of Women's Studies* 15(3), 295–311.

Kasten, P.A. (2014) *Making Sense of Saints: Fascinating Facts about Relics, Patrons, Canonizations and More*. Our Sunday Visiting Publishing Division, Huntington, Indiana, USA.

Kunz, M., Seifert, B. and Trueb, R.M. (2009) Seasonality of hair shedding in healthy women complaining of hair loss. *Dermatology* 219, 105–110.

MacNiven-Johnston, G. (2009) *Rita of Cascia: Saint of the Impossible*. Catholic Truth Society, London.

Martin, J. (2006) *My Life with the Saints*. Loyola Press, Chicago, Illinois, USA.

Mayblin, M. (2014) People like us: intimacy, distance and the gender of saints. *Current Anthropology* 55(10), 271–280.

Papalini, M. (1997) *Blessed Maria Teresa Fasce, Abbess of the Augustinian Monastery of St. Rita of Cascia: Her Life, Her Spirituality*. Augustinian Monastery of St. Rita Publications, Cascia, Italy.

Rotelle, J. (2000) *The Book of Augustinian Saints*. Augustinian Press, Villanova, Pennsylvania, USA.

Tari, M. and Vanni, I. (2008) On the life of San Precario, patron saint of precarious workers and lives. *Fibreculture Journal* 5, 1–7.

Trueb, R.M. (2009) St. Agnes of Rome: patron saint for women with hair loss? *Dermatology* 219, 97–98.

Winstead, K.A. (2011) *The Life of St. Katherine of Alexandria*. University of Notre Dame Press, Notre Dame, Indiana, USA.

15 Conclusion

Kevin Griffin[1]* and Fiorella Giacalone[2]
[1]*Dublin Institute of Technology, Dublin;* [2]*Department of Political Science, University of Perugia, Perugia, Italy*

As stated in the introductory chapter, this book is primarily derived from the proceedings of a meeting of Francophone anthropologists, the XXVIII Colloque Eurethno du Conseil d'Europe, on the theme of pilgrimage in Europe, which was held in Perugia and Assisi in 2014. As such, the publication of these papers in English brings to the Anglo-centric academic community many unique and fresh contributions from primarily French and Italian authors in relation to religious tourism and pilgrimage, thereby bridging a range of academic disciplines, cultures, languages and perspectives, and thus, providing a unique and eclectic multicultural treat. This short chapter brings together some concluding observations on the individual chapters and their overall contributions to the aims of this volume.

In proposing this book, the established aim was to explore themes such as globalization and even glocalization in relation to the evolution of 'popular' pilgrimages in Europe. The thesis of the project is that local level pilgrimages, when based on strong expressions of faith can have much wider local, regional and international appeal. This idea was elucidated through a range of sociological and ethnographic studies that illustrate the evolution of pilgrimage sites and saints, while also dealing with a range of theoretical issues and themes. A subtext of many of the chapters is the central role of ordinary people in the popularization of faith-based practices, thus illustrating religious tourism as an expression of cultural identity, the interrelationship of cultural groups and the overall formation of culture and society. The multidisciplinary nature of the text is paramount for generating holistic perspectives when exploring and understanding these complex and challenging themes, and this is achieved through the multidisciplinary assemblage of both themes and author disciplines.

A further aim of the book is to provide students, managers, scholars and others who are interested in religious tourism and pilgrimage and societal development with a collection of current perspectives on the growth, development and evolution of faith practices surrounding contemporary and historical sites and saints. In reaching out to a range of audiences, the editors of the volume are cognisant of blending strong sociological, ethnographic and tourism theory with sound practical cases of an applied nature. Thus, the book should act as an invaluable reference for academics, students and practitioners on the evolution and development of faith-based tourism and pilgrimage.

Through the inclusion of cases where issues such as conflict and/or inclusion of diaspora are presented, the book also deals with themes

*Corresponding author. E-mail: kevin.griffin@dit.ie

and issues that are of international interest. The volume therefore, honours the diversity of international spiritual traditions while seeking common ground among them. The book will hopefully open a dialogue that is global in conception by being responsive to common challenges of inclusion and coexistence within and among the world's many traditions. It thereby considers the importance of peace agendas being defined by broad cultural experiences, not just the beliefs and ideals of a particular nation or culture.

While doing this, the text also challenges the ever-widening gap between specialists within the sociological, ethnographic and religious tourism sectors. The book provides practical case studies, and illustrations of religious tourism and pilgrimage development from a variety of perspectives, bringing together for the first time a range of cases and perspectives presently located in disparate sources, in the areas of social and cultural development, linked to pilgrimage and religious practices.

Contemporary Pilgrimages, in Specific Local Circumstances

Some of the contributions in the volume are concerned with *contemporary pilgrimages, in specific local circumstances*, and these chapters are primarily the result of ethnographic research that highlights the dynamics that develop between institutions and popular cults. An example of this is Spitilli's analysis of the cult of the 'Madonna del Alno di Canzano', which examines a blending of local folk activities and liturgical practices, to create a complex local cult. This resonates with Lamothe's work in the Landes region of France, which focuses on the blending of very local sport traditions with religion to create local cults with national or even international appeal. Meanwhile, in the south of Italy, Bellio examines the construction of new places of worship associated with fortune telling. This has significant importance in this region where many supernatural figures are ascribed mystical qualities. A practical case study by Paola De Salvo demonstrates how a cult following is fostered in the development of the Way of St Francis, with the support of local political and religious authorities. The final example in this category of contemporary pilgrimages in specific local circumstances is

Fournier's analysis of local pilgrimages in Provence (France), where ritual battles have become an instrument of tourism development, with religious and civil authorities exploring opportunities to capitalize on this ritualistic heritage.

Creation of dynamics that expand cults to other places

A second main theme that weaves between many of the chapters is the *creation of dynamics that expand cults to other places*. The force whereby this occurs can occur at either the behest of the ecclesiastical authorities or by the will of the devotees who export and transform symbolic practices, according to specific contexts. Running contrary to institutional desires, but driven by popular practices is the cult of Saint Sarah in Saintes Maries de la Mer, in the Camargue (France), where the gypsy saint is not recognized by the Church, but is the subject of strong devotion for various Roma communities as described by Gaëlla Loiseau; of further interest is the export of this particular ritual by tourist-pilgrims to Brazil, where Sarah has become a black saint of the marginalized. Julliard in discussing the cult of St Nicholas of Bari (Italy), notes that this saint curiously attracts both Catholic and Orthodox pilgrims – Italians and Slavs.

A further aspect of this process is the manner in which migrant populations bring with them their own gods, and their own cults, often reinforced by the distance from home and the risks associated with migration. Cults and pilgrimages find different expressions in western Europe, through the migration of Catholics and those of other religions. In illustrating this, Cruzzolin reflects on the worship of the Señor de los Milagros in Italy by Peruvian immigrants, which is manifest in Perugia and Rome where pilgrimages take place. In a similar way, Guillaume writes about the way Portuguese immigrants in France follow the cult of Saint Solvang on Pentecost Monday – an important element of life for the French-Portuguese community. Such blending of ethnicity and culture with religion is also reflected in Parbuono's chapter about the Temple of the Buddhist Association of the Chinese community in Prato, which hosts a range of important Chinese festivals thereby forming a locale for 'complementary cultural worship'.

The large numbers of migrants render the contemporary religious landscape in Italian cities ever more complex, with the presence of Chinese Buddhists, Latin American Catholics, Muslims, Greek and Russian Orthodox rites, and Christian and Muslim Roma. At a time when interfaith dialogue appears more relevant and important than ever, this volume aims to highlight the many different contexts in which religious tourism is expressed, in both western and eastern Europe, in terms of exchanges between the many ways of being European, and ways to accept new citizens from other continents and religions.

The final section of the book brings together the two main strands, exploring the idea of glocalized worship of an international saint in a local manner – reflecting the spread of the particular cult to other locations. The worship of St Rita of Cascia, one of the most widespread Catholic icons of the twentieth century, venerated not only across Europe and Latin America, but also in the Middle East (such as in Lebanon), is interpreted with reference to local perspectives. The relationship between the saint and the town of Cascia, with which she is identified, and an analysis of the pilgrimage to Roccaporena, with a reflection on the boundaries between pilgrimage and tourism is undertaken by Giacalone, who also seeks to investigate the meaning of the relationship between pilgrims, the saint and local identity. Also dealing with St Rita, Kuzma emphasizes the emergence of the cult of the saint in Poland, in Krakow in particular, where the post-communist era has seen the development, especially in Catholic areas, of new processional routes associated with transnational cults. Kiely further elucidates these themes in exploring the evolution and anatomy of devotional practice among a predominantly female congregation in Ireland, who attend a weekly novena Mass, to seek favours and support from a saint who is simultaneously a figure from medieval Italy and an ordinary woman like them, who understands their ongoing practical worries.

Discussion Questions

Chapter 2 Discussion Questions

- Measure the validity of an interpretive approach that applies the ethnological perspective to the European context, together with the methodologies of historical research and religious anthropology aimed towards Christianity studies.
- Consider the festive and ritual disposition in particular as a site of negotiation, and conflict between various cultural, political and social levels.
- Decodify the interconnection between the legendary system and ritual system paying particular attention to the mediating function of some animal and plant categories.
- Take into consideration the historical significance of the legendary protagonists and their configuration in relation to the history of the cult and the political use of the founding legend.
- Explore the nuances that Christianity assumes in suburban and rural contexts as forms of 'local religion'.

Chapter 3 Discussion Questions

- Do features of post-modern tourism justify one continuing to differentiate between pilgrimages and religious tourism?

- Do the renewed interests/demands of tourists/pilgrims and their secular dimension impoverish the spiritual dimension of pilgrimages?
- Can religious itineraries reinforce the significance of bonds between the religious attractor and the place being visited?
- Can a religious itinerary become a tourism marketing tool?

Chapter 4 Discussion Questions

- How have the forms of pilgrimage changed over time (i.e. transformation from pilgrimage to religious tourism)?
- Which transformations have suffered during the past few decades of Calabrian society?
- What impact did the figure of Fratel Cosimo have on religious phenomena in Calabria?
- What role did the Church develop as an institution in the contemporary transformations of religious phenomena?
- What patrimonial actions and management of collective religious practices are implemented in southern Italy?

Chapter 5 Discussion Questions

- Discuss how pilgrimages have changed from traditional to contemporary societies.

- Explore how ritual battles and violence are universal features in traditional pilgrimages.
- Discuss the reasons why traditional pilgrimages were so often the place where factionalism and rivalries were expressed.
- Consider the ways traditional rivalries could be valorized in religious tourism today.

Chapter 6 Discussion Questions

- Explore the construction and reconstruction genesis of religious sensitivities inside the historical and urbanistic events of cities strongly impacted by migration flows.
- Reflect on the relationships among migration contexts, spaces and practices of worship.
- Highlight some of the central elements in the religious practices and beliefs Chinese residents in China (Wenzhou) and in Italy (Prato) have in common.
- Define relationships, integrations and differences among the pilgrimage forms practised by migrant believers.

Chapter 7 Discussion Questions

- The appropriation of the figure of Sarah is not met with resistance in that her recognition activates a universal signifier (Sarah as gypsy symbolic). Discuss this lack of conflict between stakeholders, while considering local issues, power plays and unexpected alliances.
- The role played by this universal gypsy identity is forged around the allegory of seduction, and thus questions the modalities of categorization and production of her identity. Is Sarah used by gypsies themselves in certain contexts of clothing as they seek to attain an 'assumed exoticism'?
- While they worship the same figure, gypsies and non-gypsies appear to be situated in different communication registers. However, the cult of Sarah recognizes their gypsy in both the Camargue (French) and Brazilian contexts, but there is no singular trajectory in this globalized universe. Does Sarah's value lie in the recognition that a singular

trajectory for her worship and development in a globalized space is not practical?

Chapter 8 Discussion Questions

- Discuss how migration is reshaping Catholicism.
- Consider the devotion as a symbolic tool useful to redefine one's presence in the world and to build a sense of community.
- Review the ways in which the image of the migrant partially coincides with that of the pilgrim.
- Explore the way in which religion can redefine the concept of power.

Chapter 9 Discussion Questions

- To what extent can a phenomenon shift from being a threat to an asset for a pilgrimage? How can the Church disentangle the double bind involved in the expansion of the pilgrimage?
- Will there be a shift of opinion to clarify the presence of new groups attending the pilgrimage (e.g. the 'Africans')?
- How do the questions raised by the pilgrimage relate to more global political and social issues?

Chapter 10 Discussion Questions

- What factors have led to the development of 'sport pilgrimages' in the southwest region of France?
- How do these sports chapels assist in the development of local cultural identity?
- Is there potential for local communities in this region of France to leverage their religious sites in the development of tourism?

Chapter 11 Discussion Questions

- How do breaks in the pattern of work and leisure influence the experiences of the pilgrim in their worship?

- How do individuals (tourists, pilgrims or both at the same time) display quite a different social/personal 'reality' when they are present within a sanctuary?
- How are the material and immaterial properties of St Nicholas's heritage understood by both tourists and pilgrims?

Chapter 12 Discussion Questions

- What are the mechanisms of transformation whereby a private and grassrooted cult develops into a formal and organized institutional ritual?
- Discuss the contextual specificities of local representations and interpretations of an international cult.
- How are the cultural, social and historical characters of a space considered as factors in the development of a cult?
- How do urban spaces operate as religious spaces?

Chapter 13 Discussion Questions

- In Catholic culture how is the use of websites and the internet changing the cult of the saints?
- With what methodology can cults and ex-votos be studied online?
- What relationship is created between the local cult and transnational dynamics in the cult of miracle-worker saints?
- How has the tourism economy changed the forms of pilgrimage?

Chapter 14 Discussion Questions

- Why is St Rita followed with such passion in Dublin?
- What are the particular features of devotion to St Rita, and how are these manifest in the daily lives of her followers?
- Are there other forms of female worship that compare with the devotion to St Rita by women in Dublin?
- Does devotion to St Rita mirror society and culture in the city of Dublin?

Index

Note: bold page numbers indicate figures and tables; numbers in brackets preceded by *n* are chapter endnote numbers.

CABI – who we are and what we do

This book is published by **CABI**, an international not-for-profit organisation that improves people's lives worldwide by providing information and applying scientific expertise to solve problems in agriculture and the environment.

CABI is also a global publisher producing key scientific publications, including world renowned databases, as well as compendia, books, ebooks and full text electronic resources. We publish content in a wide range of subject areas including: agriculture and crop science / animal and veterinary sciences / ecology and conservation / environmental science / horticulture and plant sciences / human health, food science and nutrition / international development / leisure and tourism.

The profits from CABI's publishing activities enable us to work with farming communities around the world, supporting them as they battle with poor soil, invasive species and pests and diseases, to improve their livelihoods and help provide food for an ever growing population.

CABI is an international intergovernmental organisation, and we gratefully acknowledge the core financial support from our member countries (and lead agencies) including:

 UKaid from the British people

Ministry of Agriculture People's Republic of China

 Australian Government Australian Centre for International Agricultural Research

 Agriculture and Agri-Food Canada

Ministry of Foreign Affairs of the Netherlands

 Schweizerische Eidgenossenschaft Confédération suisse Confederazione Svizzera Confederaziun svizra

Swiss Agency for Development and Cooperation SDC

Discover more

To read more about CABI's work, please visit: **www.cabi.org**

Browse our books at: **www.cabi.org/bookshop**, or explore our online products at: **www.cabi.org/publishing-products**

Interested in writing for CABI? Find our author guidelines here: **www.cabi.org/publishing-products/information-for-authors/**